THE EMPIRE IN THE WORLD

THE EMPIRE IN THE WORLD

A STUDY IN LEADERSHIP AND RECONSTRUCTION

By

SIR ARTHUR WILLERT, K.B.E.

B. K. LONG

H. V. HODSON

Edited by

E. THOMAS COOK

OXFORD UNIVERSITY PRESS

LONDON   NEW YORK   TORONTO

1937

OXFORD UNIVERSITY PRESS
AMEN HOUSE, E.C. 4
London Edinburgh Glasgow New York
Toronto Melbourne Capetown Bombay
Calcutta Madras
HUMPHREY MILFORD
PUBLISHER TO THE UNIVERSITY

11899

PRINTED IN GREAT BRITAIN

BIOGRAPHICAL NOTE

Sir Arthur Willert, K.B.E.

Before his resignation in March 1935, Sir Arthur Willert was Chief of the Press Department at the Foreign Office, to which post he had been promoted from Councillor in November 1925. The greater part of his career has been spent on the staff of *The Times*, and during the War, except for one break during which he acted as secretary at Washington to the British War Mission, he was the Chief Correspondent of that newspaper in the United States. There are few, if any, diplomatists and statesmen in Europe or in America with whom, at one time or another, Sir Arthur Willert has not been in close contact. His last volume, *The Frontiers of Europe*, was published a little over a year ago.

H. V. Hodson

Since 1931 Mr. Hodson has been connected with the *Round Table*, of which he is now Editor. He was on the Staff of the Economic Advisory Council, attended the Ottawa Conference, and has travelled widely throughout the Empire. He is a frequent broadcaster in the Home and Empire programmes. He was formerly a Fellow of All Souls, and his publications include *The Economics of a Changing World*.

B. K. Long

Mr. Long for nearly fifteen years was Editor of the South African *Cape Times* and retired in 1935. For many years previously he was connected with *The Times*, acting first as Colonial and later Dominion and Foreign Editor. Between the time he left Oxford until 1913 he was called to the Cape Bar and was a member of the Cape House of Assembly and later of the first Union Parliament. He helped to draft the Constitution of the Union of South Africa. In 1920 he went as *The Times* correspondent to Australia with the Duke of Windsor when Prince of Wales. In 1932 Mr. Long attended the Ottawa Conference as the representative of the *Cape Times* and its associated newspapers of South Africa.

E. Thomas Cook

Mr. Cook is Assistant Editor of the *Empire Review*. In 1935 he edited a volume *Conservatism and the Future*, which was prepared with the help of Lord Eustace Percy, Mr. W. S. Morrison (now Minister of Agriculture), and other leading Conservatives.

PREFACE

THIS volume was planned two and a half years ago. A number of events of world-wide importance have intervened and delayed its appearance.

None of these events have altered the fact that there is no subject of greater importance to us than the British Empire Overseas, its tradition, its future, and its capacity to keep together in a world apparently determined to fly into fragments.

When selecting the essential factors which must guide the future conduct of Imperial relations, I was not unaware of the immense range such factors must be expected to cover. That very immensity has been most difficult to bring within the pages of a single volume. The original subjects were: the Foreign Policy of the Empire, the Constitution of the Empire, and the Economics of the Empire. Within these the authors have endeavoured to bring all matters relating to inter-Imperial government and organization.

The co-ordination of the material in the pages which follow has, in one sense, been my task; but the authors who undertook the work at my invitation have also been at considerable pains, while retaining their individual viewpoints, to make the volume a complete and continuous diagnosis of Imperial problems.

The Empire in the World is presented as a free, untrammelled expression of opinion with any collective responsibility resting upon my shoulders. It must not, therefore, be read as a joint declaration of policy although it is clear that each author is conscious of an urgent need for the British Government to give a lead in all matters relating to Imperial policy, especially in the sphere of Foreign Affairs.

E. THOMAS COOK

BROOKS'S, ST. JAMES'S,
LONDON, S.W. I.

CONTENTS

PART I. THE WORLD AROUND US

By SIR ARTHUR WILLERT

PART II. THE EMPIRE: NOW

By B. K. LONG

PART III. ECONOMICS OF THE EMPIRE

By H. V. HODSON

CONTENTS

PART IV. FOREIGN POLICY

By SIR ARTHUR WILLERT

PART I

THE WORLD AROUND US

THE SLUMP IN DEMOCRACY

THE Imperial Conference of 1937, meeting to take stock of the affairs of the Empire and of the relations of the Empire with the outside world, was convened in circumstances contrasting strongly with those which attended its two immediate predecessors of 1926 and 1930.

In 1926 the world seemed to be in a fair way to recovery from the shocks and dislocations of the Great War. In Europe the Pact of Locarno had been signed, and the League of Nations, under the wise guidance of M. Briand, Herr Stresemann, and Sir Austen Chamberlain, seemed to be coming into its own, and victors and vanquished to be coming together. In the Far East there was no indication that within a few years Japan would lawlessly attack China and deal the League the first of the series of great blows which have brought it to the ground. Across the Atlantic the United States was rushing into her post-war 'boom', and nobody dreamed how soon the bubble of that 'boom' was to be pricked. Democracy, having won the War, seemed in a fair way to consolidate the Peace. Most things, except the economic situation in Great Britain, never good since the War and aggravated by the great strikes of that year, looked satisfactory and encouraging.

By 1930 the economic tempest had broken and all the world was battered by its blast. But no one as yet foresaw how disastrously it was destined to develop or how decisively to influence politics both national and international. It was still believed that it would blow itself out as other similar storms had done before, and that then the liquidation of the War could be comfortably continued. Nobody is now so sanguine. Many things have been changed, generally for the worse. Among the Great Powers of Europe only England, with the other countries of the Empire standing unshaken behind her, has, in spite of the collapse of sterling in 1931 and of the constitutional crisis of 1936, come through with her political and economic system fundamentally unimpaired and unchallenged. That fact the Imperial Conference of 1937 will be entitled to put on the bright side of its ledger. It can also place there, first, the emergence of the United States under the leadership of the second President Roosevelt from the depths into which the panic of 1929 plunged her, and, secondly, the general, if slow and often tentative, improvement of international economic conditions, due partly to the currency agreement reached in the autumn of 1936 between the United States, France, and Great Britain.

In high international politics little can be found that is encouraging, except once again in those territories which are controlled or influenced by the English-speaking peoples and the democracies of north-western Europe. The League of Nations remains prostrate; the democracies have lost the initiative to the dictatorships in the field of diplomacy; all nations are rearming, and the danger of war is on all men's lips. The more the situation is studied, the more it compels the conclusion that the person who first said that in the last few years we have passed from the post-war period into another pre-war period was guilty of no particular exaggeration.

Thrice in modern times England has fought and triumphed in Europe at the head of a great alliance to save the Continent from a hegemony which would not have suited her. Each of the three wars ended in the opening period of a century. The Peace of Utrecht closed the long struggle against the ambitions of Louis XIV of France in 1714; Napoleon was sent to St. Helena and the Peace of Paris finally signed in 1815; the Treaty of Versailles, with most of its ancillary agreements, was concluded in 1919.

The real reactions of the first two wars took about twenty years to indicate themselves. As we look back upon the eighteenth century, we see that by 1737 the Peace of Utrecht had already become no more than a truce before the series of great contests which raged over Europe and out over the world during much of the rest of the century, and were only ended at Waterloo. The Peace of Paris was, on the other hand, considered by our forebears a hundred years ago to be fairly certain to endure as a guarantee against universal conflict, in spite of the way in which it had ignored the tide of nationalism and liberalism let loose by the French Revolution and by the impact of Napoleon upon Europe. Otherwise England would not, during the fourth decade of the last century, have allowed her army to continue to 'sleep upon the laurels and recollections of the Peninsula' and would not, with a sure instinct for the future, have ignored as irrelevant a specialist's agitation about the 'extremely reduced state of the Navy' in the face of a possible Franco-Russian alliance.

This century, on the showing that its fourth decade has so far made, threatens to go the way of its eighteenth rather than of its nineteenth forerunner, with the difference that, whereas the Empire sprang triumphantly out of the eighteenth-century contests, there is no possible chance of further twentieth-century warfare doing us anything save grievous harm. The decade has been a period of increasing anxiety and strain. Each of its years has begun under a stormier star than that of its predecessors. They have witnessed the progressive dissolution of the Treaty of Versailles and the progressive disillusionment of those who had hoped that, in spite of its manifest imperfections, it was somehow or other going to bring into being a better international system. They have seen the underpinning, upon which it was hoped that that system would be reared, battered into alarming instability.

We fought the Great War primarily to prevent Europe from falling not merely under a hegemony but under the hegemony of an essentially anti-democratic nation. A principal purpose of the War was thus 'to make the world safe for democracy'. The War, as it progressed, was discovered to be immeasurably more destructive and savage than the worst of its predecessors, and, long before it was over, it was everywhere agreed that its repetition on anything like the same scale would indeed be Armageddon. A principal purpose of the Peace was, therefore, the protection of the world from the possibility of such a catastrophe. The world was to be made safe for peace as well as for democracy.

The instrument devised for this end was, of course, the League of Nations. The League of Nations has been well described as having been called into being to create a 'better understanding, particularly between the Great Powers', than the 'old diplomacy' had been able to establish and to 'restrain reckless or criminal policies in world affairs'. The central feature of the 'old diplomacy' had been the grouping of the Great Powers in shifting alliances for the purpose sometimes of keeping the peace and sometimes of winning a war against an ambitious aggressor. This meant at the best an uneasy equilibrium and at the worst war. It was a possible system so long as big wars were not disastrous to losers, winners, and neutrals alike; so long, that is to say, as force could be regarded as a tolerable alternative to diplomacy. It was hoped that the League of Nations would replace this competitive Balance of Power system by a co-operative system under which the nations would work together to settle disputes peaceably, and would combine to restrain, by force if necessary, any of their number that 'ran amuck' and tried to use force for the furtherance of its ambitions. The League was also to be the guardian of the organic law of the world as rewritten at the Peace Conference.

By the beginning of 1937 these hopes had, for the time being at any rate, been definitely stultified. A series of cumulative and closely connected discomfitures had reduced the League to the position of an unregarded cipher in the high affairs of the world. Japan had flouted it with impunity when she took Manchuria by force of arms in 1931 and 1932. In Africa it had failed to protect Abyssinia from the rape of her independence by Italy. In Europe the collapse of the Disarmament Conference, which came between those two events, had started a race in armaments the pace and dangers of which had been enhanced by Germany's obliteration of the penalty clauses of the Treaty of Versailles, first by launching her tremendous rearmament programme in 1935 and then by sending her troops back into the demilitarized area of the Rhineland almost exactly a year later. To these infractions of the public law of Europe the League and the League Powers opposed nothing more effective than Notes and Resolutions.

Germany, Japan, and Italy had reintroduced into diplomacy the principle and practice of 'power policy', the other characteristic of the bad old order. 'If you don't like what I am doing, come and stop me by force.' Such was the typical gesture of power policy; and it had been successfully made first by Japan towards Great Britain, the United States, and the League over Manchuria, then by Germany as against the League countries when she smashed the Treaty of Versailles, and again by Italy when she dared the League Powers in general and Great Britain in particular to fight her over Abyssinia.

Nor does that close the catalogue of the League's discomfitures. The moderation with which France was treated after the Napoleonic War may not have sufficed to prevent France from sympathizing with the forces of nationalism which subsequently undid the work of the Peace Settlement in Belgium, Italy, and Germany; but it did do much to secure for Europe the immunity which it enjoyed from universal warfare during the last century. Credit for this belongs to England, or rather to her Foreign Minister, Lord Castlereagh, who, backed by the Duke of Wellington, persuaded his less imaginative colleagues in the British Cabinet and the Prussians, who wanted among other things to take Alsace Lorraine as protection against France, that the merciless penalization of France was bound to produce a war of revenge, and that, if Europe wanted peace, the Powers should accept her as an equal with as little delay as possible, now that Napoleon had been eliminated. Lord Castlereagh's success in this matter would entitle him to a high place among British Foreign Ministers, even if he had done nothing else to win it.

In the Treaty of Versailles moderation, so far as the actual liquidation of the war was concerned, was not achieved at all. Germany, after being excluded from the negotiations, had forced upon her a treaty which she was to a great extent justified in holding to be impossibly hard and contrary to some of the conditions of the armistice, that is to say, to various of President Wilson's Fourteen Points. One reason for this was the excessive, if understandable, bitterness of the French against a foe who, after deliberately and deceitfully attacking them, had for four years been in ruthless occupation of part of their country.

Another reason was the change that had come over the circumstances both of warfare and of peacemaking since Lord Castlereagh and the Duke of Wellington successfully withstood German vindictiveness in Vienna and Paris. War, during the Napoleonic era, was still mainly an affair for specialists. It was conducted with comparatively little regard to the opinions of the peoples of the countries concerned. Propaganda, though practised at times with limited objectives, especially by Napoleon, had not assumed a tithe of the importance which it acquired in the last war. Neither universal suffrage nor universal education existed in those days, and it did not seem to the belligerents worth while to expend any large amounts of time and energy in fortifying the spirit of their own populations and in sapping that of their opponents. Diplomacy was also an affair for specialists. The great majority of those who went to international conferences in those days belonged to a cosmopolitan governing caste and were able to settle things quietly among themselves without much reference to public opinion. Statesmanship was still its own master.

It was different at Paris in 1919. Popular passions dominated the Conference. Delegates whose countrymen were clamouring that the Kaiser should be hanged and that Germany should be forced to pay for the expense of the War were hardly in the position of plenipotentiaries. The atmosphere in which they met was contaminated by the hatreds, distrusts, fears, and ambitions which had come down to Europe through the centuries, stirred up by the War and by war propaganda and reinforced by the new distempers which the War had produced. The crust of European civilization was quaking beneath their chairs. In some places it had broken, and anarchy and famine had come to the surface. Everywhere there was dislocation, political, financial, and commercial. It was feared that, if the Peace Settlement went slowly, huge portions of the Old World might fall into chaos through which Bolshevism, then a menace of unplumbed potentialities, might stalk disastrously.

Hence there could be no delay until constructive statesmanship could have a chance. Some sort of code for the stabilization of Europe had to be produced as quickly as possible. Reparations, the most burning question of all, was left for later settlement, and for years contaminated the atmosphere of Europe in general and of Franco-German relations in particular. Empirical and other imperfections were allowed to stand in the treaties in the hope that, after passions had cooled, they would be ironed out by the League of Nations and by that new system of international co-operation of which it was to be at once the executive and the symbol. That hope has not been realized, for reasons to which we will return later in this book. The worst disappointment has been over disarmament, or, more correctly, the limitation of armaments. Germany was to a great extent disarmed by the Treaty of Versailles. It was indicated by the victors, in the Treaty and elsewhere, that the compulsion of the vanquished would be followed by their own voluntary disarmament at some not too distant date. Hence the bitterness of Germany at the failure of the Disarmament Conference, and hence Herr Hitler's subsequent defiance of the disarmament clauses in the Treaty. Germany felt that she had been kept waiting intolerably long for the restoration of her equality with other nations, and history is unlikely to blame her over-much for the actions to which this opinion led her.

In other ways, too, the League has been unable to mitigate the extravagances of the Treaty of Versailles and to cope with their results. The territorial maladjustments of the settlement remain unaltered in spite of Article 19 of the Covenant, which empowers Geneva to advise the 'reconsideration of treaties which have become inapplicable and the consideration of international conditions whose continuation might endanger the peace of the world'. The Peace Conference disbanded without implementing the third of President Wilson's Fourteen Points, which demanded 'the removal so far as possible of all economic barriers and the establishment of an equality of trade conditions among all nations'. It did not even insist that the new States of central and eastern Europe should accept as a condition of their creation the obligation of free trade, at any rate among themselves. The League of Nations, despite the efforts of

M. Briand and other statesmen, has failed to remedy the resultant state of affairs or that orgy of economic nationalism which has so much increased the embarrassment of Europe.

Economic nationalism has increased the embarrassment of Europe largely by helping to compress to a dangerous degree of explosiveness the dynamic nationalism of the dictatorships. Economic hardship combines with German exasperation at the failure of the Disarmament Conference and at the continuation of the servitudes of Versailles to explain the rise of Herr Hitler. The difficulty of finding trade in tariff-strangulated Europe exacerbated Italian discontent with the Peace Settlement, and especially with the fact that she was the only one of the four victorious Great Powers not to be given mandated territories to hold. This rendered it easier for Signor Mussolini to win his double victory over the Abyssinians and the League of Nations. Herr Hitler and to some extent Signor Mussolini are the result less of the direct impact of the War than of a peace badly drawn and worse administered. In the patter of the Freudian school, the two figures that now bestride the Continent were at the start the incarnation of national inferiority complexes as much as anything else.

So it is that, nearly twenty years after the Peace, the world still awaits that 'better understanding between the Powers' which the League was to have created; 'reckless and criminal policies' remain unrestrained, and in all the disturbed parts of the world dictatorial or at any rate militarist and anti-democratic governments are in control and are maintaining the initiative which, as we have seen, they have won for themselves in high affairs since the beginning of this decade. The discomfiture of democracy encircles the earth even more conspicuously than its successes did a generation ago. Country after country which in the old days looked to Washington, London, or Paris for light and leadership now gazes admiringly or with apprehensive respect at Berlin and Rome. From Moscow another anti-democratic creed seeks recruits in other lands and is proclaimed by Fascism to be the arch-enemy, a challenge which Communism throws back with equal violence.

The impingement of this conflict upon international affairs increases the embarrassments of the democracies and the impotence of the League of Nations. In eastern Europe the organization of peace is held up by the strain existing between Moscow and Berlin, a strain enhanced since the end of 1936 by the so-called anti-Communist Treaty between Germany and Japan. That Treaty is officially depicted as dealing only with the means of thwarting Communist propaganda in the territories of the signatories. But Russia and the other countries that fear war between Russia and Germany are to be excused if they regard it as a potential alliance of two Fascist States against a hated enemy whom it is thus hoped to immobilize.

In the west of Europe the same confrontation of creeds has aroused, and may again arouse, grave fears of international strife. The aid which the Russian Communists have given to the forces of the Left, and which the Italian and German Fascists have given to those of the Right, in the Spanish Civil War has shown how hopeless it is to expect either side to observe the rules of international decency and honour when it suits them not to do so. Russia, Germany, and Italy all subscribed to the agreement which, under the leadership of France and England, the European Powers had made at the beginning of the trouble to do their best to prevent men and munitions from reaching either side. This agreement was meant to minimize the danger of a clash between Fascism and Communism and even between Fascism and Democracy such as active partisanship in the Civil War might well bring about. Unfairly as it penalized the Spanish Government, it did, at first at any rate, diminish the amount of help given by the outside world to the Spaniards in their fratricidal savagery, in spite of dictatorial 'volunteers' and gun-runners. But, by the end of 1936, it had not prevented Spain from becoming the cosmopolitan battle-ground of the rival 'ideologies'. If Germans, Italians, and Russians were fighting there in numbers with the inevitable connivance of their governments, French and British volunteers were also in the field on the sides they favoured. Thus the diplomacy of the democracies seemed once more to have been too weak to implement the intentions of its authors, excellent as those intentions were.

In any case, and whatever their denouement, the Spanish tragedy and its international reactions show that we are faced with the additional dangers of a conflict of rival political and social 'ideologies' both within and across the frontiers of the nations, a conflict which may further increase the difficulties of the peace-loving and war-fearing nations.

Those 'ideologies', moreover, though now bitterly antipathetic to each other, have much in common. They are based upon the break-down, in the countries which profess them, of the free individualism we believe in. They are buttressed by the conviction that no individualistic system can any longer cope with the intricate and interwoven problems of modern government and business. Berlin, Moscow, and Rome both despise democracy and believe that its race is run. The internal well-being of the British countries belies this contempt. On the other hand, the contemporary showing of British foreign policy tends to justify it.

The failings of British diplomacy in counsel and execution are saddled both abroad and at home with a large share of the responsibility for the discomfiture of the democracies. This may be unfair, but there are unfortunately circumstances which make it natural. In all the major crises in recent years the British Government has taken an energetic but unsuccessful part. At least half the blame for the Manchurian fiasco is commonly placed at its door; its industrious attempt to bring France and Germany together at the Disarmament Conference brought it nothing but disappointment; its constant efforts, since the failure of the Conference, to take the lead in the reconstruction of Europe have—like the Franco-British effort to secure neutrality in Spain—been brushed aside by the dictatorships. Its share in the Abyssinian business belongs to another portion of this book. Here it need only be said that it revealed the calamitous consequences of foreign policies of which divided counsels and bad advice are among the ingredients. It was marred at first by lack of alertness, or procrastination, or both. Then, after Sir John Simon had left the Foreign Office, there supervened a period of jerky and ill-considered precipitancy culminating in the advocacy of sanctions at far too late a date and followed by timidity and half-measures and, in the end and not unnaturally, by a resounding defeat. And, if his failure to make good intentions prevail earned for Mr. Eden as bad a rebuff as has ever fallen to the lot of any British Foreign Minister, one of the by-products of Abyssinia was as humiliating an experience as has ever fallen to the lot of a British Cabinet.

During the short course of the incident of the so-called Hoare–Laval proposals the Cabinet betrayed in succession one of the most important promises which they had given in the general election a few weeks before, a fundamental principle of British foreign policy, and a colleague. They ignored public opinion one week in a way which made people wonder whether cynicism or lack of sophistication was the principal cause of their blindness, and next week capitulated to it by throwing Sir Samuel Hoare to the wolves with an explanation even more abject than the act which it failed to white-wash. One result of this transaction, not without bearing upon the present diplomatic situation, is that foreigners in general were left with more respect for Sir Samuel Hoare than for the other principal participants in the incident. Sir Samuel Hoare, it was felt, might have been badly advised to join with M. Laval in what at the time was condemned as a betrayal both of the League and of the Abyssinians, but he at any rate faced the resultant music with consistency and courage and was in a sense not unjustified in his judgement by subsequent events.

The year 1936 thus witnessed the decline of the influence of the democratic countries in Europe to the lowest point since the War. Yet, sombre and threatening as the dawn of 1937 was, it did not, as already said, lack gleams of encouragement. France appeared to be regaining strength and poise after the bout of political, social, and economic distempers which had been weighing so heavily upon her. The potential prestige of Great Britain was also far higher than the discomfiture of her diplomacy would seem to indicate. The calm common sense with which she, like the other countries of the Empire, had come through the anxious days which culminated in the abdication of Edward VIII had enormously impressed the world, and had done much to restore the damaged reputation of the National Government and especially that of Mr. Baldwin. Mr. Baldwin, it was on all sides proclaimed, had triumphantly emerged from the shadows which the Hoare–Laval affair had cast upon him. He had brought to bear upon the crisis human and political qualities of the most enviable order, and had (to quote a contemporary American press comment) 'rationalized calamity into triumph' with a sureness of touch and judgement such as no other man in British public life could have brought to the occasion. The same people, too, who were contemptuously brushing aside our diplomacy were the first to admire the steadiness with which the British countries continued to recover from the depression. It was noted everywhere that better times had returned first and most emphatically to those parts of the world which map-makers are in the habit of colouring red, that Australia led the way out of the crisis, that we and South Africa followed neither slowly nor unsuccessfully, and that Canada stood up better than the United States to the cyclone which devastated the American continent.

There have been other slumps in the prestige of our external policy. The most notable was that which we experienced more than 150 years ago, when the surrender of Lord Cornwallis at Yorktown made it finally apparent that we had lost the American colonies. The sun, Europe proclaimed, had set upon the fortunes of the English people. It was not then long before the sun rose again. This time the recovery of our influence would be even quicker if we could find a policy which would enable us to take a lead with France in restoring to the democracies the initiative which they have lost.

The foreign policy of the Empire has so far been based upon the League of Nations, that is to say upon the organized collective co-operation of the nations in the interests of peace and equity. Ought that still to be its policy? Why in particular has British policy failed so signally in recent years? Is it a case of bad conception, or bad execution, or both? Can the League of Nations be rescued from its impotence and made to function as its founders meant it to function? Or must it be relegated to the limbo reserved for lost causes and unattainable ideals and be replaced by some other international system? Or is it that the nations are not yet ready for any effective system of co-operation? Must they then return to the old system of alliances and the Balance of Power? Or, again, is there a half-way house between the old system and the new? Or is there some untried system which could supplant both old and new? To what extent, if any, does the conflict of Communism and Fascism alter the assumptions upon which the League system was grounded? If the League of Nations is to be resuscitated what should the responsibilities of the Empire be under it? What should the Empire do, if the League fails and the old diplomacy rules again?

Such are some of the forms in which one of the two great questions confronting the peoples of the Empire can be posed. The other question concerns their own inner affairs. Are those affairs so ordered as to give the Empire first a maximum of internal harmony and prosperity and secondly a maximum of influence in any effort which it may decide to make on behalf of peace and prosperity? If not, how can they be altered? Can they be so ordered as to withstand the political and economic strains which are bound to continue if that effort fails or if it is not made at all?

The best approach to these and cognate questions lies perhaps through a survey of the state of the world with reference both to the League of Nations and to Imperial expediency. It is to be hoped that we shall never lose that streak of sentiment, that faith in free institutions, which made the elder Pitt, the most aggressively patriotic of statesmen, take the side of the American colonists during the Revolutionary War, which prompted Burke to dedicate his eloquence to the same cause, which inspired our support of Italy and Greece and other nationalities striving for independence, and in more recent times so quickly secured appeasement between Boer and Englishmen after the South African War. But, especially in these stark days, idealism unsupported by a lively and accurate sense of expediency can well be the worst of counsellors. Canning, more than a century ago, said that 'the generous and high-minded disinterestedness which immortalizes the hero cannot or ought not to be considered a justifiable motive of political action between nations'. President Wilson discovered the truth of those words when the American nation repudiated his signature of the Treaty of Versailles and the Covenant of the League of Nations on the ground that membership of the League carried with it responsibilities which seemed to it to run contrary to its true interests and real policies. The Empire would equally discover their truth if, on the one hand, it stubbornly insisted in its loyalty to an impracticable League, or, on the other hand, dropped the League prematurely and abandoned the cause of world peace and reconstruction in quest of some glowing but intangible vision of Imperial self-sufficiency.

II

THE PAN-AMERICAN ANSWER

THERE are to-day three principal theatres of diplomacy in the world. There is Europe, with which, so far as high international affairs are concerned, most of Africa and the contiguous parts of Asia may be associated; there is the Far East, and there is the American hemisphere. How do they and their problems concern the Empire? How does the authority of the League stand in them?

Let us take the western hemisphere first. The two Americas are of the greatest importance to the Empire. Canada, the second largest of the British countries, covers a great area of one of them; they contain the richest and most powerful of modern nations, namely the United States; their market for finished goods and raw materials is of great value to us, and much British capital is sunk in them. It is therefore satisfactory that in the western hemisphere the democratic system and peaceful intercourse between nations should be safer than they are anywhere else. For this, however, the League can claim no credit. Its writ does not run either in South or in North America. In North America the United States is not a member of it. In South America its membership is large and important; but peace and security there rest not upon its distant authority but upon the immanent and overpowering strength of the United States, who is rearming as vigorously as any European Power. Were the Empire to break up and Canada to be thrown on her own resources, the United States would resist her invasion from across either ocean as firmly and for the same defensive reason as we have always opposed the conquest by some ambitious Power of the shores of the Continent over against our island.

In Latin America the Monroe Doctrine compels the same resistance by the United States to the foreign aggressor. The American creed of foreign policy has three main articles. The first is that no extra-American Power should be allowed to gain new footholds or interfere in the politics of her

C

hemisphere. That is the Monroe Doctrine. The second is that the United States should avoid political entanglements in the Old World. That is the logical complement of the Monroe Doctrine. The third is that in the general adoption of principles and practices, such as those for which the League stands, lies the best hope for the organization and preservation of peace. The third article is, of course, cancelled out by the second so far as American membership of the League and direct participation in European affairs go, though, as will be shown later on, not necessarily where indirect assistance is concerned. But in the western hemisphere, especially since the Pan-American Congress at Buenos Aires in December 1936, all three articles work together to secure that the ideals and principles of Geneva shall be guarded from outside attack. Their conjunction also means that the United States would go a long way in co-operation with the larger Latin-American States to secure them from local attack as well.

Like his predecessor and political tutor, Mr. Woodrow Wilson, during the crisis of the War, President Roosevelt, in this new crisis of human affairs, is working to secure that the countries of the American hemisphere shall so organize their relations as best to ward off the troubles besetting other parts of the globe. The story of Mr. Wilson's moves in that direction is told in the narrative of Colonel House, to whose advice and assistance his diplomacy owed so many of its successes. A few months after the outbreak of the War, Colonel House began to feel that the time had come for the inauguration of a positive and permanent Pan-American policy of conference and co-operation. He thought, in the words of his biographer,[1] that the 'bankruptcy of European diplomacy' in the summer of 1914 had 'resulted primarily from the lack of an organized system of international co-operation'. Colonel House describes as follows, in his diary, the proposition which he put before President Wilson:

'It was my idea to formulate a plan, to be agreed upon by the republics of the two continents, which in itself would serve as a model for the European nations when peace is at last brought about. . . . My idea was that the republics should agree to guarantee

[1] *The Intimate Papers of Colonel House* (Ernest Benn, London), vol. i, p. 213.

each other's territorial integrity and that they should also agree to government ownership of munitions of war.'

This suggestion President Wilson translated into a draft treaty providing for a common and mutual guarantee of territorial integrity and of political independence under the republican forms of government. There were also provisions for the peaceful settlement of disputes and an undertaking not to allow revolutions to be helped from the territories of the contracting parties. The project failed, for various reasons, though some of its ideas find their place in the Covenant of the League. One reason for its failure was that President Wilson's predilection for republican government was of the crusading variety, and Latin America never quite forgave his interference in Mexico against a revolutionary ruler of dictatorial tendencies, in spite of the fact that, at one period of the trouble, he paid the leading South American countries the compliment of calling them in to co-operate towards its settlement on equal terms with the United States.

President Roosevelt is hampered by no such past. On the contrary, the cordiality of the atmosphere of the Buenos Aires Conference and the readiness of Latin America to work with the United States is largely due to the 'good neighbour' policy which the President and his able Foreign Minister, Mr. Hull, have steadily pursued. That policy was in point of fact originated by President Hoover. Under it the diplomacy of the 'Big Stick', originated by the first President Roosevelt before the War and carried on, as we have seen, by President Wilson towards Mexico and by the Republicans during the first part of their long term in office after the War, has been finally abandoned. The last American marines were withdrawn from Nicaragua just before President Roosevelt went to the White House in 1933, and a year later he brought to an end the other military protectorate which the United States had been exercising in the Caribbean over the coloured, French-speaking Republic of Haiti. During the same period the United States surrendered her treaty right to interfere in the domestic affairs of two of her other neighbours. She cancelled the so-called Platt amendment, under which, after freeing Cuba from Spanish misrule at the end of the last century, she had reserved, and on one occasion exercised, the right to intervene if the Cuban Government seemed to her to be functioning inadequately. She cancelled a somewhat similar right to interfere with the affairs of Panama, which she had assumed when the first President Roosevelt had somewhat roughly encouraged Panama to separate herself from Colombia in order to facilitate the acquisition by the United States of the rights over the Isthmus which she needed for the building and administration of the canal; and neither President Hoover nor President Roosevelt used the American right to intervene in their finances when Haiti's neighbours, Santo Domingo and Salvador, defaulted on their foreign debts.

At the Pan-American Conference held at Montevideo in 1933 the United States gave fairly definite promises that in the future the Latin American countries need not fear any attempt at single-handed intervention on her part. It was said at the time that in making these assurances Mr. Hull, who deservedly enjoys in Latin America popularity achieved by none of his predecessors, had opened a new era in the Pan-American relationship. That relationship was still further consolidated by Mr. Roosevelt, again with the assistance of Mr. Hull, at the 1936 Pan-American Conference. Mr. Roosevelt made it clear in his speech at Buenos Aires that the Monroe Doctrine was no longer to be considered as implying the assumption by the United States of unilateral responsibility for the safety of the Latin-American Powers at its doors. The peace and prosperity of the western hemisphere must in the future be the affair of all its nations acting together.

'We in the Americas make it at the same time clear that we stand shoulder to shoulder in our final deliberations, that others who, driven by war madness or land hunger, might seek to commit acts of aggression against us will find a hemisphere wholly prepared to consult together for our mutual safety and our mutual good. I repeat what I said in speaking before the Congress and Supreme Court of Brazil: "Each one of us has learned the glories of independence. Let each one of us learn the glories of interdependence." '

The American republics, Mr. Roosevelt continued, must

be an example to the rest of the world in the exercise of democracy.

'The lack of social or political justice within the borders of any nation is always a cause for concern. Through democratic processes we can strive to achieve for the Americas the highest possible standard of living conditions for all our people. Men and women blessed with political freedom, willing to work and able to find work, rich enough to maintain their families and to educate their children, contented with their lot in life, and on terms of friendship with their neighbours, will defend themselves to the utmost, but will never consent to take up arms for a war of conquest.'

Mr. Roosevelt's renunciation of any unilateral responsibility on the part of the United States for the affairs of her neighbours was implemented during the Conference by American participation in an undertaking subscribed to by the other American republics not to intervene in each other's internal affairs. A foundation for Pan-American political co-operation already existed before the Buenos Aires Conference in the shape of a nexus of four treaties for the settlement of disputes by investigation, mediation, and arbitration, for the outlawry of war, and for the non-recognition of territorial changes brought about by other than peaceful means. At the Buenos Aires Conference the treaties were reinforced by the signature by all the republics of a treaty providing for consultation and co-operation between them, if war should threaten or break out between two or more of them or if war outside their continent should render joint action advisable for the maintenance of peace in it.

When the Buenos Aires Conference met there was some talk of the possibility of an American League of Nations and of the establishment of an American Court of International Justice. Nothing, however, came of those ideas. The American Government is against a separate court for the western hemisphere, and by no means all the Latin-American countries are ready to abandon the League of Nations; for in spite of the developments already mentioned they like to discover in their continued frequentation of Geneva a sort of counterpoise to the dominating authority of the United States, which no amount of protestation about the new-found 'collectivity' of the Monroe Doctrine can entirely destroy, so long as the last word in international affairs comes from armaments and the money and material behind them. Nor have the American republics been able to evolve a complete collective neutrality policy against an outside war, if only because the United States had not at the time of the Buenos Aires Conference evolved a permanent policy of her own. But if Pan-American solidarity is not yet fully attained, everything in Pan-American politics shows that the Americans are more than ever disposed to draw out of direct participation in the politics of the outside world and to cultivate the tender and threatened plants of democracy and peace in the seclusion of their own gardens.

Dislike of direct participation does not mean that the United States in particular may not still have great indirect influence on the affairs of the world. We are at this moment feverishly increasing our armaments. The usefulness of these armaments may easily depend upon the United States, in spite of her present tendency towards isolation. This is a subject to which we will return later. The American neutrality policy is likely to remain essentially malleable, even if definite laws are enacted about it. It will continue to respond within certain limits to the general drift of American opinion towards the outside world, and of course will be in the last resort influenced by the American judgement of the merits of any contest in regard to which it has to be exercised and by American feeling towards the contestants. In the struggle between democracy and dictatorship that feeling is strongly on our side. Mr. Roosevelt is never tired of proclaiming so. He has excoriated the dictatorships in a Message to Congress with a roughness not usually to be found in State Papers. In his speech to the Pan-American Conference he said:

'We know, too, that vast armaments are rising on every side and that the work of creating them employs men and women by millions. It is natural, however, for us to conclude that such employment is false employment, that it builds no permanent structures and creates no consumers' goods for the maintenance of lasting prosperity. We know that nations guilty of these follies inevitably face the day either when their weapons of destruction must be used against their neighbours or when an unsound economy, like a house of cards, will fall apart.'

The Americas, Mr. Roosevelt continued, would suffer on account of war, even if they succeeded in remaining neutral. They could, however, help the Old World to avoid war. They could set an example of a great community of nations living at peace. They could help to lower the trade barriers between nations, the height of which are at once a symptom and a cause of bad relations.

Towards us the development of American feeling will partly depend upon factors which are far from intangible. Neither the goodwill which exists between the English-speaking peoples nor specific instances of good fellowship, such as that symbolized by the 3,000 miles of unguarded frontier between the United States and Canada, should blind us to the fact that these relations still have their sore spots. One such spot is the war debt. Sophisticated Americans might like to scrap it and have done with it, but the American public in general is not of that opinion. It does not see why, with all our vaunted prosperity, we should not pay something and thus relieve the American taxpayer of a fraction of his burden. It argues that if Europe, including ourselves, can finance vast armament programmes then it can afford to pay creditors. The obvious economic counter-arguments make no effect on the average voter or indeed the average Congressman.

And if the debt affects public opinion, the tariff policy of the Empire and notably of Great Britain affects political opinion. The present American Government, thanks largely to the enlightened enterprise of Mr. Hull, is, unlike its predecessor, working for lower tariffs. President Roosevelt also, as we have just seen, thinks that freer trading is essential to world recovery, political as well as economic. Congress passed, in 1934, an Act which allows the Government to negotiate, until the summer of 1937, reciprocal trade agreements for the betterment of the American export trade. About fourteen such agreements have been concluded, and it is likely that the life of the Act will be extended and its terms improved. The American trade agreements extend the reciprocal concessions they make to all countries which do not discriminate against the United States. This compromises the preferential results of the bilateral bargains less than might be expected, as each treaty naturally concerns products of which the signatories are the chief producers. Washington considers that we, by the manner in which we promote our bilateral trade treaties and above all by our quota system, are on the contrary working for preferential advantages rather than for the general expansion of trade. The results of the Ottawa Conference were also regarded as a step in the wrong direction. But, though there was at the time a certain movement in Congress to protest that our intra-Imperial agreements constituted discrimination on the part of the countries of the Commonwealth of a nature that the United States ought to resent and which might now be considered as discrimination within the meaning of the Reciprocal Trade Agreements Act, the general feeling of friendship and sympathy for the Empire prevented the movement from maturing.

Mr. Runciman's visit to Washington in January 1937 was therefore of great value and significance, despite the fact that no more than general and tentative approaches could be made towards an Anglo-American trade agreement. At least it cleared away doubts and suspicions by showing that the will to co-operate in economic affairs existed on both sides.

Proceedings at the Buenos Aires Conference and, still more, American comment upon them make it clear that the United States is out for all the trade that she can get in Latin America. So does the fact that about half of the American trade treaties are with Latin-American countries. This is a perfectly legitimate attitude. But it is also legitimate, and is recognized by the United States to be legitimate, for Great Britain and the other units of the Empire to do what they can to preserve and foster their own trade with that part of the world. In 1935, 15 per cent. of American exports, 22 per cent. of American imports, and 19 per cent. of the total American foreign trade was with the Latin-American countries. The Latin-American countries as a whole sent to the United States 28 per cent. of their exports in 1934, and received from that country 30 per cent. of their imports. For the countries of the Caribbean the figures were 55 and 57 per cent. The writer of the treatise from which the above figures have been taken[1] comments on them to the effect that the expansion of inter-American commerce is likely to be from now onwards the major economic problem for the western hemisphere in general and the United States in particular. 'The United States', he continues, 'is especially eager to rebuild its commerce with the Latin-American nations, reduced by the depression to less than pre-war figures. The growth of German and Japanese trade with certain countries of the area has also awakened apprehension in the United States.'

Mr. Neville Chamberlain in a speech towards the end of 1936 at Leeds[2] warned British manufacturers not to neglect trade with foreign countries in their preoccupation with domestic orders that a return of prosperity—and, he might have added, rearmament—are bringing them. Export trade, he said, when once lost was much more difficult to recover than home trade. In connexion with this warning the failure of the American commentator just quoted to mention Great Britain with Germany and Japan as a rival of whose competition the United States had to be afraid in her own hemisphere does not, if the bull may be allowed, make pleasant reading, especially in view of the fact that the British share of imports into South America dropped between 1913 and 1929 from about 25 per cent. to about 15 per cent., while the American share rose from about 25 per cent. to nearly 40 per cent.

[1] Charles A. Thompson, 'Towards a new Pan-Americanism', *American Foreign Policy Association Report*, 1 Nov. 1936.
[2] Reported in *The Times* of 20 Nov. 1936.

III

THE PROBLEM OF JAPAN

IN the Far East the League of Nations is as impotent as it is in the western hemisphere. But there the parallel ends. In the western hemisphere the League is superfluous because, as was shown in the last chapter, its principles and precepts are being effectively practised under other leadership than that of Geneva. In the Far East its writ fails to run because the controlling country there has no use for it.

Japan is even more definitely hostile to Geneva than Germany or Italy. Whereas Italy is still a member of the League and Germany has talked of coming back to it in certain circumstances, Japan has shown, so far, no sign of cancelling the resignation which she tendered in 1933 as the result of the protests which the League had made, in conjunction with the United States, against her seizure of Manchuria. On the contrary, her spokesmen have intimated that the guardianship of international peace in the Far East is her affair and not that of the League.

The United States was actively interested in the Manchurian business because Japan's coup had broken the Washington Nine Power Treaty signed at the Washington Naval Conference in 1922, of which she was a signatory, as well as the Covenant of the League. It broke the Covenant because Japan was pledged by her signature of it to respect and preserve the territorial integrity of China, who was a member of the League. It broke the Washington Nine Power Treaty because under it Japan had specifically undertaken to respect the territorial and political integrity of China in common with the United States, the British Empire, China herself, France, Italy, Holland, Belgium, and Portugal. The Washington Treaty also stipulates that all nations shall have equal rights in trade and industry in China. In Manchukuo the rights and opportunities of foreigners in those matters are now by no means equal to those of the Japanese; and, in regard to China as a whole, Tokyo has made it clear that it considers that its nationals are entitled to any preferential treatment that can be secured for them there. It has further sought to strengthen its position by denouncing (quite legally) the Washington Naval Treaty of 1922 under which Japan, in common with the United States, Great Britain, France, and Italy, undertook to limit the size and number of her large war-vessels.

Japan proposes to work both politically and economically to secure for herself a special position in the Far East and in China. Various factors impel her to this course, notably the economic pressures that are discussed later in Chapter V. So far, however, her penetration of China has not gone as well as it might have done. The Mongolian venture was in any case bound to bring but slow returns, and, however well it is consolidated, will never satisfy the economic needs of Japan. In northern China Japan seemed towards the end of 1936 to be in danger of something like a rebuff. The semi-independent Chinese Provincial Government which exists at Peking showed a marked reluctance to dance to tunes called in Tokyo. It seems to prefer those of the Chinese Central Government at Nanking. As this is written, not long after the Sianfu incident, with its hazy background of personalities and Oriental psychology, anti-Japanese feeling, and Communism, much in regard to the political future of China is obscure. The political crisis in Japan has only increased the fog through which the Western observer views the Far-Eastern scene. In both countries developments seem to be moving towards a show-down, in which the military resolution or otherwise of Japan would be matched against the political solidarity or otherwise of China.

All that can be said is that Japanese fear of Russia has slowed down the practical application of what has been called Japan's Monroe Doctrine for the Far East. The Japanese, like the Germans, now almost their allies, are essentially military-minded, and they have been disconcerted by the strides that Russia has made towards vast and apparently efficient armaments, by the discovery that she has unexpectedly strong forces in her eastern possessions, and, above all, by the realization that the Russian base at Vladivostok makes Japan particularly vulnerable to air attacks. But, if slowed down, Japanese expansion will not be abandoned. In fact, the more it is slowed down in the Far East, the more it may branch out into more distant channels. The economic urge behind it, strong enough in itself, is emphatically reinforced by national pride and by that same belief in the national destiny that is driving modern Germany and modern Italy into similar postures of explosiveness.

Japan, like those two countries, has not been kindly handled by the political circumstances of recent years. Like them, she came, from her own point of view, none too well out of the liquidation of the Great War. Or rather, she came badly out of the final liquidation; for in her case there were two peace settlements, one good and the other bad. The first was at the Paris Conference in 1919. The second was at the Washington Naval Conference. In the twenty-odd years between 1894 and 1918 Japan fought three wars. First she beat China; then at the beginning of the century she beat Russia; and, finally, she was with the victors in the Great War. Out of much of the fruits of her Chinese victory she was defrauded by Western, though not by British, diplomacy; her triumph over Russia gained her much prestige but less than she had hoped in territory. The Great War, on the other hand, seemed at first to have brought her profits out of all proportion to the risks and energy which she had put into it. While Europe was bleeding itself white upon its battlefields, Japan had captured the markets of her allies in the Far East and even outside it, and had gone far towards establishing a special position for herself in China. The Versailles Treaty consolidated her gains so thoroughly that China refused to sign it.

Japan's triumph and the great expectations which it generated were short-lived. Her industrial 'boom' went the way of other war prosperity; the Chinese made things difficult by their curious power of half-organized, half-instinctive popular resistance which they afterwards used against the British until Sir Austen Chamberlain added to the laurels which he gathered for himself at the Foreign Office by giving them tangible proof that we meant well and liberally by their national aspirations. Soviet Russia unexpectedly consolidated herself in the Far Eastern possessions of her Imperial predecessor.

And then came the Washington Conference. There, under the adroit leadership of Lord Balfour and Mr. Hughes, the American Secretary of State, the United States and Great Britain had one of their all-too-rare spasms of complete and effective co-operation. They arranged the Far East to suit themselves and their ideals. Japan was deprived of her Alliance with Great Britain, which since 1902 she had regarded as her certificate of membership of the Concert of the Great Powers. Great Britain had gone into that Alliance largely that she might concentrate her fleet in European waters to meet the then-nascent menace of German naval competition. That menace vanished when Germany signed the Treaty of Versailles, and Great Britain felt herself free to gratify the American desire for the abandonment of the Alliance. Then under Anglo-American pressure suavely applied Japan saw her position in China disappear, her special rights in Shantung, which the Peace Conference had confirmed, given up, her claim to a preferential treatment in China denied in the Nine Power Treaty, and finally her navy limited in the Washington Naval Treaty to the tune of three large ships for every five which the English-speaking Powers allowed themselves each to possess.

Morally and materially the Washington Treaties were as bitter a blow to Japan as two friendly nations have ever delivered against a third. The Japanese took it well. They had no choice. They were too weak to resist, and shortly afterwards their weakness was increased by the terrible earthquake of 1923. In 1924 came another humiliation. Since 1907 Japanese immigration into the United States had been limited by a so-called 'Gentleman's Agreement' under which the Japanese had loyally kept their emigration to the low level stipulated by the United States. Congress, however, suddenly in 1924 passed a law which replaced this agreement by regulations which the Japanese found extremely damaging to their pride. Canadian provincial legislation struck them a similar blow. In 1926 a further embarrassment began to threaten. There seemed a chance that China might go Bolshevist. The ferment, it is true, bore most hardly upon British interests and rather helped Japan by deflecting to her some of our trade. But the Japanese took a long view. Their future, they felt, depended upon their position in the Far East and upon the maintenance and development of their trade with China, both of which would be compromised if Moscow controlled China. A new tariff law recently passed in the United States heavily penalizing their products strengthened that view.

Nevertheless, then and for some years afterwards Japan continued to be a model citizen of the world. She was at least as patient as the United States and Great Britain towards the Chinese disturbances; she worked hard to promote her trade abroad by good political relationships; she was an admirable member of the League of Nations. Then the violently patriotic element, helped by the growth of grievance and discomfort, gained the upper hand; admirals and generals imposed their will upon the liberal and patient statesmen who had been ruling the country, and the people were made ripe for their piratical leadership by the dislocations and despairs of the economic depression. What justification, it was asked, when Geneva invoked the Covenant of the League, and London and Washington the Nine Power Treaty, against the rape of Manchuria, had the Western world, after barring Japanese settlers from its territories, to turn round and deny to Japan her right to exploit her own corner of the globe in any way she liked? Why should not Asia be for the Asiatics as much as North America for the Americans and Canadians or Australia for the Australians? Why should the white races sprawl at will all over the world and deny to an Oriental race the right to expand across a narrow sea into another Oriental land?

The admirals and generals may to-day be less powerful than they were a few years ago. Japanese plans in regard to China may not be maturing as had been hoped. But Japanese expansionism has come to stay. It has the sanction of economic necessity. The sense of racial and national destiny behind it is just as strong as that which exists in Germany or in Italy. Its advocates preach not that Japan is the equal of the white races but that she is their superior, just as German 'racialism' proclaims that of the chosen Aryan race Germans are the chosen tribe.

'Only the realization that the one and absolute sovereignty is vested in Heaven, and that on behalf of Heaven, a certain nation shall be entrusted with the performance of this sovereignty for the benefit of all mankind, can pave the way to final world peace and international co-operation.'

These words were penned not by a Nazi propagandist but by a Japanese philosopher.[1] China has already felt the impact of this expansionism. The British Commonwealth, the United States, and the Soviet Union may all find their vital interests threatened by it. What is the answer to the threat? It is not the League of Nations, for the League of Nations was brought to nullity in the Far East when the United States and Great Britain showed at the time of the Manchurian affair that they were not prepared to defend by force of arms the *status quo* which the League and the Nine Power Treaty guaranteed. Nor does it seem as likely as it once did that Japanese plans might be wrecked by the armed opposition of the Soviet Union. The steadily growing strength of Russia tends to drive the Japanese southwards. A continuation of that tendency might in the end mean war between Japan and the United States or the British Empire or both, brought on by a Japanese threat to Hong Kong and Singapore, the Philippines and Hawaii, and upon all that lies behind those outposts. Such an event would indeed portend the final bankruptcy of the Pacific policy of the Western Powers. There is, however, no reason why it should be inevitable if the Western Powers in general and the British Empire in particular would approach the Japanese problem in a positive, constructive, and sympathetic fashion. Japan's economic difficulties must be recognized. It must be recognized that she, like Germany and Italy in Europe, came late

---

[1] Quoted in *The Fortnightly*, Jan. 1936, from *Japanese and Oriental Political Philosophy*, by Chakao Fujisawa.

into the race for the possession of the wider and emptier parts
of the world with the result that she is hard pressed for elbow-
room and feels herself the victim of inequitable restrictions.
It must be recognized also that recently these restrictions,
if relieved at any rate in theory by the acquisition of Manchuria, have been aggravated by the tariffs, quotas, and other
impediments which the countries of the Empire in common
with the rest of the world have placed in the way of international trade.

The examination of what the Empire can do to that end,
both alone and in conjunction with other countries, belongs
to subsequent chapters in this volume. Here it need only be
pointed out that, if Japan could be given the same freedom
of entry into the markets of the world as we, also, need if we
are to acquire anything like a permanent and full measure
of prosperity, two things might well supervene. Her pressure
on China might relax and her nationalism become less
dangerously dynamic. Strong as the almost mystical urge
towards a pan-Asiatic policy has become, there is still in
Japan a large party who might be able to allay the present
dangerous wave of emotionalism if they could point out that
the Western Powers were ready to abandon the dog-in-the-
mangerish policy of which Japanese opinion now accuses
them.

IV

OUR STATE IN EUROPE

EUROPE is the heart of our civilization. Expectations, held especially in the Dominions and the United States after the War, that the Pacific would soon vie with it as the centre of gravity of international politics have not been realized. It remains the economic pivot of the globe. India and China may be more populous, the United States may be as rich, but the demands of the continental countries upon the outside world are still the heaviest. For that reason they alone, or rather their prosperity, are of the greatest moment to the Empire. Should the confusion of their politics, to say nothing of economic nationalism, continue to impede the slow economic recovery that some of them are now enjoying, then the industrial prosperity of Great Britain will also be impeded and the problem of the disposal of their raw materials be doubly aggravated for the Dominions.

Despite her troubles, Europe actually, at this moment, takes more of our goods than any other part of the world. She is to us what its home community is to a great department store; and, if they are wise, the directors of such a store expend hardly less thought and energy upon promoting the prosperity of the community than they do upon their own business. Should another great war come to Europe, its effect upon the Empire might, after perhaps a burst of delusively prosperous war trade, be disastrous. It would mean either a long-drawn struggle with victory for nobody and chaos, social, political, and economic for everybody, or it would mean swift victory for some well-prepared aggressor. The second contingency would leave the Continent under the dominance of a single ambitious Power, a situation which it has always been our policy to avoid, by war if necessary; the first contingency would mean a grievous loss of trade for the whole Empire, and for Great Britain the added danger of slipping into the chaos.

Great Britain is an integral part of both Europe and the Empire. She is and for a long time must be the centre and leader of the Empire. She holds this position by virtue of wealth and population. Hard upon half the white population of the Empire still lives within her narrow limits. If Europe is the Empire's best customer, a great part of what the Empire sends to Europe goes to Great Britain. London, too, remains the centre of Imperial finance.

In the present state of Europe and with the League of Nations as weak as it is, the chances of localizing a war would certainly be no better than they were in 1914. And if a general war started England would almost certainly be drawn in, however remotely its origins might have touched her interests. In any case, as has just been said, she would share its disastrous social and political consequences. Her weakness would be the weakness of the Empire. Without her the Empire would tend to degenerate into a collection of minor States. In the Pacific the United States and Japan would then be the two countries to count. Over much of the rest of the world the United States would be the dominant Power. In Asia and in the waters and lands to the south of Asia the forward party in Japan would be in an immeasurably better position to turn into a reality their dream of an Asia for the Asiatics. The Empire is thus vitally concerned in the peace and prosperity of Europe, and in the continued ascendancy of Great Britain as an effective European Power.

If in times of stress like the present Europe is the danger-centre of the world, so even in quieter times she is and must remain its nerve-centre. In 1931 the collapse of the pound sterling and exaggerated accounts of mutinous discontent in a few British warships in a secluded Scottish inlet was the signal for the first overt move by the Japanese towards the separation of Manchuria from China. Italy's dissatisfaction with things in Europe caused war in Africa and roused the Empire to anxiety for the safety of its great line of communication through the Mediterranean. Scarcely had tension between ourselves and Italy been relaxed than civil war in Spain renewed this anxiety in a different form. And so it is bound to be now that science has closed up distances as a man closes up a telescope.

The 'power politics' of the dictatorships are the immediate, though by no means the sole, reason for the major distempers of Europe. The picture of the Continent divided into approximately the same armed camps as those from which the nations marched to war in 1914 has been too often painted to demand detailed reproduction. It is enough that Germany, discontented and expansionist, teaching her people that they are a race marked out by Providence for leadership, strong in spirit, armaments, and industries, and growing quickly stronger, has been in the last few years conducting a diplomacy as provocative and as disquieting as she did in the years preceding 1914; that Russia and France are again nervously banded together in a posture of defence which Germany again interprets to her people as being one of deliberate encirclement; that both sides are jockeying for allies and competing ruthlessly in their military preparations; and that once more Great Britain, though sympathizing with France, and through France linked in uneasy friendship with Russia, is anxiously trying to ease the tension.

Germany has a considerable degree of right on her side. The inequalities of the Treaty of Versailles were not such as she could be expected to continue to bear, and she still has colourable economic grievances. Italy had justification for the discontent and restlessness which led to the crowning illegality of her attack on Abyssinia. Nor would it be fair to accuse either country of deliberately planning a European war. Though they glorify force and drill their youth by the million to practise it, though they sneer at peace and at the League of Nations, both Herr Hitler and Signor Mussolini constantly assure the world that the last thing that they want is such a war. There is no reason to doubt the sincerity of those assurances. They and their countrymen know just as well as we do the destructive horrors of modern intensive warfare. But neither that nor anything else that the spokesmen of Berlin or Rome can say alters the fact that power politics are dangerous. It is said that after he had announced in 1935 his first great infraction of the Treaty of Versailles in the shape of his decision to have all the Army, Navy, and Air Force that he needed, Herr Hitler and a group of his confidants sat up all night fearing a message that the French had crossed the frontier to apply sanctions. It is said also that after the second great German infraction of the Treaty almost exactly a year later, when Herr Hitler marched his troops into the demilitarized zone of the Rhineland, Paris did for a moment seriously consider some such action. On either occasion the moving of French troops across the frontier would have meant war. That is the peril of power politics. Sooner or later a country or countries may refuse to be bluffed. Then war is almost inevitable; and, if the bluffer climbs down, he is likely to do so only in order to prepare a bigger, better, and more dangerous bluff.

The stability of Europe was, for the first fifteen years after the War, based upon the weakness of Germany or, to put it the other way round, upon the strength of France and her allies. The drive and efficiency with which Herr Hitler and his party have built up the material and military strength of Germany and the cool courage with which they have conducted their foreign policy has destroyed that stability. For the present an uneasy Balance of Power may keep the peace. But even if it is not destroyed by some power policy explosion, that equilibrium must at best remain precarious. The speed of Germany's recovery has been astonishing. At home, when Herr Hitler came into office four years ago, her plight seemed desperate. Trade and industry had gone to bits; six million unemployed walked the streets; hundreds of thousands of upper- and middle-class youth felt condemned to hopeless idleness. Abroad, Germany was of comparatively little account in the high affairs of Europe. She was ringed round. On the west France watched her with hostility and suspicion. In the east Poland and the countries of the Little Entente, Czechoslovakia, Yugoslavia, and Rumania, were all allied with France. Italy was not particularly her friend. Even in 1934 Signor Mussolini turned away from the meeting which he had with Herr Hitler in Venice with a gesture of contemptuous superiority. In central and south-eastern Europe France was still in the ascendancy, with Italy coming up, and the Powers were scolding Herr Hitler for making propaganda in Austria just as a farmer might scold a boy who was hanging about his orchard.

How different is the situation at the beginning of 1937. Internally, Germany is vibrant with controlled and purposeful energy. Unemployment has been reduced to manageable proportions. A formerly dispirited and humiliated population have for the most part been given a militant belief in their country's future. Abroad, Herr Hitler's diplomacy has advanced from objective to objective with what has been called a 'majestic and measured tranquillity'. The description may seem inapt in view of the blatant trappings in which that diplomacy is invested, in view, for instance, of the vituperative fireworks with which even the Führer does not at times scorn to illuminate it. But it is essentially just. Having smashed the worst inequalities of the Treaty of Versailles by official rearmament in 1935 and by his Demilitarized Zone coup early in 1936, Herr Hitler turned to eastern and south-eastern Europe. He sided overtly with the Nazi Government of Danzig in its controversy with the League of Nations. He sent his chief economic authority, Dr. Schacht, upon a tour of the Balkan and Danubian States and later to Turkey and even Persia in order to make propaganda and collect trade. His Propaganda Minister, Herr Goebbels, has been equally active and is said among other things to have bought for Germany the friendship of some three-score newspapers in eastern and south-eastern Europe. Helped by these and other measures of carefully calculated prestige propaganda and also by subsidies, German trade and influence along the Danube have increased in a manner highly encouraging to Berlin and highly disconcerting to the French, who have lost in those parts much of their old ascendancy. It has been estimated that in subsidies for her exports to these and other places Germany spent in 1936 not far short of £100,000,000. This is about the sum which she would have been paying in reparations under the Young scheme. In other words, she is now exporting abroad at her own expense and for her own good just about the same amount of goods as she would have been doing had she still been paying reparations.

Italy also has been made to play second fiddle to Herr Hitler's tunes. Signor Mussolini, in spite of the fact that the main motive of his European policy had so far been to minimize German influence in Austria and to keep her closely tied to Italy, was forced to bless the Austro-German reconciliation, with its possibilities of increased Nazi influence in Austria, as a 'notable step forward on the road to the reconstruction of Europe and of the Danubian countries'. That was in the summer of 1936. During the preceding winter Germany had registered sympathy with Italy's Abyssinian adventure. Her exports to Italy of materials useful for war increased considerably, and on the trucks that took them across the Alps messages friendly to Italy were sometimes scrawled. Italy on her side modified her embargo upon exports, notably in the case of hemp, in favour of Germany. Later on in the year two Italo-German conventions were signed, one for the benefit of trade between the two countries and one for the improvement of air travel between them and for the exchange of certain privileges in aviation matters. In the autumn there was a joint declaration in which Germany recognized the Italian Empire of Abyssinia, and Italy and Germany both noted the concurrence of their interests and their desire to collaborate. There was also a statement that in regard to the Spanish War the two countries stood together as backers of the revolutionaries. A little later Austria and Hungary also recognized the Abyssinian Empire.

Whereas three years ago Herr Hitler used German ambitions in Austria as a spur to German patriotism and Signor Mussolini used the necessity of safeguarding Austria from Germany as a spur to Italian patriotism, now both dictators point to Russia as the enemy outside the gates and to Communism as the enemy within the gates. But the possession of a common bugbear need not mean any real sympathy, and it is probably accurate to interpret the new German-Italian friendship as an indication less of a dictatorial alliance than of the growing supremacy of Germany. Signor Mussolini was, of course, encouraged to attack Abyssinia by the impunity with which Japan and Germany had defied the League, but it is also possible that the attack was in part prompted by the realization that Germany was eclipsing him in Europe and by his desire to distract attention from his discomfiture by a spectacular colonial venture. In Germany, contemptuous memories of the Italian 'betrayal' of 1914, when Italy, in spite of her place in the Triple Alliance, refused to join the Central Powers, are by no means dead; and it would be surprising if in Italy anything but anxiety were felt at the activity of Nazi propagandists in the Tyrol and other limitrophe Austrian provinces and even, it is said, among the German population of the Italian Tyrol.

But, though the cement of real friendship may be absent from Italo-German relations forceful power is what counts in these days, and the more Germany dominates the European stage the more likely Italy is, especially now that she has the pacification of Abyssinia on her hands, to march in step with German diplomacy.

We do not grudge Germany her progress. She is entitled by virtue of her size, strength, efficiency, and geographical position to a place in the front rank of the Powers. Her recent infractions of the Treaty of Versailles are not seriously held against her by the British peoples. When she decided to rearm the general feeling throughout the Empire was that we should have done the same in her place. When she marched into the Demilitarized Zone not an Englishman would have marched to turn her out again. It was felt that to tell Germany that she was to be the equal of other nations as the Versailles Powers had been doing for some time past and at the same time to deny her the right to quarter troops in part of her territory was out of date to the verge of absurdity and provocative to the verge of danger. Still less was resentment felt at Germany's repudiation, towards the end of 1936, of the control established by the Treaty of Versailles over the navigation of the Kiel Canal and certain of the great German rivers which are international waterways.

Nor is her internal government any concern of ours, incompatible as its form is with our political philosophy and abhorrent as many of its methods are to our sense of humanity. Tolerance of other forms of government abroad is the complement of our love of free institutions at home. All that we ask is that the authoritarian States should not try to export their creeds where they are not wanted, and we are not prepared to take very seriously such encouragement as Nazis or Fascists may have been giving to the antics of Sir Oswald Mosley.

Germany's neighbours, unfortunately, take, for reasons with which we are bound to sympathize, a less complacent view of the rise of the Third Reich. One is reminded as one examines the relations of France and Germany and of Germany and Russia of Lessing's remark that the 'essence of tragedy is not a clash between right and wrong but a clash between two rights'. The average German is convinced that Russia means to try to smash his country, certainly by Communist penetration and, if she gets the chance, by arms as well; secondly, that both Russia and France are concentrated upon ringing it round and keeping it out of the economic sun. In that connexion it must be remembered that every German believes that Franco-Russian encirclement was the cause of war in 1914 and that Russian mobilization made war inevitable. The French people are certain that they are right in fearing a war of revenge. They note that Herr Hitler in *Mein Kampf* speaks of their country as the 'deadly enemy'. The Russians note that Herr Hitler and his propagandists are for ever harping upon Germany's need for sources of raw material and food. They read in *Mein Kampf* Herr Hitler's dictum that, if Germany ever does need new lands to give her such things, she must carve them out of Russia. They see Germany rearming; they hear Herr Hitler and his mouthpieces shrieking in speech after speech and article after article that Russia is the enemy; they see him drawing closer and closer to Japan, an equally expansionist and military nation, equally ruthless in its methods, and their declared rival in the Far East; they read that he has concluded a treaty with Tokyo of which the terms are overtly offensive to them and the spirit covertly menacing.

For France especially the situation is tragically disquieting. Three times in the last 150 years the French and Germans, sworn enemies through the centuries, have been at each others' throats. On the first two occasions the French were beaten; on the third they won after a terrible ordeal, splendidly endured. And now the fruits of their victory are crumbling away into discomfiture and doubt. Though they took territory from her and otherwise tried to weaken her, Germany is to-day as strong and menacing as ever. Undoubtedly the French have made mistakes in their treatment of her. Poincaréism was a terrible handicap to the Weimar Republic; during the Disarmament Conference several chances of compromise were missed. But it is no use telling Frenchmen that. Most of them do not believe it and those who do consider not without some justice that their mistakes were largely our fault—an argument which, with its background, will be dealt with later. For the present we are only concerned with the immediate results of this deadlock of convinced dislike and suspicion.

It is a deadlock that has to be faced. There are those who think that it may be solved by the collapse of Nazi Germany, probably for economic reasons. That is possible but not probable. Nor is it a contingency to be light-heartedly desired. Its realization might well render the present confusions worse confounded and even more dangerous, for a stable Germany is essential for the stability of the Continent. The Nazi Party, moreover, is very strongly entrenched, and if economic calamity threatened it, it might prefer the gamble of a war of aggression to a tame acceptance of domestic defeat. The constant harping upon their need for colonies, for sources of supply, and for markets by the most efficient propaganda machine in the world has convinced the German people that they would be justified in exploding if nothing is done by other countries to relieve the pressure. The speeches of Sir Samuel Hoare, Mr. Eden, and others to the effect that Germany's claims for more economic elbow-room should be sympathetically examined, carefully phrased though they have been, have increased this belief. Nothing so far has come of them, and German opinion more and more feels that the British statesmen lack either sincerity or the authority to make the French and the other 'hemmers-in' listen to them.

That we may be unable to persuade France and the frightened countries to make economic concessions to Germany as things stand is indeed only too possible. Those countries argue that the weakness of the League of Nations leaves them no choice but to strengthen their defences. And what, they ask, is the good of strengthening themselves against a potential enemy if at the same time they strengthen that enemy by increasing his wealth and economic resources? Here, again, is Balance of Power politics in its purest form, as dangerous to the peace of Europe as the German and Italian policy of doing a thing and daring the other side to undo it.

If in Europe half Germany's energy goes to the welding of a zone of influence in the centre and south-east, the other half has been expended in diplomatic efforts to break up what she considers to be the opposing *bloc*, to weaken the Franco-Russian entente, to discourage Great Britain from taking an interest in central Europe, and to drive wedges between Great Britain and France. She has used the Spanish Civil War to try to stir up a Communist scare in western Europe and to persuade British and French opinion that Russia cannot be trusted, that the real function of Germany is to spread herself and her influence across the Continent as a bulwark against Bolshevism, just as she has tried to immobilize Russia by her anti-Communist treaty with Japan.

And all the time the race in armaments gathers speed and intensity. In the last twelve months Russia has strengthened her already vast forces against Germany's colossal programme; the Left Government of France has followed its predecessors of the Right and Centre in increasing the effectiveness of the French armaments and has been courting Poland, who had been leaning towards Germany; Signor Mussolini, stimulated by his Abyssinian success, has said things to the effect that 8,000,000 Italian bayonets were the best contribution he could make to the cause of peace; Belgium and the smaller countries, not excluding the remote and peaceful democracies of the north-west, are refurbishing their defences. All this enhances the menace of both planned and accidental warfare. Lord Grey of Falloden has recorded his considered opinion that the 'real and final account of the origin of the Great War' is to be found in armaments. He wrote also as follows:

'. . . great armaments lead inevitably to war. If there are armaments on one side, there must be armaments on other sides.

While one nation arms, other nations cannot tempt it to aggression by remaining defenceless. . . . Each measure taken by one nation is noted and leads to counter-measures by others.

'The increase of armaments that is intended in each nation to produce consciousness of strength and a sense of security does not produce those effects. On the contrary it produces a consciousness of the strength of other nations and a sense of fear. Fear begets suspicion and mistrust and evil imaginings of all sorts till each Government feels it would be criminal and a betrayal of its own country not to take every precaution, while every Government regards every precaution of every other Government as evidence of hostile intent.'[1]

Nor is it only the sense of insecurity and fear that breeds war as armaments grow. The stronger nations believe themselves to be, the more inclined some are to bluff and others to call their bluff, a process which, as just said, may easily produce war. And though for the moment the manufacture of armaments is producing prosperity in many countries and especially in Germany, what will happen when Europe is fully rearmed? The time must come sooner or later when factories will be closed and men laid off and dividends passed. Then may follow an economic crisis which might produce an aggressive war or a chaos almost as bad as war. Herr Hitler, it must be repeated, has often, and with a sincerity which cannot be questioned, said that the one thing which he wishes to avoid is another war. But on the very first page of *Mein Kampf* there appears this passage: 'Only when the Reich contains the whole German race and can no longer assure all its people their food, will the needs of the people establish the moral right to win foreign soil. The ploughshare can then be beaten into the sword and from the tears of war will spring for posterity its daily bread.'

Mein Kampf was written long ago and it would be unfair to hold its author to all that he says in it. But the above passage, like the others here mentioned, has been so often paraphrased and repeated by the moulders of modern German opinion that it cannot be ignored. Its threat is, of course, against Russia. But it is not only Russia whom German

[1] Lord Grey of Falloden, *Twenty Five Years*, vol. i, p. 91.

expansionism in the east and centre of Europe might concern. It might concern the Empire almost as directly as a German thrust to the Channel and the North Sea would do. Herr Hitler, it is true, did not, when he wrote *Mein Kampf*, think that colonies were important. 'Expansion', he said, 'must be in Europe rather than over sea. Shouting for another fleet or for the winning back of the German colonies worries England, whom Germany needs as a friend.'

It is possible that those are still his views—on the Navy question, anyhow, he has come to terms with us—and that, as some think, the current agitation for colonies among his countrymen has been designed partly to stimulate German nationalism and partly to give Germany something she may renounce to please us if she wants to try to buy our tolerance for another forward move on the Continent, and to furnish an excuse for that move.

Be that as it may, the situation might become menacing were Germany, by the peaceful continuation of her present tactics or even by successful war, to consolidate her hegemony over those parts of Europe between the Baltic, the eastern Mediterranean, and the Aegean. It would not be a question of picking up a few colonies, which all sensible Germans know would not do them much good economically. It would once more be the vision of 'world dominance or downfall' which was one of the things that urged the pre-War German expansionists to risk and lose the gamble of 1914. Once more Herr Hitler's hands might be forced by the extremists as those of the Kaiser were in those days. Germany would then be at least as strong as she was in 1914 and we should be among those whom her move would menace, even if it were confined to the south-east of Europe and the Near East.

Mr. Eden told the House of Commons not long ago that the Mediterranean is for the Empire 'not a short cut but an arterial route'. As everybody knows, it has long been the centre of a continuous struggle between the Powers for strategic posts. All through the last century, even before the Suez Canal existed, our diplomacy was constantly engaged in preventing Russia from gaining free access to it in the East and thus putting herself athwart our communications. We hold Gibraltar to guard the western entrance of the sea, and our relations with Egypt for the last two generations have been dominated by our desire to be in a position to protect the Suez Canal. Until recently France, our firm friend and trusted ally, was the only other country that has counted on the Mediterranean. Now Italy has come into the picture.

Italy, said Signor Mussolini, in a speech[1] not long after his Abyssinian triumph, is an island which stretches into the Mediterranean.

For Great Britain, that area was but one of many routes—'indeed a short cut by which the British Empire can reach its outlying territories'. To which Mr. Eden replied that 'freedom of communication in these waters is a vital interest in a full sense of the word to the British Commonwealth of Nations'. This exchange was the signal for the opening of discussions in Rome which culminated, at the beginning of 1937, in the publication of an Anglo-Italian accord on the Mediterranean policy. The accord declares that the two countries

'Recognize that the freedom of entry into, exit from and transit through, the Mediterranean is a vital interest both to the different parts of the British Empire and to Italy, and that these interests are in no way inconsistent with each other;

'Disclaim any desire to modify, or, so far as they are concerned, to see modified, the *status quo* as regards national sovereignty of territory in the Mediterranean areas;

'Undertake to respect each other's rights and interests in the said area;

'Agree to use their best endeavours to discourage any activities liable to impair the good relations which it is the object of the present declaration to consolidate.

The accord, and the accompanying undertaking by Italy to eschew territorial change especially in the Balearics, as a result of the Spanish war, useful as they may have been, must not be taken at more than their face value. They left the strategic needs and political principles of the British Empire in the Mediterranean unchanged. They equally left unrescinded all that Signor Mussolini has said or caused

[1] At Milan, 1 Nov. 1936.

to be said about the Mediterranean being once more the Roman sea that it used to be in classical days, and above all in the light of his obvious desire to see established in Spain a sympathetic, and if possible subservient, government. It means that, until conditions in Europe are stabilized and until the rule of international decency is secured in its remoter parts, our Mediterranean front is just as open, perhaps more open, to attack than what Mr. Baldwin has called our new defensive frontier on the Rhine. As things are going to-day, Germany may come down to the Aegean and the Dardanelles prepared to march towards the East, and, whatever may have happened to Spain, Italy will be at least as strongly entrenched in the centre of the Mediterranean as she was when the threat of her armed displeasure deterred the National Government from advocating effective sanctions for the defeat of her attack on Abyssinia.

However much we may strengthen the Navy and the Air Force, the fact remains that Italy can keep all her forces in the Mediterranean while we shall have to keep no inconsiderable part of ours nearer home and also, in present circumstances, in the Far East. Considerations of security as well as of trade and prosperity thus compel the Empire to regard as a paramount interest the peaceful stabilization of the whole of Europe, after such changes have been made as are necessary to meet the legitimate demands of the dissatisfied countries.

V

THE ECONOMIC BACKGROUND

THE present crisis in world affairs, as we have seen, is a tangle of economic and political troubles. The merest glance at recent history shows how closely those two groups of causes are entwined. Post-War economic history may be divided into three phases, each of them five or six years in length: the aftermath of the War, unstable recovery, and depression. Political history followed precisely the same general course. In the early phase, while currencies were collapsing, while war-time distortion of industry was bearing its fruit of mass unemployment, while the new States were struggling to maintain themselves in adverse economic circumstances which the peace settlement itself had helped to create, the outstanding events in European politics were the Ruhr invasion, the Fascist revolution in Italy, and a series of minor threats to peace which were more than once bought off at the price of justice. It was a world still dominated by the emotions of the War and the dislocations of the Peace.

Then came a period of hope and calm. Typical on the political side were the Locarno settlement, the admission of Germany to the League, and the preliminary efforts towards general arms limitation. Typical on the economic side were the stabilization of currencies (the Reichsmark in 1924, the French franc in 1926–8), the expansion of international trade, and the enormous flow of capital from creditor to debtor countries, both in Europe and in the New World. But the economic recovery was unstable, partly because of the normal swing of the trade-cycle, but more especially because of the distortions and disturbances of the economic system that had been caused by the War or its consequences, and had often been exaggerated rather than relieved by the terms of the peace. On the economic side the post-War settlement was thoroughly bad. The ignoring of President Wilson's Economic Point when the map of Europe was redrawn and the League of Nations created meant giving a free hand to economic nationalism in a hothouse of national egoism. The multiplication of sovereign States, the partition of former economic unities, the unemployment and loss of capital due to the collapse of inflated war industries, all these things entailed more and higher barriers to world trade. By contrast, the payment of reparations and war debts even on a moderate scale required comparative freedom of world trade if it was to be economically possible. The scale of reparations actually demanded was not moderate but fantastically high. Not only was default inevitable; the consequences of the effort to pay and of the distraint when payment could no longer be made spread disastrously through the whole economic system.

These troubles were merely hidden by the blanket of apparent prosperity from 1925 onwards. Reparations were indeed moderated, but they were in effect paid by Germany, not out of her own resources, but out of the money she borrowed abroad for industry and public works. Other countries, too, glutted themselves on the stream of American and British capital. But the whole structure was artificial, because the borrowed money served to inflate and distort the tariff-bound economies of the borrowers, while the tariffs of the lenders ensured that the service of loans could not be paid except from the proceeds of further investment. And so *ad infinitum*. Free capital movement and barricaded trade spell disaster sooner or later, and this was no exception to the rule. It was the boom rather than the crash on the American stock exchange that pricked the bubble; for it dried up the stream of lending, forced monetary restriction and still higher tariffs on every borrower, and laid the seeds of the British monetary failure of 1931.

With the economic collapse came political disorder. Japanese and Italian aggression, the Nazi revolution, civil war in Spain, these were typical of the depression phase. What comes next? Let us not be too optimistic, for a start, about the political consequences of the recent improvement in trade, production, and finance. By itself, world economic recovery cannot solve the major problems of current world politics. It does, however, give us a far better opportunity for solving them. Economic improvement cannot, for instance, do away with Germany's militarism and faith in force, which seem to be permanent national characteristics; but in company with the relaxation of economic nationalism that it makes possible it can lessen the sense of constriction and injustice on which that militarism fattens. And if economic recovery proceeds faster outside Germany's financial and economic barricades than inside—which seems very likely—it may enhance the attraction of freedom and democracy themselves.

This was surely the real significance of the Anglo-Franco-American currency agreement of September 1936 as a factor in world politics. It was not a snook cocked at other folk who choose Saturdays for sudden pounces of policy; but it did offer an opportunity for proving that international co-operation, relative freedom of trade, and political neighbour-liness are able to produce economic prosperity beyond the grasp of nations that live by self-sufficiency at home and threats abroad. Unhappily, there is still some danger that the British Government may turn its back on this oppor-tunity, for no better reason than a narrow-headed insularity that poses as nationalism, even as imperialism. But of that more later.

The more hopeful opportunity opened up by world re-covery is the positive aspect of the link between economics and the political crisis. The negative aspect is the degree in which adverse economic factors have caused that crisis and are still intensifying it. Much of the common argument on this point is caused by confusion between immediate and distant causes. Thus it may be true at one and the same time that war is inevitably caused by economic troubles (the Marxist would say by the inherent defects and contradictions of capitalism), and that no major war ever arose out of an economic dispute. Looked at in one light, the chief conflicts of national purpose that threaten war to-day are not primarily conflicts of economic interest. Germany is not quarrelling with Russia over markets, nor yet (despite Herr Hitler's covetous phrases about the Ukraine) over sources of economic wealth. Intervention in Spain or Czechoslovakia does not betray a competitive quest either for purchasing power or for materials to purchase. And so on for other danger-spots.

E

But go back a little farther along the chain of causes. Is it only a coincidence that the present phase of world-wide danger began in the worst moments of the economic crisis, between 1931 and 1933? How much of his power does Herr Hitler owe to the inflation of 1923, to the later deflation (both aggravated by the reparations pressure), and to the drying-up after 1929 of the stream of foreign loans that for five years had enabled Germany to live on the wealth of the world? Economic difficulties may not, indeed, be the proximate causes of war; but they create conditions under which dictatorships rise and flourish, and later the dictators can persuade their people and themselves that war is better than economic stagnation and the menace that economic discontent points at their own régime.

The force and immediacy of economic causes are not uniform, but vary widely in different patches of the world crisis. Economic difficulties appear nearer to the surface in the problem of Japan, for instance, than in the problem of Germany. Japan has a population of 70 millions at a density per square mile of rather more than two-thirds of the density in England and Wales. But in order to get the comparison right we must remember that a large part of Japan is barren and mountainous, that the population is increasing at the rate of 800,000 a year compared with something approaching stability in Great Britain, that Japan is even less well provided than Great Britain with industrial raw materials, having little iron or coal, that outside Korea with its 23 million inhabitants she has but a very small colonial empire to afford her privileged markets, and that, although her mercantile marine is substantial, her invisible income from overseas is tiny compared with the quarter of a billion sterling annually gathered in by Great Britain in shipping earnings and interest and dividends on capital abroad.

These facts make it clear, to any one who knows Great Britain's own periodical anxiety about her balance of trade, that the pressure upon Japanese economy is heavy and continuous. Her endeavours to secure export markets reflect, not spite against commercial rivals, but an urgent and compelling need. Her low standard of life is not so much a cause of her economic success as a result of her economic difficulties. National standard of life is only another name for national income per head, and Japan can maintain and increase her national income only by maintaining and increasing her external trade, both inward and outward. The greater the difficulties she finds in exporting, and therefore in paying for her imports, the lower will her standard of life be driven. Only through an expansion of her external trade can Japan develop a larger market for imported goods and raise her national standard closer to the level maintained by her competitors.

The precise connexion between economic forces and the Manchurian adventure can be estimated only by an expert historian of the Far East. Few people would deny an indirect connexion, that is to say, a manifestation of general economic difficulty in an impulse to break out somehow. But a direct connexion is a more doubtful matter; for not only has the adventure been frowned upon by the manufacturing and merchanting interests who would have been the first to welcome it had the objective really been economic; the results themselves have so far confirmed them in their antipathy. In Manchuria and Mongolia, Japan has indeed brought under her control new markets, in which she can assure herself a privileged position, and new sources of certain raw materials. Yet this has spelt no obvious relief to her economic problem. Why? In the first place, the resources of the provinces she has occupied, though substantial, are not such as to cause a sudden revolution in the economy of the Japanese empire. This is one of the reasons for the continued pressure outwards through Mongolia against the ramp of Soviet influence; for the great reserve of industrial raw materials in 'east Asia' is in the north Chinese provinces of Shensi and Shansi, and its exploitation in the interests of Japan demands a strong strategic frontier to the north and west.

In the second place, the resources available are not ready to be plucked like ripe fruit from trees. Their exploitation needs time; it needs heavy capital equipment and continuous expenditure. Inside or outside the Japanese military ring they have to be paid for, in real costs and in money. That means, in effect, sending goods in return—which brings us to the third reason why Japan's economic problem has not been solved by her conquest of Manchuria. The invaded territories are no exception to the rule that in order to import a country must export, unless the balance is made up by 'invisible' transactions (i.e. services, interest payments, capital borrowing). If Manchukuo and north China turn out to be a disappointing market, they must also be disappointing in relation to Japanese needs for raw materials.

At this point it seems necessary to set the economic facts of the Asiatic problem in proper perspective. For the British Empire it is far less important than the parallel problem of Europe, which, as has been pointed out in an earlier chapter, remains the political and economic focus of world affairs. In 1935 British exports to China and Japan totalled less than £10 millions, whereas British exports to European countries exceeded £140 millions. Even for Australia, from whom Japan and China buy a great deal of primary produce, east Asia is a less important market than north-west Europe outside Great Britain. At the same time, for Japan herself east Asia means much less, in economic terms, than is sometimes imagined. In 1934 the whole of China accounted for barely 5 per cent. of Japanese foreign trade, both imports and exports. British India was twice as important as China on either side of the account. Japan sold well over three times as much to the United States as to her great continental neighbour, and bought from her over five times as much.

Unless, therefore, China and Manchukuo can themselves be made very much wealthier, they can help only fractionally in easing Japan's economic task. With the steady increase of her population, that task certainly grows no lighter. Should it become oppressive, the reactions in the form of lowered standard of life, unemployment, and capital losses are likely to produce a fresh eruption of aggressive national ambition. The forward policy in east Asia is not, fundamentally, an alternative to Japanese expansionism in other directions. In its economic aspect it is a symptom—for Europe, a relieving symptom—of deep-seated trouble that by itself it cannot cure, and that may produce like symptoms elsewhere.

There is a plain lesson here for the rest of the world—particularly for the British Empire and the United States, who would be the first to feel the strain if Japanese expansionism were to veer southwards. To raise fresh barriers to Japanese trade is economically futile and politically suicidal. The continuous aim should be a mutual relaxation of obstacles to trade, both tariffs and quotas.

Our Chinese policy is equally important in the same connexion. China is perhaps the greatest of the undeveloped markets of the world. Provided its political consolidation continues, its prime need will be capital, which Great Britain and the United States can supply but Japan cannot. If those countries invest their money in China, and direct their Far Eastern policy towards enabling China to borrow, they will naturally expect a return advantage in the shape of increased markets for their goods. As far as capital goods are concerned, they will almost certainly obtain such markets while the investment is proceeding, and will continue to sell to China in the face of competition from all quarters.

When, however, China's increased prosperity enables her to buy more consumable goods, she will probably buy them from Japan rather than from the countries whose capital will have supplied the initial impulse. This may cause some resentment in the British Empire and the United States. But the resentment will be misplaced. Unless and until Japan herself becomes a large creditor country, her exports and imports will approximately balance, as they do now (from 1931 to 1935 her average annual excess of imports was 50 million yen, on an average total trade of 3,685 million yen). That means that if Japan sells more to China she will *pro tanto* buy more from abroad (including prominently the Empire countries and the United States), or else relax her selling pressure in other markets—such as the British colonies—where she competes with European or American goods. The path of economic and political wisdom for the English-speaking world in its Far Eastern policy is overwhelmingly plain.

In Europe the issue is not so clear cut. As Mr. Roosevelt said, in his speech to the Buenos Aires Conference on 1 December 1936, it is no accident that the nations that have carried furthest the raising of barriers to trade 'are those which proclaim most loudly that they require war as the instrument of their policy. It is no accident that their attempts to be self-sufficient have led to falling standards for their people.' If there is economic 'suffocation' in Europe it is 50 per cent. self-inflicted. Japan, indeed, is far from blameless in this respect, but she has never pursued economic self-sufficiency as the main thread of her national policy. She has not wholly subordinated her economic policy to her strategic plans. Germany is in a different case. Her economic position is as much the product of her political and strategic objectives as the other way about. While Japan's external trade has been rising, Germany's has been stagnant or falling, and the blame is not wholly upon her neighbours; for Germany's policy in trade and finance, let alone in politics and armaments, has done nothing to ease the barriers that oppose her dealings with the rest of the world. Every step towards self-sufficiency, by increasing her industrial costs, makes it more difficult for her to sell abroad. And so the vicious circle spins, with the German people pacing inside like a white mouse in a treadmill, fooling itself it is making progress.

Germany, more than any other country, seems to have deceived herself with the illusion that the employment created by making armaments means real economic prosperity. Prosperity is a function of the material welfare of the people. If forces of capital and labour are diverted from making food or boots or houses to making armaments, which do not afford economic welfare, then belts must be tightened and prosperity recedes. Armament inflation is just a particularly vicious form of living by taking in one's own washing.

But when all that has been said, and when it is realized that the completest answer to Germany's economic difficulties would not solve the problems set by her political ambitions, by her dictatorial system of government, and by her faith in Nazidom as a missionary religion, there remain, nevertheless, vital points of sympathy between the economic diagnosis of the Far Eastern problem that has been given above, and the fundamental ills of Europe. Japan, Germany, and Italy—to name the three countries that have most loudly voiced their grievances and have violently thrust back —possess this at least in common. All three are industrial countries, maintaining their standard of life by means of large-scale manufacturing industry, and being in greater or less degree dependent on outside sources for food to maintain their population (though the degree of such dependence is immaterial to the present argument). Their industry needs raw materials that they cannot themselves produce. Self-sufficiency is only relative; for even the United States with its vast and varied area cannot supply itself with such things as rubber, indeed tropical products of every kind, and all Herr Hitler's efforts cannot create nickel mines or lodes of iron ore in Germany. That being so, each of the countries in question must export at least enough to pay for its necessary raw materials. Moreover, modern large-scale industry sooner or later finds that it cannot work with maximum efficiency on the basis of the home market alone, but must seek expansion in export trade. Every rise in exports of manufactures increases equivalently the need for imported raw materials. In brief, foreign trade is absolutely essential to the life of Germany and Italy, as it is to the life of Japan.

Equally, and for the same reasons—in most particulars magnified—foreign trade is essential to the life of Great Britain. So it is to France, Czechoslovakia, Austria, the United States—every country whose fortunes rest upon manufacturing industry. The difficulties of living in a competitive world are not peculiar to the sabre-rattling dictatorships; the depression did not hit them alone, true as it may be that their mode of government, while able to force the economic system into an official strait-jacket, enhanced the danger of imprudent government spending, and repressed the recuperative power of private initiative. On the other hand, Great Britain—to draw the comparison that concerns us most—has two great advantages, a privileged market in the Empire and a large income from her overseas investments, in spite of the losses and realizations resulting from the War. To that extent, less fortunate or poorer countries are subject to the greater economic pressure and have the better excuse for raising barriers to imports.

Of investments abroad—if we rule out compulsory liquidation or compulsory transfer between one nation and another —there is only this to be said in the present connexion: that they are a temptation to the possessing countries to support policies of restriction of output, which, though nominally non-discriminatory, in effect discriminate in their favour, since they are compensated for having to pay more for raw materials by receiving more in dividends on their investments in the raw-material-producing industries. This aspect of the problem is discussed in greater detail in a later chapter in this book. As for the privileged market, there are really two separate questions: reciprocal preferences in the self-governing Commonwealth, and self-awarded preferences for the imperial Power in its dependent colonies. The first is much the more important, measured by the volume of trade involved, but it is the second that causes a grievance for the non-colonial Powers. Both questions are fully discussed in the appropriate section below. Here, in relation to the economic causation of European and Asiatic war-threats, it need only be said that to restore the open door in the dependent colonies seems to the naked eye to be the first main contribution that the British Empire could make to world appeasement.

What, then, of Germany's demands for the return of colonies? For her leaders scoff at the suggestion that the generalization of the open door, which is already enforced in most of her former colonies, would be an adequate substitute for territorial transfer. As an earlier chapter has suggested, there are reasons for suspecting that her colonial demands are really a piece of political and diplomatic card-play, and that the economic arguments with which they are ostensibly supported are only part of the poker. Whether that is so or not, the unmistakable fact is that colonial transfer would be almost insignificant as an economic solvent. And this applies as much to Italian conquests and reputed designs as to German claims for the undoing of the colonial clauses of Versailles.

If Germany absorbed the whole of the output of her former colonies, on the basis of 1934 figures, they could fully supply her requirements of a single industrial material only, sisal. They might, with a certain encouragement, provide all the mineral phosphates she needs to import. They could furnish her with a certain quantity of cocoa, tropical woods, gold, diamonds, and a number of other things. But as regards the supply of copper, tin, manganese, nickel, petroleum, rubber, cotton, wool, not to mention other important raw materials, the former German colonies are right off the map. Moreover, however rich they were in unexploited raw materials, in order to buy from them—short of confiscation in some disguise or other—Germany would have to sell to them. That is just as much her problem to-day, and could not be miraculously solved by any extension of her 'currency area'.

While colonial markets, and colonial resources, are in the aggregate important, they are only one part, comparatively small, in the whole economic complex. It does not really enhance the appeal of Germany's case that she deliberately distracts attention to a side-issue from her genuine economic problem—how to live in a world of cut-throat competition and intense economic nationalism. But that distortion of her case does not absolve other nations, particularly Great Britain, from their duty to help in finding an answer to that problem, which is also the problem of Japan, of Italy, of Austria, indeed of every country in the world, ourselves included.

Why particularly Great Britain? Great Britain is probably the richest country in the world, per head of her people, poor though some of them are; she has the greatest volume of investment in other lands; economically, the world is her parish, and she lives only by trading. She stands to lose most, in a merely material sense, by economic or political collapse in other parts of the world, even if she could draw in her own skirts from it. She stands to gain most by economic and political recovery. She has, at the same time, the greatest responsibilities and the greatest opportunities. It is one of the most depressing facts in a grim international picture that she seems to be shirking responsibility and letting opportunity slip.

Great Britain, for instance, is financially dominant over a great part of the world—the Empire, the rest of the 'sterling area', Argentina, everywhere that trade is financed by the sterling bill and London is the main source of long-term or short-term credit, even to a certain extent in France, so long as France's home credit market is not self-reliant but turns to London in a crisis. That position gives her a unique chance to further the international monetary and exchange policy best suited to the world's needs. Stabilization on a reformed gold standard, says Great Britain officially with an Empire chorus at her back, is the ultimate objective. But it is a case of 'jam yesterday and jam to-morrow, but never jam to-day'. Over and over again Mr. Neville Chamberlain repeats that Great Britain cannot stabilize unless and until a list of conditions is fulfilled. Yet those conditions themselves are at least partly her responsibility. They include a lowering of barriers to trade and a settlement of the war debt problem—as if the initiative on these matters was entirely out of Britain's hands, and she was the necessarily passive victim of other nations' errors.

There are very few people in Great Britain who think that (in the absence of reparations payments from Germany or substantial payments on the other and originally much larger inter-Allied debts) the whole of the instalments due under the Baldwin-Mellon agreement ought to be paid. If American opinion is set to demand that or nothing, nothing it will be, and perhaps the whole subject is better left alone. But many more people in Great Britain than present policy would suggest feel intensely unhappy at the supine attitude apparently adopted by the Government. It is for the debtor, not the creditor, to propose a settlement if he feels that payment in full is impossible. What basis of settlement might be put forward is a complicated and technical question. Some suggest that the whole capital sum should be repaid, though without interest; but even on such a basis there is room for wide variation as regards the number of years over which repayment should be spread. Opinion differs even among the best informed as to the annual amount that can be reasonably found by taxation and transferred across the exchanges. The important thing is that a fair and sensible offer, understandable of the people, should be made while American politics present a favourable opportunity. Obviously any settlement ought to be made the occasion for a general reconsideration of international economic relations. For Great Britain's ability to pay, in the sense of ability to find the necessary foreign exchange, is clearly conditioned by her ability to secure a sufficient surplus on her balance of trade and services; while at the other end the United States cannot be paid unless she is willing in the last resort to take payment in goods.

The onus, however, is not entirely on the United States. Great Britain's capacity to pay, having regard to her great invisible income from abroad, is almost as much a function of her total external trade as of the balance that she strikes between imports and exports. Her receipts in dividends and interest on foreign and imperial investments were still about £50 millions less in 1936 than at their peak before the slump. This represents clear, net loss to the national income, whereas loss of trade, apart from incidental unemployment, causes a net loss of national income only to the extent of the profits forfeited. If by her trade policy Great Britain could enable her own commercial and public debtors to pay interest in full or higher dividends, by receiving their goods, and if she could at the same time extend her markets in the United States and elsewhere through compensating reductions of tariffs, she would not find a reasonable payment on war debt account beyond her economic means.

Hopes were raised by the statement made when the Anglo-Franco-American currency pact was announced, to the effect that the success of the policy of monetary co-operation was linked with the development of international trade. Here was opportunity ready to be grasped. A few days later a spokesman was sent to express the British Government's views in the economic and financial committee of the League Assembly, and next morning *The Times* headlines ran: 'Lower Trade Barriers: British Lead at Geneva.' The opportunity was actually being grasped. A rude disappointment, however, awaited the reader who perused the column underneath; for the Government had given no lead whatever in lowering trade barriers (the suggested colonial materials inquiry having been on the *tapis* for a year). On the contrary, he had hinted that Great Britain would be forced by devaluation of the gold currencies to raise her tariffs unless other countries lowered theirs. Again the familiar passing of the buck, the smug assumption that other countries must move first.

It is true that Great Britain's balance of trade is not on the face of it in a very satisfactory condition. But the rise in the excess of imports in 1936 was chiefly due to the rising prices of raw materials and semi-manufactures, not to abnormally high imports of fully manufactured goods subject to protective tariff. High prices for the raw materials of industry do not suit Great Britain unless they are associated with a liberal régime in world trade (not excluding her own). The best way of rectifying her balance of trade is through a general expansion both of imports and of exports.

But this is wandering rather far from the main theme of this chapter, which is to paint the economic background of the world crisis. Great Britain is not the only country to blame for present inertia, either within the Commonwealth or beyond. Nor, even if she takes the initiative that it lies with her as the world's richest country to take, can she safely act unilaterally. Comparison with the disarmament problem is commonplace—but there is this vital difference, that whereas action must doubtless be multilateral in economic disarmament, it need not be universal. Some countries, perhaps for political and strategic reasons, perhaps through obstinate adherence to an outworn economic creed, are unlikely to join in any movement for steadily liberating world trade. Very well; let them see and envy the benefits of freer trade in the world outside. Thus the international political strain may be doubly relieved: by a relaxation of the general economic pressure out of which the political strain itself has partly arisen, and by a wider popularity for peace and democracy through the example of prosperity among the free and peace-loving States.

PART II

THE EMPIRE: NOW

I

IN 1914

IT is all very well to take it for granted that the Empire will automatically say 'ditto' to anything that Great Britain takes it into its head to do in world affairs. But a forest of questions springs up when this facile and reassuring assumption is looked into. What, for one thing, is meant by 'the Empire' in this connexion? Is it likely to function as a unit? Can it so function?

Similar questions about the Empire were being asked when war broke out in 1914.

In 1914 the Empire had settled down into very much its present form. The days of Colonial struggles for individual rights that had been a matter of course for centuries in the United Kingdom were long over. Canada had been federated for nearly fifty years. The Commonwealth of Australia dated back to the beginning of the century. South Africa, only just emerged from the years of reconstruction that had followed the end of the Anglo-Boer War, had been swept by a surprisingly powerful Closer Union movement in 1907 and 1908, and had accomplished the union of its four States in 1909. New Zealand, free from the racial antagonisms that had racked South Africa, had forgotten what it was to be divided.

By 1914 the nature of the main Imperial current—in the four united colonies which were to become Dominions, that is to say—had changed. It had been immensely impetuous, surmounting natural obstacles, wide-spreading. In Canada it had absorbed the Prairies and put them under wheat. In Australia it had turned the southern coast-belt, which broadens out far into the interior of that great continent (larger actually in area than the United States of America), into a land covered by superb stations rich in cattle and sheep. In New Zealand, on a smaller individual scale, the same impulse had cleared the woodlands and turned a mountainous wilderness into a settled country, where the price of land mounted continually. Gold discoveries had brought a flood of adventurers into Australia. In South Africa, first diamonds, then the wonderful riches of the Transvaal gold-fields, had transformed the population from one of poor, struggling whites and swarming, hardly tamed natives, into a flourishing community of prosperous farmers and of townsmen absorbed in the pursuit of wealth; both with natives doing their manual labour for them.

In all four, the routine of life had settled down into an adapted form of European habit. The rule of law was established; courts functioned; municipalities controlled urban communities and local authorities country areas; Parliaments debated and legislated; stock-exchanges fluctuated. The period of material settlement was over. An era of consolidation had set in. The tendency was towards more and more complete concentration on local affairs. Europe was far away. The old irritation against Downing Street control had faded. Though Germany was building battleships and bringing her conscript army to a pitch of drastic efficiency never aimed at before, and though her network of railways clustered ominously against the Belgian frontier, few thought that there need be any fear of war in Europe. If there was, it had already been authoritatively announced in Canada and more than hinted in South Africa, that a colony need not be involved unless its Parliament deliberately decided to fight on the British side. No one had thought out the implications of this vague doctrine of passive belligerency; and it had become sporadically current in Canada and South Africa more because local conditions favoured its nebulous reassurance against being dragged into European complications than because anything like a majority of the Canadian or South African people contemplated the possibility of letting Great Britain fight a European war without helping her.

Canada had had years of peaceful life side by side with the United States. The frontier between them was unfortified. Men and money moved freely to and fro. Canada was accustomed to rely instinctively on the power of the United States

to protect her against aggression, either on the Atlantic or on
the Pacific side. The normal reluctance of the American to
take any interest in the quarrels of Europe was as natural to the
Canadian, especially in the Western Provinces. Yet fears
in the United Kingdom that Canada would drift away from
the British family of peoples towards a formal association
with the United States were shown to be groundless whenever
they were tested. Any proposal by a Canadian statesman
to work out schemes for closer trade relations with the United
States by means of reciprocal tariffs had been violently resented in Canada. Canada was jealous of her right to settle
her own tariff policy; but she was much more jealous of her
fiscal independence of the United States and much more
determined to guard herself against being swamped by the
tide of United States business interests.

In South Africa the political school which advertised
habitually its repudiation of British obligations in foreign
policy was more aggressive, more powerful, and more specific
in its tenets than in Canada. It was still in what has been
called the 'attacking phase' of its development as an element
in the population of a British Dominion. After the brief
period, from 1900 to 1910, when both Dutch and British
South Africans felt a simultaneous impulse towards Union,
considerable numbers of Dutch South Africans began again
to brood over memories of the Anglo-Boer War. They
had let themselves be persuaded, in the short fervour of
the Union movement, that Great Britain and their British-
descended fellow citizens had forsworn all thoughts of domination from outside South Africa or of supremacy within it
for the English language and English ways of thought and
life. Union had been founded on the most formal assurances
that English and Dutch were both to be official languages,
with absolute equality between them. But the first Union
Cabinet, of which General Botha was Prime Minister and in
which all the ministers but one were Dutch by birth, had
hardly been in office more than a few months when General
Hertzog, the Minister of Justice, began to accuse General
Botha of being lukewarm in asserting Dutch rights, both in
the use of the Dutch language and in official appointments.

F

The quarrel soon became acrimonious. General Hertzog carried it into the country districts and made a series of speeches in which he denounced his Prime Minister with great bitterness. A breach became inevitable. General Botha resigned and reformed his Cabinet, leaving General Hertzog out. General Hertzog founded the Nationalist Party, with championship of the Dutch language, Dutch culture, and Dutch individual rights as its sole creed.

Thus, at the beginning of 1914, South Africa was the one part of the self-governing Empire in which bitter race enmity was the predominant influence in local politics. The doubt about Canada, if Great Britain was involved in a European war, was not a doubt about the loyalty of every element in her population. It was a doubt whether there would be general support for active participation in a European war. The doubt about South Africa was far more serious. How large an element in the South African population did General Hertzog and his Nationalists represent? Would their antagonism to Great Britain, about which there could be no illusions, go far enough to drive them into actual rebellion against General Botha's Government if it gave active support to Great Britain? General Botha was Dutch himself. A part of Dutch South Africa would follow him. But how large would that part be? How many South Africans of Dutch descent were there who would follow General Hertzog rather than General Botha, and would have to be reckoned hostile if war actually broke out in Europe and Great Britain was dragged in?

This was the most anxious and disconcerting question that the statesmen of Great Britain had to ask themselves about Empire support for British foreign policy at the beginning of 1914. But there were other questions. No Empire community had gone the length of General Hertzog and his Nationalist followers in making antagonism to Great Britain the first article in a political creed. But others had carried independent ideas pretty far. There had been a general revolt in all the self-governing Empire communities against British free trade. They had all established their right to settle their own fiscal policy; they had all committed them-

selves to protection; they had all granted preferences to
British goods; they had all, at repeated Imperial Conferences, done their best to convert British political leaders
to a plan for a system of Empire trade organization through
reciprocal agreements; they had all failed in that attempt;
they all shared a deeply felt, though a sternly repressed, resentment at the contemptuous rejection of their overtures by
the Liberal Cabinet that had been in power in Great Britain
since 1906.

In Navy defence, too, some of the Dominions had displayed
an independence of view and a disregard for the opinions
of the Admiralty which were disconcerting. Germany was
building a battle fleet that could hardly be anything but a
threat to British sea power. Canada and Australia had
refused to follow what seemed to British statesmen and
Admirals the self-evident wisdom of the example of New
Zealand, the Cape, and Natal in contributing to the cost of
the British Navy. Instead, the two chief Dominions had
insisted that it was their own business to protect their own
shores and commerce by navies built and owned by themselves, though dedicated to instant identity with the British
Navy if war came. The Navy of Canada, it was true, was
insignificant; for Canada relied on the tacit protection of the
United States. But the Australian Navy was an affair of a
battleship and cruisers, powerful enough, if it had been under
Admiralty control in peace time, to have been a substantial
asset in the sea-rivalry with Germany. The cold logic of sea
strategy was unanswerable intellectually. Where your peril
was, there should your Empire sea strength be also; and that
was in the North Sea. But Australia had insisted that her
cities were vulnerable from the sea-board. She must be able
to protect them against bombardment by any stray outlier
of a hostile fleet, if war broke. This, to British statesmen
in 1914 and earlier, seemed yet another example of the queer
blindness of the Dominions to their true welfare and of their
perverse reluctance to follow the advice of British experts in
trade or defence matters.

Doubts in British political and official circles about the
value of the Empire to Great Britain in peace or war were

no new thing either. As the colonies had progressed in self-government, and as four of them had consolidated their separate governments into one, British public opinion had been inclined to conclude that their ultimate destiny was separation. The process of colonial development coincided, in the latter half of the nineteenth century, with the period of Great Britain's greatest prosperity. It seemed to many anxious-minded contemporaries that not only must white communities in other continents which had reached the stage of governing themselves, without control or direction from the centre, want in the end to sever themselves from all connexion with the Old Country, but the Old Country herself, in the full tide of her accumulating wealth, must find them a burden rather than a reinforcement. This conviction dogged most thoughtful minds in England all through the period of the industrial revolution. There was no vision of an Empire which would hold together and grow in strength even though it had no central focus formally in the British Isles. The pessimistic view of the future of the Empire still persisted at the beginning of 1914, though much less confidently, for it had been attacked and shaken by Joseph Chamberlain.

There would be nothing palpably absurd in a reading of the history of the Empire as a series of reactions to tides of political sentiment in the United Kingdom. The Reform Acts of the 1830's were certainly followed by the grant of responsible government to Canadian, Australian, and South African communities. The Anglo-Boer War was the climax of years of rich prosperity in Great Britain, when British good fortune had begun to seem to be established so firmly that there was something laughable in the thought that it could be defied by a handful of farmers in the Transvaal and Free State. British pride, on the other hand, after it had been chastened by the long endurance test of the Anglo-Boer War, saw nothing derogatory in the grant of free self-government to the two Boer ex-republics within five years of the Peace of Vereniging. Another five years afterwards, the Union Constitution of the four South African States was hailed at Westminster as the triumph in South Africa of enlightened British statesmanship. These are all reasonable interpretations of trends in Empire history. But it would be distortion to ignore the influence of such a personality as Joseph Chamberlain. He went to the Colonial Office when it was the Cinderella of Whitehall. He turned it into a rostrum from which his actions as much as his speeches announced a new view of the Empire and its peoples. He gave the best of his talents to being their interpreter to the people of Great Britain. He saw the future of the Empire in terms of the growth of its communities. He sympathized with them and understood their minds as no Colonial Secretary before him had been at the pains to sympathize and understand. His great plan for consolidating the Empire politically and by an Empire tariff system broke under the remorseless analysis applied to it, in all its novelty and crudity, of detail, by the Asquiths and Winston Churchills—unrivalled in that day at expounding the one-sided benefits of what passed as free trade. Chamberlain himself was broken in the failure of his plan to carry the country. But his influence on the Empire stood. He had raised faith in it to the status of a creed. He had discredited the scepticism about its endurance and its value that had been a recurrent fashion in British politics. No interpretation of Empire tendencies can overlook his work, which must rank among the major forces that supervised the growth of the Empire as a community of free peoples and prepared the way for the appearance of the Commonwealth after the European War.

The enthusiasm which his work at the Colonial Office bequeathed to his disciples set them on a trail which seemed not only in his best tradition but to point straight towards undeniable benefits for the United Kingdom as well as of the colonies and dependencies. Common sense, they believed, told them that a scattered Empire of separate governments and of peoples in an endless variety of stages of development would be more secure, would have its progress stimulated, would reach a new harmony between its distant parts and its multitude of political institutions, if it could be fitted together under a single Imperial Parliament. The major colonies had no sooner established themselves securely on a basis of free institutions than they had begun to draw together in their respective continents and to form themselves into unions under one Parliament and Government. Even in South Africa this need for union had been felt so strongly that it had been able to unite the four States, though the race animosities that the Anglo-Boer War had left were still hardly cooler than they had been at the end of the war. There was everything in the experience of these unions to encourage a movement towards a similar union for the whole Empire. Imperial federation became the aim of many of the ablest and most public-spirited citizens of the Empire. New Zealand statesmen had preached it in more than one Imperial Conference. In contrast to it, the growth of colonial nationalism, which found an eloquent exponent during these years in Mr. Richard Jebb, seemed alarmingly and inevitably a disintegrating force. If the colonies were to develop their individualities as communities without check what would become of the Empire? Its dissolution would be as unavoidable as disastrous. The natural prophylactic against this insidious pernicious anaemia was to tighten the ties between the component parts of the Empire and to top the new structure with an Imperial legislature to which each responsible community would send its allotted number of representatives. That would counteract nonsense about a colony having its own fleet or deciding for itself whether it would join in an Imperial war. There would be an Imperial budget in which each self-governing part of the whole would pay its contribution to the expense of running and protecting the whole. The blessings of Great Britain's free-trade system would be spread over the Empire, and the colonies which had committed themselves to protection would see the error of their ways. A wide career would be opened to ability from every part. A world which had begun to sneer at the illogical looseness of the British Imperial system and to predict its dissolution at the first whiff of grape-shot would see that there underlay the system a strength, and that it was held together by a cohesion, which had only to be challenged to assert itself, and to be questioned to clothe itself in a constitutional garment of universally recognized shape.

The Imperial federation movement started off with great enthusiasm. Its intellectuals, working in various parts of the Empire, produced a literature which demonstrated beyond intelligent doubt the disadvantages of an unorganized Empire and the blessings of a federal alternative. But there it stopped. Some stubborn instinct, common to Canada, Australia, and South Africa, and discernible even in New Zealand, clogged its progress. The mechanical difficulties in the way of an Empire Parliament and Government began to seem more insuperable the more logically they were exposed as rather imaginary than real. The old fear of the colonist that Downing Street control would obstruct his progress revived, though inarticulately in contrast to the reasoned volubility of the advocates of Imperial federation. It became increasingly apparent that, inapt and informal, weak for defence and clumsy in counsel, as the current Imperial fabric was— and no one was at pains to deny these defects—the people of the colonies preferred it so. Their hearts, they knew, were in the right place; that being so, the Empire was as safe against voluntary dissolution as it could be if its institutions were systematized and centralized. System and centralization, they suspected, were so alien that they would do more harm than good. Things Imperial were well enough as they were, in essentials that was to say. To exaggerate potential ills which might result from the current state of affairs was to be alarmist; and they sniffed suspiciously for the motive of an attitude so un-British. Imperial federation, as a preventive against the risk of Empire dissolution from inside, thus never became more than a plan of theorists.

But the champions of Imperial federation wanted it as much to equip the Empire to resist aggression from outside as dissolution from inside. They were alarmed by the unpreparedness of the British peoples for war. The years, however, that followed the end of the Anglo-Boer War were all against them. Boer resistance had shaken confidence in the British arms, but they won through in the end. From 1906 war seemed a more and more remote possibility. Britain's reply to the threat of the German fleet seemed sufficient, even if

Germany refused repeated overtures for a truce in Navy building. Diplomacy, tackling serious international crises one after the other and always succeeding in smoothing out the differences between the Powers, won unjustified confidence from British public opinion in its adequacy for even the last emergency. Just as in the British Isles themselves it was vain to preach conscription during the years between 1900 and 1914, so all through the Empire there was stubborn scepticism about war as a contingency worth contemplating, combined with a dumb confidence that if the improbable did happen and war came, the Empire would manage somehow to do its share at sea and in the field. But the failure of the Imperial federation movement did not reassure British statesmen. When war challenged the Empire they had nothing safe to go on in estimating the help to be expected from the Dominions. It came abundantly and with far less delay than pessimism would have predicted. In Canada and South Africa Parliament was called on to decide whether each should join with Great Britain. Even in South Africa, in spite of the sullen resistance of the Nationalists, there was never any doubt about the answer of Parliament. The Nationalists were in a very small minority. They were to wait ten years before they succeeded in defeating the Botha Party, then led by General Smuts in succession to General Botha. Rebellion did break out in South Africa when it was known that Parliament had decided for an invasion of German South-west Africa, where a large wireless station was inconvenient for British control of the seas and the small German force might at any moment organize a raid against South African territory. The Nationalist leaders refused General Botha's appeal to discountenance rebellion, which attracted to its leadership more than one of the veterans who had led the Boers in the field. But the response to General Botha's appeal to his own people for volunteers to crush the rebellion was excellent. The rebellion fizzled out and General Botha was left free, first to invade and conquer German South-west, then to send General Smuts with an army to harry the Germans in German East Africa, and finally to reinforce the British line on the Western Front in Europe with

a contingent which, though small in numbers, excelled itself
in heroic service.

If the precedent of 1914 can be relied on for answers to
the questions set out in the first paragraph of this chapter
there is little cause for uneasiness. But is it a precedent for the
Empire now; and, if it is, is it reliable?

II

IN 1937

SINCE 1914 the Empire, especially the Commonwealth, has been transformed. India, too, had then hardly thought of the possibility of self-government. In 1937 the Montagu-Chelmsford reforms have worked out their ten-year period, and, as this is being written, the Provincial elections under the new Federal Constitution are being held. The Commonwealth is usually understood to mean the association of the United Kingdom (including Northern Ireland) with the five Dominions—Canada, Australia, South Africa, the Irish Free State, and New Zealand—within the Empire. Newfoundland, which was reckoned as a Dominion at one time, has since had its constitution suspended and is now itself suspended constitutionally somewhere between the status of a self-governing colony, to which no doubt it will ultimately return, and a Crown colony.

The advance of the Dominions from the semi-dependent condition in which the War found them in 1914, not domestically, but in their external relations, to complete autonomy, both internal and external, has been the predominant fact in the change of the Empire. The same current is carrying India, Ceylon, and Burma steadily onwards. But the Dominions have been the leaders in the movement and the Empire now comprises, in the Commonwealth, a group of States, equal to each other in what jurists call status, though still in varying stages of strength and international prestige. This the jurists have agreed to know as stature, in contrast to status.

The end of the War saw the movement well on the way. In 1918, in the month of June, when the last German offensive was at its height, Sir Robert Borden, then Prime Minister of Canada, addressed the Empire Parliamentary Association in London. For the second year in succession he and the other Dominion Prime Ministers, or their deputies, were attending the Imperial War Cabinet. Empire change was his subject. The meeting of the Imperial War Cabinet, he said, was 'a very great step in the constitutional development of the Empire. . . . We meet there on terms of perfect equality. We meet as Prime Ministers of self-governing nations. We meet there under the leadership and the presidency of the Prime Minister of the United Kingdom. After all, . . . the British Empire, as it is at present constituted, is a very modern organization. It is perfectly true that it is built up on the development of centuries, but, as it is constituted to-day, both in territory and in organization, it is a relatively modern affair. Why, it is only seventy-five years since responsible government was granted to Canada. It is only a little more than fifty years since the first experiment in Federal Government—in a Federal Constitution—was undertaken in this Empire. And from that we went on, in 1871, to representation in negotiating our commercial treaties; in 1878 to complete fiscal autonomy, and after that to complete fiscal control and the negotiation of our own treaties. But we have always lacked the full status of manhood, because you exercised here a so-called trusteeship, under which you undertook to deal with foreign relations on our behalf, and sometimes without consulting us very much.

'Well, that day has gone by. We come here, as we came last year, to deal with all these matters, upon terms of perfect equality with the Prime Minister of the United Kingdom and his colleagues. . . . If I should attempt to describe (the Imperial War Cabinet), I should say it is a Cabinet of Governments. Every Prime Minister who sits around that board is responsible to his own Parliament and to his own people; the conclusions of the War Cabinet can only be carried out by the Parliaments of the different nations of our Imperial Commonwealth. Thus, each Dominion, each nation, retains its perfect autonomy. I venture to believe . . . that in this may be found the genesis of a development in the constitutional relations of the Empire which will form the basis of its unity in years to come.'

Sir Robert Borden thus defined on behalf of the Dominions the progress in their relations with the United Kingdom that had been the effect of the European War. The War was still in its most doubtful stage when the Imperial War Conference of 1917 met in London on the invitation of the new Prime Minister, Mr. Lloyd George. He gauged the popular instinct accurately when he summoned the Dominion Prime Ministers to this conference, which, as Sir Robert Borden said, became to all intents and purposes the War

Cabinet of the Empire. Dominion troops were fighting for the Empire all over the world. It was right that the Dominion statesmen should be called to London to share in the highest direction of the War. When Mr. Lloyd George proceeded to invite General Smuts—who had come to London to represent South Africa at the Imperial War Conference, leaving General Botha to handle the dissatisfied element of Dutch South Africans—to join the permanent Imperial War Cabinet, there was immediate and general approval. Without Dominion help in the field, the fortunes of the Allies would have been less propitious even than they were in the dark days of 1917. Their help in counsel should prove, the popular instinct had it, as valuable. The Dominion leaders themselves felt strongly that the war record of their men had made it ridiculous for their countries to be still in the leading-strings of Great Britain. But if they were not in leading-strings where were they?

The secret history of the discussions which took place between the Dominion leaders in 1917 has still to be written. Sir Robert Borden, Prime Minister of Canada, had a precise idea of what the new ranking of his Dominion within the Empire should be. He had brought with him to London a brilliant, experienced, and far-sighted unofficial lieutenant, Mr. John Dafoe, editor of the *Winnipeg Free Press*. Whether it was from Mr. Dafoe's brain that the conception of Dominion status first sprang—Sir Robert Borden himself made no secret of his debt to Mr. Dafoe at the time—or whether the conception had been forced by events upon the minds of the two Canadians and of General Smuts simultaneously, may never be known. In any case, Dominion status it was to be—a stilted and ugly combination of words, which nevertheless expressed better than any alternative that was available then or has been suggested since the new position of the Dominions. Dominion status, as it was conceived by the Canadian and South African leaders in 1917, was to mean that the Dominions were to be equal partners with Great Britain in the Commonwealth. They were to be wholly free from control. The Parliament at Westminster was not to legislate for them without their consent. The old Crown right, already almost obsolete in practice, of reservation and disallowance of Dominion legislation was to be done away with, except where it was enshrined in a Dominion Constitution to safeguard some special provision.

Before the world, the Dominions were to stand as self-sufficient nations, with all the inherent privileges and rights of States in the community of peoples. In foreign policy they were not to be committed by Great Britain against their will and without their consent. The difficulties of Dominion status in actual working were not hidden from these Dominion leaders even as early as 1917. But their faith was that it would lead to an immense outflow of mutual goodwill between the States of the Commonwealth, would reassure sensitive racial feelings in Canada and South Africa, and would prove competent to surmount the inevitable difficulties as they arose. Sir Robert Borden, Mr. Dafoe, and General Smuts were thinking at that time much more of the relations between Great Britain and the Dominions within the Commonwealth than of the international position which their countries would have under their new status. They feared friction within the Commonwealth unless the complete autonomy of the Dominions was recognized as firmly established directly the War was over. They were sure that the fullest degree of looseness in the Commonwealth framework was the best guarantee of its indestructability by internal dissension.

Doubtless these ideas were communicated to the other Dominion Prime Ministers and to British ministers. They were approved, for no British statesman at that stage in the War, least of all Mr. Lloyd George, failed to understand the change that had come about in the standing of the Dominions within the Empire. Possibly British ministers did not think out the full consequences of Dominion status, as Sir Robert Borden, General Smuts, and Mr. Dafoe thought them out. British ministers were busy men in those days. But it is certain that the Dominion status idea, as conceived by the Canadian and South African leaders in 1917, looked forward to all the results that have followed since. Complete autonomy within the Commonwealth could not, even at that stage, imply, in the mind of any one with enough imagination to foresee its possibilities, limitation in any sense. The conception of Dominion status comprehends all the shapes that it has taken in any Dominion, the Irish Free State included; and if some British ministers were to show in later years that they had not foreseen all those shapes, they and their successors, when it came to the point, always acquiesced, in detail, in what was accepted in principle in 1917.

So the Imperial War Conference of 1917 quietly included among its resolutions a decision that as soon as possible after the end of the War there should be a special Imperial Conference about the future constitution of the Empire. It did more. It laid down in broad outline what it conceived to be the main principles of the new constitution. The Dominions, it said, should preserve all their existing powers of self-government and unfettered control of their own affairs. To that should be added a clear recognition of their standing as autonomous nations of an Imperial Commonwealth. (The use of 'an' is significant. It suggests that 'Empire' was no longer, in 1917, a proper term for the association of the United Kingdom and the Dominions, but it shows that 'Commonwealth' had not yet established itself as the more suitable alternative.) The 1917 Conference also mentioned India as 'an important portion' of the Commonwealth, and went on to state the proposition that the right of the Dominions and India to an 'adequate voice' in foreign policy must be recognized and that there must be 'effective arrangements for continuous consultation in all important matters of Imperial concern, and for such necessary concerted action, founded on consultation, as the several Governments may determine'.

The special conference on the new constitution of the Commonwealth was never held. At first, during the proceedings in Paris when the Versailles Treaty was being negotiated, co-operation between Great Britain and the Dominions, on terms of mutual equality and common responsibility for foreign policy, seemed much simpler and more practical than before. But this impression soon faded. The new ideas about the equal partnership of Great Britain and the Dominions began to lead almost at once to incidents which looked much more awkward and ominous than they were.

It was better, both British and Dominion ministers came to believe, to let the new Commonwealth system work itself out for a while than to try to reduce it immediately to the formula which the Conference of 1917 had contemplated. It was more in the British tradition as well. And there were numbers of intensely patriotic, well-meaning, and not too well-informed people in Great Britain whom it would have been impossible, at that stage, to convince that formal recognition of Dominion autonomy and equality did not presage the speedy dissolution of the Empire. The Dominion Prime Ministers, especially the Prime Ministers of Canada and South Africa, had to reckon, too, with the considerable sections of their own people which were constantly interpreting innovations in Imperial relations as grievances exploitable for local political purposes, and the not less considerable sections which were perpetually active, on the other side in local politics, in exploiting the contrary grievance—that the Empire was precisely as it had been before the War and that all the talk about innovations was treacherous humbug.

At Versailles the Prime Ministers of the Dominions signed the Treaty each for his own country—a token to all the world that Great Britain no longer spoke for her Dominions as well as for herself. Dominion representatives had taken a by no means negligible part in the negotiations. In a leading role, General Smuts had produced for the Peace Conference a subtle opinion on the justification of including claims for civilian losses in war damage which had clinched an intellectual reputation second to none, though it left men wondering how he could have brought himself to give it and lessened unhappily the effectiveness of his protest against the vengefulness of the Treaty in its final form. The Dominion Prime Ministers returned to their own places. It remained to be seen how the new Commonwealth system would work out in practice. They must have been less easy in their minds about that than about its essential wisdom and soundness in theory, of which they had no doubt, though New Zealand was afterwards to shy at the working out of the new scheme and to say that she for her part had always been, and remained, content with her pre-war status *vis-à-vis* the United Kingdom.

India shared with the Dominions the separate signing of the Peace Treaty as well as membership of the League of Nations.

From that, in a process to be described in the succeeding chapters, the Commonwealth progressed to the stage at which definition of the new system of interrelation between its members became not only desirable but imperative. That stage was reached when the Imperial Conference of 1926 assembled in London. A committee on Inter-Imperial Relations was appointed at the beginning of its meetings, with Lord Balfour as chairman. Its report was adopted by the Conference. The first sentence recorded the committee's opinion that 'nothing would be gained by attempting to lay down a Constitution for the British Empire', because of the 'very different characteristics', and the 'very different histories' of 'its widely scattered parts' and the 'very different stages of evolution' that they were 'at'; because, too, the Empire, 'considered as a whole, . . . defies classification and bears no real resemblance to any other political organization which now exists or has ever been tried'. The committee proceeded, however, in the second paragraph, to commit itself to the statement that 'there is . . . one most important element in (the Empire) which, from a strictly constitutional point of view, has now, as regards all vital matters, reached its full development . . .—the group of self-governing communities composed of Great Britain and the Dominions. Their position and mutual relation may be readily defined.'

The famous definition of the nature of the States of the Commonwealth (including, though that is often forgotten, the United Kingdom) followed. 'They are autonomous Communities within the British Empire, equal in status, in no way subordinate one to another in any aspect of their domestic or external affairs, though united by a common allegiance to the Crown, and freely associated as members of the British Commonwealth of Nations.'

Profound in insight and felicitous in wording as this definition is, its authors flattered themselves when they preceded it by the remark that 'the group of self-governing Communities composed of Great Britain and the Dominions' had,

in 1926, 'as regards all vital matters, reached its full development' at least 'from a strictly constitutional point of view'.
The equal status of the Dominions has since been made the
basis of interpretations of 'free association' which the Imperial
Conference of 1926 never glanced at.

The committee continued, in words which are particularly
appropriate for quotation at this moment of world crisis, by
remarking that:

'A foreigner endeavouring to understand the true character of
the British Empire by the aid of this (the equal status) formula
alone would be tempted to think that it was devised rather to
make mutual interference impossible than to make mutual co-
operation easy.

'Such a criticism, however, completely ignores the historic
situation. The rapid evolution of the Oversea Dominions during
the last fifty years has involved many complicated adjustments
of old political machinery to changing conditions. The tendency
towards equality of status was both right and inevitable. Geographical and other conditions made this impossible of attainment by the way of federation. The only alternative was by way
of autonomy; and along this road it has been steadily sought.
Every self-governing member of the Empire is now the master of
its destiny. In fact, if not always in form, it is subject to no compulsion whatever.

'But no account, however accurate, of the negative relations in
which Great Britain and the Dominions stand to each other can
do more than express a portion of the truth. The British Empire
is not founded upon negations. It depends essentially, if not
formally, on positive ideals. Free institutions are its life-blood.
Free co-operation is its instrument. Peace, security, and progress
are among its objects. Aspects of all these great themes have been
discussed at the present Conference; excellent results have been
thereby obtained. And, though every Dominion is now, and must
always remain, the sole judge of the nature and extent of its
co-operation, no common cause will, in our opinion, be thereby
imperilled.

'Equality of status, so far as Britain and the Dominions are concerned, is thus the root principle governing our Inter-Imperial
Relations. But the principles of equality and similarity, appropriate to *status*, do not universally extend to function. Here we
require something more than immutable dogmas. For example,

to deal with questions of diplomacy and questions of defence, we require also flexible machinery—machinery which can, from time to time, be adapted to the changing circumstances of the world.'

These passages from the report of the Inter-Imperial Relations Committee of the Imperial Conference of 1926 are the charter of the Commonwealth. The Statute of Westminster does no more than apply the principles stated in them. They do not commit themselves to the proposition that South Africa, say, or New Zealand, is as great and powerful as the United Kingdom. But there is a recognized international equality of States, *qua* States, which does not depend on their wealth or strength; and that the Dominions have equally with Great Britain.

But in practice there were a number of laws and regulations, dating back to the days when the Dominions were not equal with Great Britain, which were inconsistent with their equality. What about them? The 1926 Conference did not shirk the issue. It recognized the inconsistencies. The King's Title, for instance, would have to be altered to recognize that Ireland was no longer part of the United Kingdom. The Governors-General would preferably now be solely representatives of the King in their Dominions, not of the British Government too, as heretofore. Though the Crown had not exercised for years its right to disallow Dominion legislation, the right remained nominally. It implied subordination of the Dominion legislatures to the British Parliament and would have to be done away with, now that the Dominions were recognized as Great Britain's equals. So would the reservation of Dominion legislation for the King's assent, unless there was some special provision in a Dominion Constitution which provided specially for the reservation of laws on particular subjects, as there was in the South African Constitution, for example. Acts of the Parliament at Westminster which said generally that any Act passed by a Dominion Parliament in conflict with an Imperial Act was invalid *ipso facto* would have to be repealed; and there were clauses in the British Merchant Shipping legislation which were not consistent with the autonomy of the Dominions. How were these anomalies to be got rid of, when the Imperial

Conference of 1926 was in the usual hurry of Imperial Conferences to get through its mass of business, so that the Prime Ministers might lose no time in returning? A committee would have to be appointed to reshape the law of the Empire so that it accorded with the equality of the Commonwealth countries. It was appointed.

But the Conference of 1926 did not disperse before it had inscribed on its records several highly important dicta about the powers and rights of the Dominions:

'It is the right of the Government of each Dominion to advise the Crown in all matters relating to its own affairs. Consequently, it would not be in accordance with constitutional practice for advice to be tendered to His Majesty by His Majesty's Government in Great Britain in any matter appertaining to the affairs of a Dominion against the views of the Government of that Dominion.'

Again:

'The constitutional practice is that legislation by the Parliament at Westminster applying to a Dominion would only be passed with the consent of the Dominion concerned.'

And:

'The appropriate procedure with regard to projected legislation in one of the self-governing parts of the Empire which may affect the interests of other self-governing parts is previous consultation between His Majesty's Ministers in the several parts concerned.'

With these maxims to guide it, the Conference, as it came to be called in preference to 'committee', on the operation of Dominion legislation met, deliberated lengthily, and produced in 1929 a momentous report, which was adopted in essentials by the Imperial Conference of 1930 and afterwards became the bones of the Statute of Westminster.

When the Imperial Conference of 1930 met, there were signs that some of the Dominions thought that other Dominions were going too far in asserting their rights. (The 1929 Conference on the operation of Dominion Legislation was criticized, too, for having exceeded its terms of reference.) Mr. Scullin, the Prime Minister of Australia, observed to the Conference that

'one of the principal tasks ahead of us at this Imperial Conference... is to advance a stage further the great task of harmoniz-
ing the real self-determination of the Dominions with the real
unity of the British Commonwealth of Nations. ... We (Australia)
hold that it is quite possible to reconcile complete and effective
autonomy of the Dominions with the unity of the British Commonwealth as a whole—but not if we attempt to dot every "I" and
cross every "T". We are a free association of peoples; and to my
mind there is nothing to be gained and perhaps a great deal to
be lost by attempting to crystallize our relations too closely within
the confines of any formal document.'

Mr. Forbes, Prime Minister of New Zealand, took the same
line. New Zealand, he told the Conference,

'valued . . . (its) close connexion with the United Kingdom and
with (its) sister Dominions, and (it would) have been well content to allow constitutional relationships to settle themselves in
the time-honoured way, in accordance with the necessities of the
position and the requirements of the time.'

But these hints were belated and had little effect on the
decisions of the 1930 Conference. The 'necessities of the
time' had a startlingly different meaning in the Irish Free
State (where the Cosgrave Government saw the de Valera influence gaining ground and knew that it would soon have
to fight for its life), or in South Africa (where the Hertzog
Government would be attacked by the republicans whom it
still kept in its political camp unless the principles laid down
in 1926 were translated into clauses of 'a formal document'),
from what they had in Australia or New Zealand. The
Dominions were making the pace in autonomy at incongruous
speeds—much faster where local conditions compelled rapid
progress than where there was no such political compulsion.
Parliamentary debates in the various Dominion Parliaments
on the proposed Statute of Westminster—which, the 1930
Conference decided, was to be the name of the Act in which
the Parliament at Westminster was to embody the conclusions of the 1929 Special Conference—were soon to exhibit
sensationally these contrasts in the onward march of Dominion autonomy.

The contrasts are important in an inquiry into the homo-

geneousness of the Empire in 1937. They point to great
differences in the interpretations which the Dominions are
likely to give of their obligations in a world crisis. New Zealand and Australia will be least inclined to insist on their
right to decide for themselves what their obligations amount
to—partly because there is no restiveness in any part of their
population against what is interpreted elsewhere as British
domination; partly because they do not flatter themselves
that they are immune from all risk of invasion. Canada and
South Africa have always had to reckon with suspicions that
partnership in the Commonwealth may mean embroilment
in European complications and will be compelled to take
them into account. Both have felt that there is little risk of
foreign aggression, though South Africa is less confident about
that now than Canada, which is shielded by the United
States. In Southern Ireland, hatred of Great Britain spurs
the ruling element in the population on to claim every right
that autonomy can give and to deny any corresponding
obligation. The principles laid down by the Imperial Conference of 1926 and embodied in legislative form by the
Statute of Westminster are the same for all the Dominions;
but they mean widely different things in different parts of the
Commonwealth because each Dominion interprets them in
a sense which its circumstances dictate. The interpretations
which some of the Dominions put on them is rejected by
others, if not in principle—and rejection in principle is by
no means out of the question—at least, and, in some instances
very energetically, in practice.

The Statute of Westminster passed the British Parliament
and took effect in December 1931. It defined 'Dominion' as
meaning Canada, Australia, New Zealand, South Africa, and
the Irish Free State. It removed the old provision that a
Dominion statute should be invalid if it was repugnant to
English law, and it gave the Dominion Parliaments the right
to repeal any British 'Act, order, rule or regulation, in so far
as the same is part of the law of the Dominion'. It exempted
Australia and New Zealand from the operation of most of its
sections unless any or each of those sections were adopted by
the Parliament of the Dominion concerned. It safeguarded

the Canadian Constitution, so far as its 'repeal, amendment or alteration' went; and it safeguarded also the constitutional rights of the Provinces of Canada and the States of Australia.

Finally, its most far-reaching clause read:

'No Act of Parliament of the United Kingdom passed after the commencement of this Act shall extend, or be deemed to extend, to a Dominion as part of the law of that Dominion, unless it is expressly declared in that Act that that Dominion has requested, and consented to, the enactment thereof.'

Much controversy, and not only academic controversy, has seethed round this clause. Does it mean that there is no longer any power in the Parliament of the United Kingdom to legislate for a Dominion without the consent of the Dominion? Admittedly, it is almost beyond belief that the Parliament of the United Kingdom would ever want to impose legislation on a Dominion. But if, in some extraordinary circumstances, it wanted to do so, has it still the power?

The circumstances of the Commonwealth make this question more than academically important. In some of the Dominions there are people who would like to see their countries break away from the Commonwealth, partly because they are unconvinced that their countries are not, theoretically at least, still subordinate to the United Kingdom. In the Irish Free State especially, republicanism is strong. It exists, too, in South Africa and is the chief doctrine of the Nationalists there—the rebels from the Hertzog camp; and they are not insignificant as a party. There are republicans in Canada. All these assume that if their country was a republic it could no longer be part of the Commonwealth; and they hold that to turn their country into a Republic would be a way, probably the only feasible way, of freeing it from what they believe to be its latent subordination to the British Parliament.

The weight of opinion which maintains that the Parliament of the United Kingdom still has power to legislate for a Dominion without its consent is considerable. Professor Berriedale Keith in his Introduction to *Speeches and Documents on the British Dominions* says firmly that 'the Imperial Parliament still possesses a pre-eminence over all the other parliaments in the Empire' and that 'the Statute of Westminster solemnly acknowledges (this), in two ways'. It 'recognizes its right to legislate for the Dominions with the assent of their governments or parliaments, whose concurrence the Commonwealth formally requires'. And it 'maintains intact the constitutional restrictions on the alteration of the Canadian, Australian and New Zealand constitutions, thus perpetuating the earlier Imperial Acts'. In addition, 'the mere passing of the Act (of Westminster), which itself is incapable of being altered by any Dominion, is a formal assertion of sovereign power'. Even, again, if the Parliament of the United Kingdom in 1931 did surrender its power of legislating for the Dominions without its consent, that was the act of a single Parliament, which could not 'limit the power of any successor'.

It is the way of jurists to postulate the existence of some ultimate single authority in any political association; and if there is a single legislative authority in the Commonwealth it must be the Parliament of the United Kingdom. Mr. R. B. Bennett, too, who was Prime Minister of Canada in 1930, and was a member of the Imperial Conference when it scrutinized and approved the clause in the Statute of Westminster about the right of the Parliament of the United Kingdom to legislate for a Dominion with its consent, made a speech on the Conference when he was back in Canada and mentioned the clause with special emphasis. The 1930 Conference, he declared, did not 'for a single moment' think 'of renouncing the supremacy of the Imperial Parliament, lest it be taken as a termination of the ties that bind together under the Crown all the overseas Dominions'.

On the other hand, the report of the Conference of 1930 contains a section which seems to suggest that some at least of the Dominion delegates at that Conference took it for granted that the clause about United Kingdom legislation, which was going to be put into the Statute of Westminster, would do away with any right of the United Kingdom Parliament to legislate for a Dominion without its consent. The Conference had inserted a verbal amendment into the clause as originally framed; and its report said:

'The delegates from some of the Dominions were apprehensive

lest the acceptance of the above amendment might imply recognition of a right of the Parliament of the United Kingdom to legislate in relation to a Dominion (otherwise than at the request and with the consent of the Dominion) in a manner which, if the legislation had been enacted in relation to a foreign State, would be inconsistent with the principles of international comity. It was agreed that the clause as amended did not imply, and was not to be construed as implying, the recognition of any such right, and, on the proposal of the United Kingdom delegates, that a statement to this effect should be placed on record.'

To the lay mind, that seems conclusive. The Imperial Conference of 1930 thus expressly denied the continuance of the old right of the British Parliament to make a law for a Dominion without its consent, and included in its report a carefully considered statement to that effect. This, too, was the conclusion that the delegates of the Irish Free State to the 1930 Imperial Conference took away with them. The Cosgrave Government was at that time almost at its last gasp. Its representatives went to the 1930 Imperial Conference knowing that Mr. de Valera would be on the alert to catch them out if they showed any weak-kneed disposition to abate a jot of the autonomy of their country. They returned convinced that the report of the 1930 Conference, and the Statute of Westminster which was to follow, had finally disposed of the supremacy of the British Parliament over the Irish Free State Parliament.

The speech in which Mr. McGilligan, Minister for External Affairs in the Cosgrave Cabinet, expounded that thesis to the Lower House of the Irish Free State Parliament is the most brilliant argument extant for the doctrine that the Statute of Westminster has extirpated all vestige of a right in the Parliament of the United Kingdom to make laws for a Dominion without its consent. The effect, Mr. McGilligan said, of the clause in the Statute of Westminster about legislation for a Dominion by the British Parliament, would be 'to destroy as a matter of law what has already been destroyed as a matter of practice, the legislative sovereignty of the British Parliament in the Commonwealth in the sense in which it existed and functioned since the foundations of the Colonial Empire were laid. The importance of that achievement is beyond question. I do not want to overstress it, but I do not want to have the effect of it minimized.'

Mr. McGilligan knew as he was speaking that, the moment he sat down, a member of the de Valera Party would get up and maintain vehemently precisely what the jurists maintain, that the Statute of Westminster did not abolish 'the legislative sovereignty of the British Parliament in the Commonwealth'. He went on to tackle the argument that the mere fact of a British statute purporting to abolish the sovereignty within the Commonwealth of the body which passed it showed that there had been no actual abolition. It was the British Parliament, he said, that had exercised sovereignty over the Dominions; therefore the British Parliament had to abolish its own right to exercise it. No other Parliament, no other authority within the Empire or outside it, could do that. The Parliament of Canada had never made laws for South Africa, or Ireland, or any other part of the Empire. The British Parliament had. It had ceased to make them for the Dominions, but its inherent right to make them had never been surrendered. The Statute of Westminster would surrender the right, in the only way that was feasible, by formal enactment of the British Parliament. And if it was said (as the jurists do say) that no Parliament could bind its successor and that some subsequent British Parliament might claim to revive the right which the Statute of Westminster abandoned—well, let it try.

At a subsequent stage in the debate Mr. McGilligan revealed something of what had passed behind the closed doors of the Imperial Conference of 1930. It had been suggested there that the British Parliaments of the future would not be bound by anything that might be done at Westminster when the Statute of Westminster was passed. On that suggestion several delegates, including General Hertzog, the Prime Minister of South Africa, had exclaimed that 'if there was ever any question of a British Parliament later repealing this Statute of Westminster, which the Dominions now wanted, the answer was that the moment that repeal was attempted the whole Commonwealth of Nations would be broken up'.

So that, though the inherent right of the Parliament at Westminster to make laws for a Dominion without its consent is never likely to be exercised and is in practice the 'figment' which it was called by a British Attorney-General as early as 1921, the question whether it survives the Statute of Westminster or not is not merely an academic question. If the right does survive, the British Parliament retains an inherent supremacy over the Dominion Parliaments and the statement in the 1926 Imperial Conference report that Great Britain and the Dominions are 'in no way subordinate to one another in any aspect of their domestic . . . affairs' is not literally true.

How much play can be made with such a theoretical superiority—and its corollary, the subordination of a Dominion to Great Britain—Mr. de Valera's record as head of the Government of the Irish Free State since 1932 has shown. His example stimulates Dr. Malan, his opposite number in South Africa, to attack the Hertzog–Smuts combination Cabinet. Sooner or later an Imperial Conference will have to confront the direct question whether the Statute of Westminster has abolished the inherent power of the British Parliament to make laws for a Dominion without its consent or not. When that happens, there can be only one answer—that it has. An amendment to the Statute of Westminster declaring in so many words that the Parliament of the United Kingdom has no power to legislate for a Dominion without its consent would settle the issue once and for all; for even republicans would find it difficult to make much of a grievance out of the putative power of a future Parliament at Westminster to undo what one of its predecessors has done.

Meanwhile, two of the Dominions, Canada and the Irish Free State, have adopted the Statute of Westminster. Two, Australia and New Zealand, have not thought its adoption necessary or advisable. The fifth, South Africa, has incorporated its provisions in South African statute law by passing the Status of the Union Act. It is taken for granted in Australia that it will be better to adopt the Statute of Westminster in the near future; but consultation with the

States will be necessary before the Federal Government asks the Commonwealth Parliament to pass the necessary resolution.

The abdication of King Edward VIII in December 1936 threw the constitutional relations of the States of the Commonwealth into sudden relief. Some conclusions from what then happened may be summarized here:

1. If there had ever been any doubt that the Government and Parliament of Great Britain would not act or legislate for any Dominion without its consent, whether the Dominion had adopted the Statute of Westminster or not, the abdication crisis removed it. All the Dominions were consulted by the British Government as soon as King Edward asked Mr. Baldwin to take the opinion of his colleagues in the British Cabinet and of the other Commonwealth Cabinets about his proposed marriage to Mrs. Simpson. The preamble of the United Kingdom Declaration of Abdication Act recites that it is passed with the consent of Canada, Australia, South Africa, and New Zealand.

2. In that crisis, the Government of the Irish Free State was in a special position, for the President, Mr. de Valera, seized the opportunity to amend the Constitution by omitting all reference to the Crown in clauses dealing with internal affairs. The Bill containing these amendments, and another Bill recognizing King George VI as entitled to 'act on behalf of the Irish Free State for the purposes of the appointment of diplomatic and consular representatives and the conclusion of international agreements', were both passed on 12 December 1936, the day after the British Declaration of Abdication Act was passed by the Parliament at Westminster.

3. The Irish Free State was thus not content to endorse the action of the British Parliament, as it was endorsed by the Parliaments of Canada, Australia, and New Zealand. Nor could South Africa, which had embodied the Statute of Westminster in its own Statute law by passing the Status of the Union Act, merely endorse the British Abdication Act. South Africa passed its own Abdication Act. Whereas the Irish Free State Act was passed on and took effect from 12 December, the day after the British legislation, the South

African Act was ante-dated to 10 December, the day on which King Edward signed the Instrument of Abdication.

4. These actions by the Irish Free State and the South African Parliaments were unquestionably deliberate and intended to show their entire autonomy in accepting the abdication of King Edward and the accession of King George as his successor. Both Parliaments were evidently determined to emphasize the fact that they were not merely endorsing the action of the Parliament at Westminster.

5. But both the Irish Free State and South Africa accepted the accession of King George VI as the next in the order of succession to King Edward VIII. And the Irish Free State has now, in the Executive Authority (External Relations) Act, recognized the King of 'Australia, Canada, Great Britain, New Zealand, and South Africa' as its King, so long as the Irish Free State is 'associated with' them, and so long as the same King continues to be King of all of them.

6. A republican amendment to the British Declaration of Abdication Act was moved in the House of Commons. The speeches in support of it were listened to hardly with patience and the amendment was supported by seven members. In South Africa, Dr. Malan, the leader of the Nationalists who oppose the Government, tried to introduce an amendment in favour of the right of secession into the Abdication Bill, but was defeated. One of the clearest morals of the abdication crisis was that, though it presented republicanism with a startlingly propitious opportunity for advocating its tenets, there was hardly a sign, anywhere in the Commonwealth, of any widespread opposition, even in theory, to the Monarchy.

III

DOMINION DEVELOPMENT: CANADA

THE Versailles Peace Treaty was signed in July 1919.
Within a year Canada, under its Liberal Prime Minister,
Mr. Mackenzie King, had suggested to Downing Street that
Canadian interests in Washington were specially important,
that it might be embarrassing for the British Ambassador
there to have to go on handling them, as he had done in the
past, and that it would be as well if Canada appointed her
own minister to represent her in the United States. The
suggestion was acquiesced in by the British Cabinet and a
Canadian minister went to Washington. A Canadian minister
has been there ever since. He is now accompanied by a
minister from the Union of South Africa and from the Irish
Free State. The United States has its own Ministers Extraordinary in Canada, South Africa, and the Irish Free State.
The new Commonwealth system had not taken long to get
under way, and Downing Street had recognized already that
when a Dominion wanted to do anything new in international relations, there was nothing for it but to agree as
gracefully as might be. Nevertheless, the next development
of Canada's new conception of her position in the world did
make Downing Street gasp. It showed, too, that the rest of
the world was thoroughly perplexed about it all. The halibut
fisheries in the North Atlantic had been a constant irritation
between the United States and Canada. Canada did not
consider that British Ambassadors in Washington had always
handled this intricate matter as skilfully and with as complete a knowledge of the Canadian case as she could have
desired. British negotiations on behalf of Canada had seldom
been strikingly successful. Canada now began to negotiate
on her own behalf with the United States about the halibut
fisheries. The negotiations prospered. They issued in 1922
in a treaty between the U.S.A. and Canada. It was signed by
a representative of the U.S.A. and of Canada. British ministers had nothing to do with it. This was startling. It meant

that the name of the King was being used and his treaty-making power employed on the advice and with the formal concurrence, not, as hitherto, of his ministers in the United Kingdom, but of his ministers in Canada. But Downing Street again raised no open protest.

It was left for the Senate of the United States to put the fat of the new Dominion status doctrine most abruptly into the fire. The Senate showed that it did not understand the position. It ratified the treaty with the reservation that 'none of the nationals, . . . of *any other part of Great Britain*' should violate the treaty provisions while engaging in fishing. There were ructions in the Canadian Parliament, where the Opposition accused the Government of ignoring the British Ambassador in Washington. But Downing Street failed to swallow this transparent bait; the Canadian Government mildly offered to prevent by law fishermen from another country (meaning by implication Great Britain) from abusing the Canadian fishing rights; the Senate agreed; the treaty was ratified by the United States. Canada had vindicated her right, implicit in her new status, to make treaties on her own behalf, without more than the formal intervention of the King's ministers in Whitehall—they had been used in this instance merely as a channel for forwarding the treaty for the King's signature—with a foreign country. A precedent had been set which was later to be followed freely by other Dominions.

When the Imperial Conference met in 1923 it was agreed that the relations of the Dominions with foreign countries and their part in the foreign policy of the Commonwealth needed some regulation. It would not be pleasant if any or all of the Dominions, or indeed the United Kingdom itself, began to go making treaties all over the place, without reference to the interests and opinions of the other partners in the Commonwealth firm. And experience had shown already that the idea that the United Kingdom could act automatically in foreign affairs for the Dominions, assuming their acquiescence and consent, would lead to trouble.

During the autumn of 1922 Mr. Lloyd George's enthusiasm for the new Dominion status—he had seen and advertised it as a funnel through which Dominion approval of and acquiescence in every move of the British Foreign Office would pour automatically towards Whitehall—had been nastily frostbitten. Having backed the Greek and antagonized the Turk, the British Government found itself face to face with a revivified and threatening Turkey at Chanak. The French, justifiably doubtful about Mr. Lloyd George's recent proceedings and ingrainedly reluctant to poke their noses into trouble which had no perceivable bearing on any immediate interest of theirs and whose outcome was uncertain, were on the point of leaving the British force at Chanak in the air, if they had not actually already done so. Here, Mr. Lloyd George must have said to himself, was a heaven-sent chance of exhibiting to the world the splendid unanimity of the Dominions with Great Britain and their eagerness to support her with all their armed might. In one of his most untimely impulsive moments the British Prime Minister fired off a cable to each Dominion, asking for its support at Chanak.

Deliberately, or through one of those failures in staff work to which Mr. Lloyd George's régime as Prime Minister was unhappily liable off and on, the summons, in some Dominions at least, appeared in the Press before it had been seen by ministers. Canada was one; and the Canadian Government was exceedingly peeved. It pointed out that a question of war was for the Parliament of Canada to decide. General Smuts was on holiday in the bush-veld and did not get the summons till some days after; but meanwhile every responsible newspaper in Capetown and Johannesburg had told the British Government that it ought to know better than to treat a Dominion with such impulsive tactlessness, to call it nothing worse. Australia, through its Government, was rather grudgingly willing to help, but also remarked on the impulsiveness of the summons and deplored the dilemma that it presented to Government and people. New Zealand alone, taking Mr. Lloyd George for granted as the mouthpiece of Great Britain because he happened to be Prime Minister, responded with instant enthusiasm both from Government and people. But this could not prevent the Chanak appeal from being exposed as a wretched fizzle, spluttering miserably before the astonished gaze of Europe's diplomatists. If the Prime Minister of Great Britain could misunderstand so conspicuously the spirit of the Commonwealth and be so publicly chided for offending against its hardly formed conventions, how could any foreigner be expected to comprehend or comply with either?

Even the Chanak fiasco, however, was not enough to enlighten the Foreign Office about the sentiments of the Dominions, and especially of Canada, on the subject of their international standing under the new Commonwealth dispensation. Peace with Turkey came under discussion at the Lausanne Conference towards the end of 1922. The Foreign Office assumed that it could be negotiated by Great Britain without the intervention of any Dominion and would be accepted by them. Canada again protested. The Foreign Office, trying to be amiable and merely succeeding in showing that it had no notion what Canada's grievance really was, observed that there could be no objection to the Canadian Parliament considering and formally approving the treaty before it was finally ratified. Canada explained that this would not meet her at all. She had no direct interest in the peace with Turkey; she had not been asked to join in the Lausanne Conference; she was not going to be just a rubber-stamp to the activities of British diplomacy.

Evidently it was time that the Imperial Conference should meet again; and it duly met in 1923. A formula for ironing out the creases that had been showing themselves in the new Commonwealth fabric was discovered and agreed to. The right of any Dominion, just as much as of the United Kingdom, to open negotiations for a treaty or an agreement with a foreign State was explicitly recognized; but it was laid down that if the treaty or agreement seemed to impinge on the interest of any other State in the Commonwealth, that State should be told about the proposed negotiations before they began, so that it could either ask to share in them or express its views in advance.

So far so good. But the Conference of 1923 did not tackle the question of the liability of any or all of the Dominions to be committed by British foreign policy. Apparently it was hoped that, as the British Foreign Office, after Lausanne, must now be assumed to have grasped the Dominion point of view about conferences and treaties entered into or negotiated by Great Britain, there would be no more trouble. It was an optimistic view; and events in Europe were soon to show that the optimism was premature. Meanwhile Mr. Ramsay MacDonald became Prime Minister and entered No. 10 Downing Street full of goodwill towards the Dominions and all the world. He sent a message to the Dominions in the middle of 1924 suggesting a number of improvements in the mechanics of co-operation on questions of Foreign policy between the United Kingdom and the Dominions. Wouldn't it be a good thing if the whole subject was discussed at an intermediate Imperial Conference? But the Dominion Prime Ministers have always found it quite difficult enough to spare the time to travel to London for Imperial Conferences every four years or so and were not enthusiastic about Mr. Mac-Donald's suggestion. Correspondence between them and the Labour Government dragged on. They were not pleased with Mr. MacDonald, whose attitude about Imperial Preference seemed to them retrograde; and they knew that his Government's existence was precarious. If he had been more firmly in the saddle, they might have treated his next overture to them with more respect. As it was, the Protocol, his effort at stiffening up the League of Nations and closing gaps in the Covenant, was rejected unanimously by the Dominions when they were asked whether they would accept it. Even New Zealand, which had been disposed to resent Canada's repeated assertions of her aloofness from British policy in Europe, was shocked by the Protocol.

Mr. Baldwin replaced Mr. MacDonald at 10 Downing Street and the new Government tried to guarantee security to France and Belgium in the Treaty of Locarno towards the end of 1925. Mr. Baldwin had noticed the signs of the times. Under him, the Foreign Office did not repeat the blunder of taking it for granted that the Dominions would endorse mechanically anything that Great Britain chose to commit herself to in Europe. The Locarno Treaty included a clause which exempted the Dominions from liability to be bound by any of its obligations without their express consent. None of the Dominions consented to be bound. Nor did India, which was expressly exempted as well in the Treaty. The principle that a British treaty, which might end in war, should not bind the Dominions unless they wanted to be bound, was established. The new Commonwealth dispensation was making the pace, but there were grave misgivings in responsible quarters.

When the House of Commons discussed the Locarno Treaty, Mr. Lloyd George quoted extracts from a speech by General Smuts. The eminent South African regretted that

'the Empire had not acted with a united front in negotiating and signing the (Locarno) Pact. . . . This case was going to be a precedent for the future. . . . More and more, the foreign policy of the British Empire would become simply that of Great Britain. The day might come when the Dominions might feel that they had little in common with such a policy and would begin their own foreign policies in their own interest. There were natural and inevitable centrifugal tendencies at work in the Empire, and he feared that Locarno had given some impetus to them.'

Mr. Lloyd George echoed and endorsed these forebodings.

'I thought', he cried, 'one of the achievements of the War was that it had unified the Empire, had brought the Dominions into the orbit, as it were, of our foreign policy, and that we should have the advantage of knowing that whatever happened to us in the future would be as the result of a policy they were just as much responsible for as we were.'

If Mr. Lloyd George really thought that in 1925 he had singularly failed to appreciate the lessons that Chanak should have taught him. All the same, the Imperial Conference, when it met again in 1926, showed that it was disturbed about the negotiation of treaties by the Commonwealth members and was not satisfied with the rules prescribed by its predecessor in 1923. It amended the rules by ordaining that when any member-State of the Commonwealth contemplated negotiations for a treaty with a foreign Power, it should notify all the other member-States; not merely, as the 1923 rules had prescribed, member-States which seemed to be affected by the proposed treaty. States so notified were directed in the new rules to 'indicate' their 'attitude with reasonable promptitude'. If the negotiating State received no comments on its intention from any other State, it would be entitled to conclude that that State acquiesced, 'so long as no active obligations on the part of the other Governments' would result from the proposed treaty.

The 1926 Imperial Conference ended its deliberations on the Locarno Treaty by recording its opinion that 'in the sphere of foreign affairs, as in the sphere of defence, the major share of responsibility rests now, and must for some time continue to rest, with H.M. Government in Great Britain'. But it added a couple of riders—that 'practically all the Dominions' were 'engaged to some extent, and some to a considerable extent, in the conduct of foreign relations, particularly those with foreign countries on their borders'; and that 'the governing consideration underlying' such negotiations 'must be that neither Great Britain nor the Dominions could be committed to the acceptance of active obligations except with the definite assent of their own governments'.

The next Imperial Conference, in 1930, endorsed these rules, adding one or two observations. It suggested that the Commonwealth Governments should not only be at pains to apprise each other when they proposed to begin negotiations with a foreign Power, but should appreciate that 'the fullest possible interchange of information between H.M. Governments in relation to all aspects of foreign affairs is of the greatest value to all the Governments concerned'. It insisted, too, that there should be no delay in expression of opinion by the various Governments when they were told that another Government meant to begin negotiations. A 'negotiating Government' would certainly be embarrassed in its negotiations if any other Government, having observations to make, did not make them 'at the earliest possible stage in the negotiations'.

There the matter stands. Any Commonwealth Government is free to negotiate a treaty with any foreign Government, but it is bound to tell the other Commonwealth Governments what it is doing, and they in their turn are bound to say what their views are about the proposed treaty,

if they have any, and to say it quickly. No Commonwealth
State is bound by a treaty made by any other Commonwealth State unless with its express consent. In most matters
of foreign affairs the British Government is expected to take
the initiative, and in doing so to keep in mind the interests
and views of each of the other Commonwealth States. The
duty of each Commonwealth Government to communicate
'information in relation to all aspects of foreign affairs', en-
joined on all by the Imperial Conference of 1930, weighs
with special emphasis upon the British Government.

In fact, the Locarno precedent of Dominion refusal to
accept obligations incurred by Great Britain in a treaty with
foreign Powers has not been followed by any means invariably. On the contrary, the more general practice has
been for the Dominions to adhere to such agreements, entered
into by Great Britain; largely no doubt because the prime
object of such agreements, since Locarno, has been to multiply the guarantees of world peace, rather than to buttress the
post-war *status quo* in Europe. They have acted with Great
Britain in signing the Kellogg Pact of 1928, in putting their
signatures to the formal acceptance of the Optional Clause
and (with the exception of South Africa) the General Act
for the settlement of international disputes. They joined with
Great Britain in the Naval Conference of 1930 and signed the
limited agreement then reached. Even the Locarno Treaty,
though all the Dominions and India refused to accept its
obligations, was praised by the Imperial Conference of 1926
in a formal resolution, which congratulated the British
Government on 'its share in this successful contribution
towards the promotion of the peace of the world'. That resolution has now a more ironic tinge in retrospect than the
refusal of the Dominions and India to bear their share of the
burden which Locarno imposed on the United Kingdom.

IV

DOMINION DEVELOPMENT: SOUTH AFRICA

CANADA took her status as a Dominion within the Commonwealth for granted after the Peace of Versailles, but asserted it in the international sphere. In South Africa, local political quarrels prevented the new status from being taken for granted, and its reality became the chief issue between the Government Party, led by General Smuts after General Botha's death in 1919, and his Dutch opponents the Nationalists, led by General Hertzog.

It suited General Hertzog's book to represent Dominion status as a sham; but probably he himself was convinced for years that it was a sham. His fight with General Smuts took two lines. In the beginning it was a fight for the survival of the Dutch language and Dutch culture. The exact equality of Dutch with English had been a prime condition of Union in 1910; but it is one thing to concede equality to a language on paper and another to make sure that it is treated as equal in every detail of a country's life. How, for example, was equality to be interpreted in terms of education? Were all Civil Servants to be required to know both languages perfectly?

The Union compact had guaranteed the posts of Civil Servants who spoke English only. They were not to be penalized for their ignorance of Afrikaans, as the Dutch language was now called in South Africa. But did this mean that the heads of the Civil Service could be allowed to be men who knew no Afrikaans? If so, how could it be said that the two languages were having absolutely equal treatment? General Hertzog had broken with General Botha on these points before the European War. The help that South Africa, under Botha and Smuts, gave to Great Britain in the War won converts for General Hertzog's Nationalist Party and set him out on his second line of attack. South Africa, he said, was being dragged at Britain's heels into a European conflict which was no business of hers. The old Boer ideal of isolation from the rest of the world was being outraged.

His Nationalist Party grew steadily stronger. He himself was almost worshipped as a champion of the Boer language, Boer culture, and the Boer's right to live remote and untroubled by international quarrels.

The logical end of this Nationalist creed was a republic cut off from the British Empire. But General Hertzog never committed himself or his party to republicanism in so many words. It was plain, for one thing, that no party which risked the hostility of the British South African could hope to govern the country. For another, the British connexion was an asset so evidently invaluable that no responsible political leader could afford to jettison it. Still, republicanism did represent an appreciable body of Dutch South African opinion, and General Hertzog was not the man to antagonize it. So when General Botha and General Smuts, after the Peace of Versailles, began to explain that South Africa was now a Dominion and had full freedom to control her own destiny, General Hertzog's reply was cut and dried. He refused to believe that Dominion status meant anything; and a long, acrimonious conflict, which persisted for years, began about the amount of freedom that South Africa actually had within the British Commonwealth of Nations. With the help of the Labour Party, General Hertzog defeated General Smuts in the General Election of 1924. Two years later he went to London with Mr. Havenga, his Minister of Finance and right-hand man, to attend the Imperial Conference of 1926.

Before he left South Africa he announced that he meant to put the reality of Dominion status to the proof at the Conference. If it was a reality, the Conference would have to say so in so many words. He was much ridiculed for his presumption in making this public demand. Who was he, local Britishers asked scornfully, to go to London boasting that he would dictate to the Imperial Conference what it was to say? Scornfully, but not wisely; for, after all, the Imperial Conference of 1917 had expressed the opinion that the new Dominion position ought to be defined and if there was a demand from any Dominion that the 1917 intention should now be implemented, why should the current Imperial Conference refuse?

It happened, too, that Canada had just passed through
a dissolution crisis and was represented at the Imperial
Conference of 1926 by Mr. Mackenzie King, intensely re-
sentful that Lord Byng, the Governor-General, should have
refused his advice to dissolve Parliament, whereas he had
agreed to a dissolution on the advice of Mr. Meighen a few
weeks later. Mr. Mackenzie King was not averse, in these
circumstances, to having the position of the Dominions within
the Commonwealth defined. The other members of the
Imperial Conference acquiesced; so that General Hertzog
and Mr. Havenga came back with the formula that they had
said they meant to get.

There the controversy about the reality of the new status,
of South Africa as well as of the other Dominions, should
have ended. But the acrimony of local political controversy
was not allayed by the Imperial Conference pronouncement.
'A substantial English element in South Africa hated the
whole idea of Dominion status. They had not forgotten the
Anglo-Boer War any more than the Dutch extremists had
forgotten it. They had always thought that they had been
cheated of the results that victory should have produced for
them; and they had blamed the Liberal Government of 1906
in Great Britain for betraying them by giving responsible
government to the two defeated republics. They still spoke
contemptuously of Afrikaans as a barbarous jargon and they
resented any process of equalizing Civil Service posts between
Afrikaans-speaking and English-speaking officials. South
Africa was a British possession and government jobs ought
to go to good Britishers.

On the other side were the Dutch extremists, who were not
particularly pleased either with the definition of Dominion
rights that General Hertzog had brought back with him
from the Imperial Conference of 1926. If South Africa was
really so free, their highest political trump-card was useless.
Moderation and race-reconciliation would be all the rage
and they would be robbed of their pleasant feeling of having
got the better at last of the English-speaking South African,
with the Hertzog Government in office as a proof of their
triumph.

So General Hertzog and Mr. Havenga had no sooner put foot on the quay at Capetown on their return from the 1926 Imperial Conference than the mischief-makers on both sides were at it in real earnest, and with all too complete success. General Hertzog was rushed by his over-fervent supporters into sanctioning a Bill to legalize a South African flag, which was to notify to all the world how independent South Africa now was, and incidentally was aiming to restrict the use of the Union Jack whenever possible upon every official building all through the Union. This enraged not only the British Jingos but all moderate-minded English South Africans. They took it as a sign that General Hertzog had gone over bag and baggage to his extremists. There was a terrific outburst of indignation, with civil disturbance and bloodshed just over the civic horizon. Neither political side really wanted that. There were protracted negotiations and a last-minute compromise, which left South Africa with a flag of her own, containing a minute Union Jack in its centre, and provided for the flying of the Union Jack, side by side with the South African flag, on a limited number of official buildings on a few specially ceremonial occasions, to remind the public of South Africa's membership of the Commonwealth and Empire.

The reluctant flag-compromise did not end the strife. Next, the Hertzog Government made a trade treaty with Germany, giving Germany most-favoured-nation treatment on the same footing with Great Britain, hoping to encourage South African exports to the Continent, and incidentally flouting the principle of fostering business with your best customer. Other Dominions had made trade treaties with foreign countries; but no Dominion had gone out of its way to extend British preference to a foreign country, and the treaty confirmed suspicions that the Hertzog Government would not mind giving Great Britain one in the eye. So did a subsidy to an Italian shipping line which the Hertzog Government granted in 1932; and as the South African Government had by then refused to follow the example of the British Government in abandoning the gold standard, to which it was sticking at a very heavy cost to its exporters, whom it was subsidizing as compensation for their losses, resentment grew and grew among the followers of General Smuts, whether they spoke Afrikaans or English. He had been away in England when Britain went off gold and had at once published advice to South Africa to do the same and do it quickly. Thereupon one side in politics said that General Smuts was nothing but the creature of England and was constantly anxious to keep South Africa in subjection to Downing Street, the other side that the sole motive of General Hertzog's Cabinet was to put a spoke in Great Britain's wheel at every opportunity. Both accusations were absurd. That they could have been launched and believed showed how bitter feeling had become. Dominion status in South Africa, instead of being a great influence for internal peace, had been distorted into a device for mutual setting of political opponents' teeth on edge.

Yet, early in 1933, the quarrel between General Hertzog and General Smuts was ended almost in a night. The Ottawa Agreements had involved notice to Germany that the trade treaty could not continue. Maintenance of the gold standard, with the bulk of the export and import trade done with Great Britain, involved continuous loss on exports and heavy increases in internal prices. Even the most ardent Government supporters began to murmur against it. Suddenly it was clear that the very existence of the Hertzog Government was in jeopardy. The gold standard was abandoned, and within a few weeks General Hertzog and General Smuts had made their peace with each other, had formed a Coalition Cabinet, had appealed to the country, and had been returned with a smashing majority.

Complete fusion of their two parties followed; but first the sign that General Hertzog's followers craved was given them, with General Smuts's explicit approval. The sign was the adoption of the Statute of Westminster as an Act of the South African Parliament. It signified the complete autonomy of South Africa as a Dominion of the Commonwealth of Nations. It made the Parliament of South Africa the 'sovereign legislative power' within the Union. It barred the application of any Imperial Statute. It vested executive power in the King 'acting on the advice of His Ministers . . . for the Union'. Criticized in Parliament by a small section of English-speaking South Africans who resented this demonstration of the reality of Dominion status in one of its most far-reaching aspects, General Smuts and General Hertzog defended the Status of the Union Act as merely a formal importation into South Africa of the Statute of Westminster.

The Status Act was passed by an overwhelming majority. A final step showed that General Hertzog and General Smuts were determined to leave no room for doubt that in every detail of executive as well as legislative procedure South Africa was immune from the least vestige of external control. Important documents of State need to be sealed with the Great Seal as well as signed by the King or his authorized representative in a Dominion. South Africa now acquired a Great Seal of her own and added to it the Signet which is used, in conjunction with the royal signature, to authenticate less important documents of State than those which require the Great Seal. The Irish Free State had acquired a Great Seal in 1932.

V

GOVERNORS-GENERAL

INNOVATIONS in the functions and duties of the Governors-General were an inevitable consequence of Dominion status. A domestic political crisis in Canada in 1926 first showed that the position of the Governor-General of a Dominion had been altered radically by Dominion autonomy. Later in the year the Imperial Conference took the question up and enumerated the principles which were to be observed by Governors-General. Rules for recommendations to the King as to the appointment of Governors-General were formulated by the Imperial Conference of 1930.

Mr. Mackenzie King, leader of the Liberal Party, was Prime Minister of Canada in 1926. There was a scandal about irregularities in one of the departments; a vote of censure was moved; the Prime Minister came to the conclusion that his Government could not carry on the business of the country properly with Parliament composed as it was. He asked the Governor-General, Lord Byng, to dissolve Parliament. Lord Byng refused. Mr. Mackenzie King, highly indignant at what he believed to be a breach of the conventions which governed the actions of a Governor-General, resigned. Lord Byng accepted his resignation and sent for Mr. Meighen, leader of the Conservative Party. Mr. Meighen formed a Government, but he had no majority in Parliament, and his only hope of carrying on at all was to evade the constitutional rule, still held valid in Canada, that ministers accepting Cabinet office must resign and go to their constituents for re-election. This irregularity was censured by the Canadian House of Commons. Mr. Meighen then obtained from Lord Byng the consent to a dissolution which had been refused to Mr. Mackenzie King, prorogued Parliament, and carried on the Government pending the general election with a Cabinet which had not a shadow of a constitutional title to be in office at all. Mr. Mackenzie

King made this the major issue of the general election and was sent back to power with a decisive majority.

The immediate issue between the Governor-General and the Liberal Prime Minister was whether the Governor-General, as the King's representative, could exercise the King's right (undoubted, though disused, in the United Kingdom) to refuse to dissolve Parliament when a Prime Minister advised a dissolution. On that comparatively restricted issue Mr. Mackenzie King was supported by the Canadian electorate and the Governor-General rebuffed. But the issue cut deeper than that. It had always been the practice for a Governor-General to ask the advice of British ministers in Downing Street when he was confronted by a political crisis in his Dominion; and it was a very open secret that Lord Byng had followed the usual practice before he refused Mr. Mackenzie King's advice to dissolve Parliament. But if the autonomy of a Dominion was a reality, advice from Downing Street to its Governor-General at a moment of domestic political crisis was an intolerable invasion of the Dominion's right to be master in its own house.

The Imperial Conference of 1926, meeting almost immediately after Mr. Mackenzie King's triumph at the elections, and with him present, addressed itself to the deeper aspects of the issue, while offering no overt opinion on the surface issue as between Lord Byng and Mr. Mackenzie King—perhaps because it thought that the Canadian election verdict against the Governor-General had better not be reopened. The position of the Governor-General of a Dominion, said the Imperial Conference of 1926, 'undoubtedly represents a development from an earlier stage when the Governor-General was appointed solely on the advice of his Majesty's Ministers in London and acted also as their representative'. The development was then defined:

'In our opinion it is an essential consequence of the equality of status existing among the members of the British Commonwealth of Nations that the Governor General of a Dominion is the representative of the Crown, holding in all essential respects the same position in relation to the administration of public affairs in the Dominion as is held by His Majesty the King in Great

Britain, and that he is not the representative or agent of His Majesty's Government in Great Britain or of any Department of that Government.'

Incidentally, this definition might be interpreted as an indication that the majority of the Imperial Conference of 1926 thought that Mr. Mackenzie King had been wrong in his controversy with Lord Byng; for if the Governor-General of a Dominion 'holds in all essential respects the same position in relation to the administration of public affairs in the Dominion' as the King holds in the United Kingdom, and, if there is no question about the King's right to refuse a dissolution (even though the right has been long disused), then Mr. Mackenzie King's indignation that the Governor-General should have usurped a right which Mr. Mackenzie King had assumed that he did not possess was misplaced. All that Lord Byng had done, in that case, was to revive a disused royal right in circumstances which he thought justified its revival; and the only real question between him and Mr. Mackenzie King was whether his judgement of the circumstances had been sound.

But that is by the way, though authoritative juristic opinion is reluctant to accept the statement of the Imperial Conference of 1926 about the position of a Governor-General in a Dominion as strictly accurate. It holds that there is a difference between the position of the King in the United Kingdom and that of a Governor-General. A Governor-General, it maintains, is not vested with the full external prerogative power of the King, that is to say, that he cannot declare war or proclaim neutrality on behalf of his Dominion. This is one of those controversial points on which the conventions of the Commonwealth are not yet crystallized, because the need to settle it has not occurred.

It followed from the principles laid down by the Imperial Conference of 1926 that the Governor-General of a Dominion should not in future be the channel of communication between the British and a Dominion Government, except at the express wish of the Dominion Government concerned, as he had been before, but that the two Governments should communicate direct; and the Conference gave explicit directions to that effect. These stand. But there was another point, to which the Conference of 1926 had not addressed itself. Advice about the appointment of a Governor-General had been given normally by British ministers to the King after the wishes of the Dominion Government had been ascertained. The practice, too, had been to appoint as Governors-General men of distinction from the United Kingdom. In the Irish Free State, however, the appointment of Mr. Timothy Healy had been successfully urged by the Free State Government before the 1926 Conference met. But it was left to the next Imperial Conference, in 1930, to assert definitely that advice about the appointment of a Governor-General must be given to the King by the Cabinet of the Dominion concerned, without the intervention of the British Government. 'The constitutional practice that His Majesty acts on the advice of responsible ministers', said the 1930 Conference, 'applies also in this instance. The ministers who tender and are responsible for such advice are His Majesty's ministers in the Dominion concerned.'

It is now well established, too, that a Dominion ministry can advise the appointment of a Dominion citizen as Governor-General and that the King will accept their advice. The Australian Government advised the appointment of Sir Isaac Isaacs in 1931. He was appointed. His successor, on the other hand, is Sir Alexander Hore-Ruthven, now Lord Gowrie, a British general. Quite recently the South African Government has advised the appointment of a long-resident, though British-born, South African, Mr. Patrick Duncan, and he is to succeed Lord Clarendon as Governor-General of the Union. By one of the queer anomalies of Commonwealth practice, the Governors of the Australian States are still appointed by the King on the advice of British ministers. Still more queer, the State Governors have more power constitutionally than the Governor-General. When, for example, Sir Philip Game, then Governor of New South Wales, dispensed with Mr. Lang as Premier of the State, he must have acted without Mr. Lang's advice, a thing which no Governor-General could have done without provoking a constitutional crisis. Again, even if the Statute of Westminster is adopted by the Commonwealth Parliament, it will not apply to the Australian States without their consent, which means, among other things, that the legislation of the State Parliaments will then still be invalid if repugnant to legislation of the Parliament at Westminster; whereas the rule of repugnancy will be at an end in its application to legislation by the Commonwealth Parliament at Canberra.

The Governors-General being precluded by the new Commonwealth system from communicating with the British Government, or acting as its agent in the Dominions, as they had done before, and the rule being that the British Government should communicate direct with the Dominion Governments, it was necessary for a channel of communication to be established. Accordingly, in Canada, in Australia, and in South Africa High Commissioners were appointed as the representatives of the British Government. In South Africa the High Commissioner has taken over the duties of the Governor-General in connexion with the Protectorates of Bechuanaland, and Basutoland, and Swaziland, on the borders of the Union. New Zealand, alone among the Dominions, is content with the old position of the Governor-General. Its Governor-General is still appointed by the King on the advice of his British ministers, though with the concurrence of the New Zealand Cabinet. He still communicates with the British Government and is its representative at Wellington.

New Zealand acquiesced reluctantly in the report of the Imperial Conference of 1926, its representative signing the report, as he said subsequently in the New Zealand Parliament, only when he was 'pressed to agree in order to preserve unanimity'. But whether this attitude towards Dominion status will be maintained by New Zealand now that a Labour Government is in power remains to be seen, for the Labour leader, now the Prime Minister, was one of the few members of Parliament who favoured the resolution approving of the Statute of Westminster.

VI

THE IRISH FREE STATE

THE reasons why the development of Dominion constitutional individuality took different ways in different parts of the Commonwealth should now be beginning to be clear. Not one of the four Overseas Dominions has insisted on its rights as a Dominion because it has wanted to make itself unpleasant to Great Britain. Each has gone to the lengths that its internal circumstances have dictated. In Canada, with its well-established consciousness of detachment from Europe and its reliance on the United States as a bulwark against aggression, the main emphasis of Dominion status has been put on freedom from automatic liability to support British foreign policy, except at League of Nations meetings when all the Empire States were acting in concert. In South Africa acute racial friction has compelled successive Governments to insist on the autonomy of a Dominion within the Commonwealth, in self-defence against the accusation of being at the beck and call of a British Government.

In Australia, Dominion status has taken another trend. The thought of possible peril by Asiatic invasion is never quite absent from the Australian mind. The automatic corollary of protection by British sea power is support of British foreign policy in general, even in European fields; for any decline of British prestige as a World Power weakens the buckler that it holds over Australia. So in Australia there has been none of the eagerness that Canada has shown to assert immunity from the consequences of British policy except with express consent, and none of the South African insistence on the formal registration of the guarantees of autonomy within the Commonwealth. But Australia has a very pronounced national individuality, and one of its marks is a tolerant amusement at the conventions of English life, at solemn forms and ceremonies, at class distinctions. This was behind the sudden assertion in 1931 of the right of the Commonwealth Government to advise the King on the appointment of a Governor-General and the selection of an Australian, Sir Isaac Isaacs, as the nominee whom the King was advised to appoint. New Zealand, more immune than Australia from the fear of invasion, with no waste of empty lands to excite Asiatic cupidities, strongly conscious of her inequality of stature with Great Britain, has felt no necessity to insist in any way on her equality of status, though she did join the other Dominions in refusing to be bound by the Treaty of Locarno.

None of the four has been actuated by antagonism to Great Britain, not even South Africa, where the Hertzog Government, which chiefly pressed for and obtained the Imperial Conference report of 1926, wanted some such declaration not as a bill of indictment against any anticipated attempt by Great Britain to restrict the freedom of the Union, but as a public demonstration of that freedom and a charter for the Afrikaans-speaking people.

The manifestations of Dominion status in the Irish Free State have been sharply different in origin and purpose. Their motive has been resentment at what are believed to have been centuries of injury by Great Britain. Their purpose has been to remove the last iota of British control. This motive and purpose Mr. de Valera, who has been their inspiration, would not deny, though he has said often that he is not hostile to the United Kingdom and would like the Irish Free State to be on good terms with it. The heritage of history and its most sensitive child, national sentiment, is evident in each stage of the operation of Dominion status in the Irish Free State, which was never a colony and did not pass through the usual colonial process of growth to Dominionhood. Self-government was granted to the colonies which have become Dominions not always willingly but always without stubborn resistance. When the Irish Free State got it at last, it was extorted rather than granted.

The long strife in the Irish Free State which followed the passage of its Constitution Act by the Parliament at Westminster in December 1922 need not be recapitulated here. In 1932 Mr. de Valera's Party, Fianna Fáil, became the largest single party in the Dáil, the Lower House of the Irish

I

Free State legislature, and Mr. de Valera took office. His majority depended on Labour support. In January 1933 he sprang another general election upon the country and came back with a majority of one over the other parties. The majority included the Speaker. Before the general election of 1933 Mr. de Valera had already repudiated liability to the British Government under the land annuities agreement of 1923. His action was denounced by Mr. J. H. Thomas, Dominions Secretary, on behalf of the British Government.

The two Governments have been at odds ever since. The British Government was prepared to submit the dispute to arbitration by a Commonwealth Tribunal. Mr. de Valera was willing to submit the dispute to such an *ad hoc* tribunal as the 1930 Imperial Conference had contemplated, but refused to comply with the provision in the relative 1930 resolution that the chairman of the tribunal should not be 'drawn from outside the British Commonwealth of Nations'. This refusal was more than the British Government of the day could stomach, and deadlock ensued. When the Irish Free State failed to pay the instalment of the land annuities due in July 1932, the British Government asked and obtained authority from Parliament to levy duties on Southern Irish exports to the United Kingdom to an amount estimated to be sufficient to make up the sum regarded as due by way of land annuities. At Ottawa, in August 1932, the British representatives would not negotiate with the Irish Free State delegation. In November of the same year imports from the Irish Free State were subjected to the same duties as those from countries outside the Commonwealth. The Irish Free State retaliated by levying specifically retaliatory duties on British goods.

So the dispute between the two Governments was well under way. But it was a much more deep-seated dispute than a difference about the land annuities. The Constitution of the Irish Free State is based on what is known as the Treaty of December 1921, between the British Government and the Sinn Féin delegation. Mr. de Valera denies the validity of the Treaty and consequently of the Constitution. The Constitution was explicitly modelled on that of Canada: it provided that the

Irish Free State should have Dominion status, and it prescribed that the Oath of Allegiance to the King should be taken by members of the Irish Free State Parliament. No sooner did he become President than Mr. de Valera proceeded to abolish the Oath of Allegiance, on the ground that it was an internal matter which the Parliament of the Irish Free State had a right to decide for itself. Article 50 of the Constitution gave the Irish Free State Parliament no power to pass amendments of the Constitution beyond the limits of the Treaty. Mr. de Valera's Constitution (Removal of Oath) Bill purported to repeal the limitation as a prelude to the abolition of the Oath. He argued that the Parliament of the Irish Free State had the same power to amend the Constitution as the Parliament of Canada—superficially an unfortunate contention, for the Constitution of Canada can be amended only by the Parliament at Westminster. On the other hand, there is no doubt that the Parliament at Westminster would pass without question or alteration any amendment properly requested by the Parliament at Ottawa. The Constitution (Removal of Oath) Bill became law in May 1933, after having been twice held up by the Senate.

Appeals from the Irish Courts to the Judicial Committee of the Privy Council came next on Mr. de Valera's programme. Under the Constitution of the Irish Free State there was no such appeal. But the right of a subject of the King in the Irish Free State to petition the Privy Council for leave to appeal was expressly maintained by the Constitution. Mr. de Valera's Bill, which came before the Dáil in 1933, purported to take away this right. It passed the Irish Free State Parliament in the same year and was assented to by the King. In a case before the Privy Council, it was argued that the Act was *ultra vires* the Irish Free State Parliament, because it violated the Treaty, which was the basis of the Constitution. The Privy Council decided that the Statute of Westminster empowered the Free State legislature to pass laws contrary to the Treaty and the Constitution, but it was silent about the moral right, not unnaturally. The Free State Government refused to recognize the jurisdiction of the Privy Council in this matter and was not represented as a party in the case.

Under Mr. de Valera's inspiration the Irish Free State
Parliament has also altered the provisions of the Constitution
relating to Free State citizenship. The Irish Nationality and
Citizenship Act of 1935 repeals the two British Acts (of 1914
and 1918) on British nationality, 'if and so far as they respectively are, or ever were, in force' in the Irish Free State. It
deprives the common law on British nationality of any effect
in the Irish Free State, 'if and so far as it is or ever was, either
wholly or in part, in force' there. It prescribes that natural-
born citizens of the Irish Free State shall not, on that account,
be citizens or nationals of any other country, thus abolish-
ing the common citizenship of natural-born citizens of any
country of the Commonwealth of Nations, so far as it applies
to born nationals of the Irish Free State. The result of this
and other legislation of the Irish Free State on the subject of
nationality and citizenship, granted its validity, appears to
be that the only persons who are entitled to be regarded as
citizens of the Free State are those who comply with the conditions prescribed by the Free State itself. All others, British
subjects or not, are aliens in the Free State. On the other
hand, under the nationality legislation of the other States of
the Commonwealth, citizenship of the Irish Free State, but
not naturalization there, confers citizenship of those other
States. In other words, whereas the rest of the Commonwealth maintains a common citizenship derived from participation in allegiance to the Crown, the Irish Free State has
asserted its own right to decide who shall have its citizenship.
The subject is complex. Its surface has been no more than
brushed here. The consequences of this Irish Free State
legislation cannot be foreseen.

Before the new Constitution was rushed through Parliament on 12 December 1936 nothing had been left undone by
the present Government of the Irish Free State to diminish
the prestige and reduce to insignificance the functions of the
Governor-General, the representative, according to the old
Constitution, of the King. He no longer had the right to
recommend money Bills to Parliament or to withhold the
royal assent to Bills. The office had been given to an individual without personal distinction. He retained a portion

only of the salary given him. The Irish Free State Government required him to return the balance.

The Irish Free State has not been behindhand in impressing on other countries its international position. It has accredited ministers to Berlin, Washington, Paris, Brussels, and the Papal Court at Rome. It joined the League of Nations in 1923 and has had a seat on the League Council. Mr. de Valera himself has been President of the League Council. As a world-notorious gesture of detachment from the British Commonwealth, it registered the Anglo-Irish Treaty of 1921 at Geneva as an international treaty in contempt of the British view that agreements between States of the Commonwealth were a domestic affair and should not be notified at Geneva.

Lastly, the consummation to which all these changes had been leading up was reached on 12 December 1936, when Mr. de Valera seized on the abdication crisis to hurry two Bills through the Irish Free State Parliament. The first of these Bills, which were both passed on 12 December, enacted a number of amendments to the Irish Free State Constitution; the second, in the words of its title, made 'provision, in accordance with the Constitution, for the exercise of the executive authority of Saorstat Eireann (the Irish Free State) in relation to certain matters in the domain of external relations'.

Mr. de Valera had given a general congress of his party a forecast of the new Constitution some weeks earlier. It was to be 'a Constitution which the Irish people would themselves freely choose if Britain were a million miles away'. Its basis was to be that 'the Irish people should be the judges of what their political institutions shall be'—'a Constitution as if there were no relationship with the States of the Commonwealth'.

The Constitution Amendment Act thus passed on 12 December 1936 takes the form of a single enacting clause and a schedule of amendments to a number of articles in the 1922 Constitution. Its precise domestic effect can hardly be pronounced upon here, for it is much in doubt, even in the Irish Free State itself. It would be premature, too, to offer any opinion about the full effect of the amendments on the position of the Irish Free State within the Commonwealth. Mr. Baldwin, as Prime Minister of the United Kingdom, was asked in the House of Commons on 25 January 1937 whether 'the claim of the Government of the Irish Free State to be a Republic as regards internal affairs and a Dominion as regards external affairs' was 'recognized by His Majesty's Government'. He replied that 'the question of the effect of the recent Irish Free State legislation on that country's relations to the British Commonwealth of Nations is now under consideration, and until the examination is complete no statement can be made on the matter'.

In general, the intention of the amendments to the Irish Free State Constitution made on 12 December is to eliminate the functions of the Crown under the Constitution. The King is no longer to be part of the legislature. No representative of the King is to be appointed. All references in the Constitution to the various duties of the representative of the Crown—such as giving or reserving assent to Bills passed by the legislature, the exercise of executive authority, summoning the legislature, appointing the President, the Vice-President, and the ministers, appointing judges, and so on— are excised from the Constitution. These duties are to be performed by the President or by the Executive Council or by the legislature, as the case may be.

The second Act, called the Executive Authority (External Relations) Act, 1936, provides that the diplomatic and consular representatives of the Irish Free State are to be appointed 'on the authority of the Executive Council'. The treaty-making power is vested in the Executive Council. But, 'so long as the Irish Free State is associated with . . . Australia, Canada, Great Britain, New Zealand and South Africa, and so long as the king recognized by those nations as the symbol of their co-operation continues to act on behalf of each of those nations (on the advice of the several Governments thereof) for the purposes of the appointment of diplomatic and consular representatives and the conclusion of international agreements, the king so recognized may, and

is hereby authorized to, act on behalf of the Irish Free State
for the like purposes as and when advised by the Executive
Council so to do'. (In the Act the words Saorstat Eireann
are used to signify the Irish Free State.)

The Act also provides that, 'upon the passing of this Act',
the Instrument of Abdication signed by King Edward VIII
on 10 December 1936 is to take effect 'for the purposes' set
out in the clause of the Act quoted above; that King Edward
VIII shall then cease to be king (of the Irish Free State) for
those purposes 'and all other (if any)'; and that 'the king for
those purposes shall henceforth be the person who', if King
Edward VIII had died on 10 December 1936 unmarried,
'would for the time being be his successor under the law of'
the Irish Free State.

VII

EMPIRE PERMANENCE

IF the new Irish Free State Constitution has turned Southern Ireland into a republic, can it remain in the Commonwealth? The Imperial Conference of 1937 can hardly avoid this question, so it may as well be faced in advance, as well as other questions about the ultimate rights of a Dominion which are being canvassed elsewhere. For example, can a Dominion secede from the Commonwealth if a sufficient number of its people want it to secede? (What would be a sufficient number is an interesting but really an irrelevant query, for unless there was practical unanimity on such a matter there would be civil war, and if it came to civil war in a Dominion on the issue of staying within the Commonwealth or leaving it, the rest of the Commonwealth could do nothing but stand aside and wait for a decision.) If, again, one Commonwealth State goes to war, can another declare itself neutral and try to get the foreign combatant to recognize its neutrality?

The answers to these questions cannot be given merely by saying that it would be unconstitutional for a Dominion to proclaim itself a republic, or to secede, or to declare itself neutral in war. They depend on the real nature of the Commonwealth—the group of countries, that is to say, which have complete equality of status, with the United Kingdom, within the Empire. The Commonwealth emerged after the War not because any one thought it out in advance or designed and constructed it, but because it was the natural result of the part that the Dominions had played in the War. Usage formed it. Usage settled into habit and became convention. Additional usages accumulated, established themselves, became conventions, and were recognized by successive Imperial Conferences. If there is any constitutional law of the Commonwealth, it is the body of these conventions, duly ratified by successive Imperial Conferences.

The Constitutional Law of the Commonwealth, that is to

say, has not preceded the conventions; it has followed on their acceptance and has been formed out of them. Whenever an existing part of the constitutional law of the pre-war Empire has conflicted with one of these conventions, it has been unhesitatingly repealed or altered to conform with convention.

The Imperial Sub-conference of 1929, which considered the Operation of Dominion Legislation in the light of the Imperial Conference pronouncement of 1926, made an attempt to find words for this process:

'The association of constitutional conventions with law has long been familiar in the history of the British Commonwealth; it has been characteristic of political development both in the domestic government of these communities and in their relations with each other; it has permeated both executive and legislative power. It has provided a means of harmonising relations where a purely legal solution of practical problems was impossible, would have impaired free development, or would have failed to catch the spirit which gives life to institutions. Such conventions take their place among the constitutional principles and doctrines which are in practice regarded as binding and sacred whatever the powers of Parliaments may in theory be.'

Any temptation to answer confidently any question about the rights of any State of the Commonwealth should be chastened by a retrospective glance at the changes which have occurred imperceptibly and have established themselves firmly before they were generally realized, far less understood. But one master-convention distinguishes the Commonwealth in its present stage from the pre-war association of the United Kingdom and what have since become the Dominions—the principle that they are all equal in status. When the Imperial Conference of 1926 put this principle and its consequences into a formula, it enumerated the then existing conditions under which the principle operated. These were: immunity of the Commonwealth communities from subjection to each other, or to any one of them, in any aspect of their domestic or external affairs; freedom of association within the Commonwealth; a unity of common allegiance to the Crown; a difference between status and stature or function—equality of status not implying uniformity in strength or in international obligation. But the formula of 1926 was no more than a formula; and if any Dominion, or the United Kingdom, for the matter of that, chooses to do something, in the exercise of its autonomy, which makes any of the conditions thus recited in the 1926 formula obsolete, not necessarily for all the Commonwealth communities but for any of them, it will be useless to attempt to restrain it by appealing to the 1926 formula, as though it were an authoritative definition for all time of the essentials of the Commonwealth association.

The upshot is that no one can lay down the constitutional law of the Commonwealth and assert that one of its communities cannot do anything specific. If some innovation, however sweeping, is embarked upon by one of the Commonwealth communities, it will, in the normal course, become a convention to which the existing laws and customs of the association will have to be made to conform. To deny the right of any Commonwealth community to pronounce itself a republic, or to secede, or to attempt to declare itself neutral in war, is to waste words. There is no authority within the Commonwealth which can restrain any member-State from doing any of these things. Whether, if any member-State does any of them, the other member-States will acquiesce in what it has done and will continue to recognize it as a Commonwealth member is another question; but if recognition was withdrawn in such circumstances it would not be because the right was denied but because the other member-States preferred not to continue association when the right was exercised.

What any Dominion may decide to do is thus utterly beyond regulation by any restrictive constitutional law of the Commonwealth. There is no such law, except in so far as usage has been accepted and ratified by any Imperial Conference. Where there are circumstances which are new, so that usage has not established itself in relation to them, no constitutional law, binding on any or all of the member-States, exists.

There is, however, a doctrine that the unrestricted freedom

of a State of the Commonwealth must be held to be limited
by what may be called moral obligations. (In practice, of
course, it is limited in various minor ways, for example,
by considerations of convenience, as in routine matters of
foreign policy, where the interests of the association as a whole
dictate that business shall be conducted by one State on
behalf of the rest.) The doctrine of moral obligation as a
limitation on the rights of individual States of the Commonwealth was enunciated soon after the War by Mr. Mackenzie
King in Canada. It seems to have been accepted by General
Smuts, doubtless because his intensely realistic mind has
perceived the bearing of inequality of stature, or function, as
between the States of the Commonwealth, on equality of
status.

Theoretically there is a clear gulf between status and
stature. In fact, the greater stature of the United Kingdom
limits the rights that her status gives her as an equal member
of the Commonwealth partnership. If Canada, say, was to
decide that rather than be involved in an Empire war she
would secede from the Commonwealth, the Commonwealth
might continue without her. But if Great Britain was to
make the same decision in the event of a war involving all
the Dominions, it is hard to believe that that would not
be the end of the Commonwealth. Inequality of stature or
function thus involves inequality of status, so far as Great
Britain is concerned. Her stature being immeasurably greater
than that of any Dominion, her status—so far as it means
complete liberty of action, external as well as internal—is
actually less, within the Commonwealth, than that of the
Dominions, because it is necessarily limited by her obligations. It might fairly be said, this being so, that, morally at
least, any theoretical right of a Dominion from the exercise
of which the United Kingdom is precluded by the responsibilities of her position should in practice, though not in
theory, be denied to each Dominion.

But the truth is plain. If any Dominion wants at any time,
through the expressed will of its people, to become a republic,
or to enforce any of the rights which have been discussed,
neither Great Britain nor any other Commonwealth State

will think of coercing it. Why then discuss these unpleasant contingencies? Because in various parts of the Empire, principally within the Commonwealth, but in India and elsewhere as well, controversy about them is always going on. Theorists like to argue on the limits, if there are any, of Dominion autonomy. Serious-minded people recoil from the thought of their country being dragged at the coat-tails of Great Britain into a European war and wonder whether, rather than that, true patriotism would not counsel secession from the Empire. Politicians play upon prejudices. If discussion of the ultimate rights of a Dominion is shirked, there are always mischievous-minded people who hint that Dominion autonomy is a sham, lip-served but not genuinely accepted by Great Britain.

On the other side in such controversies are the out-and-out Imperialists. They do not understand the changes in the Empire system since the War and still think of the Dominions as British preserves by right of conquest or colonization. Dominion status infuriates them; denial of Dominion rights is their stock-in-trade in argument, especially if they happen to be politicians. The persistence and bitterness of controversy about republicanism, secession, and the rest, in one or two of the Dominions, would shock British public opinion if it were known. All the more reason why there should be no hair-splitting in Great Britain about Dominion rights. To speak or write as though there was a phantom-tribunal of constitutional law, somewhere or other in the Empire, before which a Dominion wanting to secede could be dragged and condemned, is completely wrong-headed. Into the bargain, it is disastrous; for controversialists in other parts of the Empire lie in wait for pronouncements of that type, exaggerate their authority, and use them as political stock-in-trade, with equal gratification on either side.

It is just as tempting, and may be as calamitous, to put a finger on any one of the institutions of the Commonwealth and Empire, saying that this is of the essence and that with its destruction the Empire and Commonwealth must be dismembered. The Empire association is more than a casual alliance of peoples. But how it is more defies definition.

There is, for example, no one authority, legislative or executive, which is supreme all through it. The cohesion of the Commonwealth is weakened, not fortified, if allegiance to the Crown is insisted on as the one connecting and inviolable link. At once a people such as that of the Irish Free State is exasperated and denies that it owes any allegiance to the King of Great Britain.

Not only, either, the people of the Irish Free State. The doctrine of republicanism is stronger in parts of the Commonwealth than is usually understood in the United Kingdom. Republicans have respected the British monarchy, because the monarchs have been so devoted to their duty; and the abdication of King Edward VIII has reinforced rather than weakened that burdensome tradition. But republicanism persists. In South Africa, to single out what is perhaps its most numerously populated habitat at the moment, the avowedly republican party of Dr. Malan, who leads the rebels from General Hertzog's camp, might in the not distant future strengthen its forces greatly in the Union Parliament. In the elections of last autumn for the Provincial Council of the Cape, Dr. Malan won a very substantial block of seats against the Hertzog-Smuts combination.

Discussion and recognition of the most far-reaching Dominion rights can only do good. The unique value of the Empire in the world is that it finds room for all sorts—of opinions and doctrines, as well as of races and peoples. It is not static politically; it is experimental, and when it begins to excommunicate any political or constitutional idea, however apparently revolutionary, some of its virtue will have gone out of it. The power of the Empire to hold together is largely the power that it gets from this elasticity. That is why it is better for such a people as the Southern Irish to remain within the Empire. Better for the Empire, that is to say, which would make a great blunder if they were expelled in indignation at what seem their studied insults to the King and British institutions in general. Their sour hostility is no more formidable than that of other races who have been reconciled to the Empire by being convinced that their freedom is safe, their language guaranteed equal rights, their culture respected and expected to bring forth its fruits, their co-operation in defending liberty in the world welcomed. The French of Canada and the Dutch of South Africa could tell the Southern Irish something of these things. If the resentment of the Irish Free State is to be reconciled, the same wisdom must be used with them as with the French of Canada and the Dutch of South Africa. In substance it is being used; but under the gratuitous handicap of a method which makes it look as if it was unwilling and extorted.

VIII

CROWN AND COMMONWEALTH

M R. WINSTON CHURCHILL, speaking in the House of Commons on the Statute of Westminster, recalled a conversation with Lord Balfour. They had been talking, he said, about the Commonwealth and had agreed that 'we are bound, where the great self-governing Dominions of the Crown are concerned, boldly to grasp the larger hope, and to believe, in spite of anything that may be written in Acts of Parliament, that all will come right, nay, all will go better and better between Great Britain and her offspring.' Whereupon Lord Balfour had said, 'I do not believe in wooden guns', meaning, as Mr. Churchill interpreted him to the Commons, that 'he saw no advantage in preserving an assertion of rights and powers on which, in practice, we should not find it possible to base ourselves'.

This, as will have been observed, is the argument of the last chapter. As there is no authority in the Commonwealth which can prevent any Dominion, to say nothing of the United Kingdom, from doing anything it likes, even to declaring itself a republic or seceding, in the exercise of its unlimited autonomy; as neither the United Kingdom nor any Dominion would think of trying to coerce a Dominion which went to the farthest lengths conceivable in asserting its autonomy; and as the Irish Free State has already gone in that direction as far as any Dominion can go, short of seceding—what, in face of this formidable array of facts, is the good of trying to make out that there are definable limits to Dominion autonomy? That attempt is certainly the least effectual, as it is the most pretentious, of the wooden guns that Balfour warned Mr. Winston Churchill against.

But the attempt to put Dominion autonomy into a doctrinal strait-jacket must be taken seriously, if only because the Crown is dragged in in support of it. The argument goes this way: the Crown is an integral part of sovereignty in the Commonwealth as a whole and in each member-State: the

Crown could not, in any member-State, be a party consenting, on the advice of its ministers in that State, to a legislative act purporting to alter the form of Government from a monarchy into a republic, or to separate the State from the Empire: if so, the Crown would be a party in one member-State to the destruction, or to the abolition, of its own sovereignty. Which is inconceivable.

In a less dramatic gesture, the same argument points a more dubious finger at the established Commonwealth convention that the Crown is advised by its ministers in each member-State, irrespective of the advice given by ministers in other Commonwealth States, and asks what is to happen —in contemplation of war, for example—if ministers in some Commonwealth States advise the Crown to declare war and in others to proclaim neutrality.

These dilemmas are real; but they are inseparable from the Commonwealth experiment in the interrelation of free communities having the same Crown. It is not impossible that the King may be confronted with the necessity of acceding to advice from his ministers in one of his Commonwealth kingdoms which is contrary to the advice of his ministers in some of, or all, his other Commonwealth kingdoms. That would put the King in a most embarrassing position, though it is clear that he could do nothing but accept the advice tendered to him in each of his kingdoms, however mutually contradictory it might be. It has not happened and may never happen. Nor did either King George V or Lord Balfour—almost certainly the two wisest men, politically, of the British generation which was mature when the Commonwealth emerged—shrink from the contingency, though they must both have been perfectly aware of it. They shared a profoundly sagacious scepticism about the virtue of 'wooden guns'.

Nevertheless, the contention which denies such a divisibility of the Crown as to enable it to accept ministerial advice in one State of the Commonwealth or more contrary to the advice tendered by ministers in other Commonwealth States, or to acquiesce in ministerial advice which would nullify its own sovereignty, can cite in support of itself some

Imperial Conference authority. It summons in aid one of the recitals of the Statute of Westminster:

'Whereas it is meet and proper to set out by way of preamble to this Act that, inasmuch as the Crown is the symbol of the free association of the members of the British Commonwealth of Nations, and as they are united by a common allegiance to the Crown, it would be in accord with the established constitutional position of all the members of the Commonwealth in relation to one another that any alteration in the law touching the Succession to the Throne or the Royal Style and Titles shall hereafter require the assent as well of the Parliaments of all the Dominions as of the Parliament of the United Kingdom.'

Those who would set limits to the autonomy of the Dominions say that this recital pledges all the Dominions to continue in allegiance to the King, and not to abolish the Oath to him, or to declare themselves republics, or to secede from the Empire, unless with the consent of all the other States of the Commonwealth. They admit that the recital is not of the same efficacy as an operative clause of the Statute of Westminster, but they maintain that by it the Commonwealth States have undertaken mutually not to do anything which would interfere with the Crown, or derogate from its present position.

The recital, as it appears in the preamble to the Statute of Westminster, reproduces with verbal fidelity the draft of it included in the report of the Special Conference of 1929 on the operation of Dominion legislation; and in submitting that draft, the 1929 Conference expressly stipulated that the clause should not be taken as being 'intended in any way to derogate from the principles stated by the Imperial Conference of 1926 as underlying the position and mutual relations of the members of the British Commonwealth of Nations'. So it is hard to see how it can have the weight which those who deny the divisibility of the Crown attribute to it.

Unquestionably, too, some of the members of the Imperial Conference of 1930, which finally approved the form in which the Statute of Westminster was to be presented to the Parliament at Westminster, would have repudiated the interpretation now sought to be put on the Succession-to-the-Crown recital by the believers in limitations on Dominion autonomy. The *locus classicus* for the case against their view of the recital is the speech of Mr. McGilligan, Minister of External Affairs for the Irish Free State (and a strong anti-de Valera man), in the Dáil in July 1931. He showed how the words 'the new position' were used repeatedly in the 1929 Conference report, about the relations between Common-wealth members, and used with deliberation and intention:

'The law, the legal position, is being made to square with the central and predominant political fact of absolute freedom and unequivocal co-equality. And in the light of that conception of the matter the recital relating to the Crown is inserted. The States of the Commonwealth control the Crown and the prerogatives of the Crown absolutely. But the Crown function is accepted in the arrangement to which we have become parties. You could not, therefore, have a series of Acts throughout the Common-wealth dealing with, say, the succession in different ways. That would be undesirable. The function of the Crown may be exer-cised in a different way here from that in which it is exercised in Canada; that is a matter of the substance and form of the advice given here and that given in Canada. You could legislate for the Crown here in a way different from that in which it is legislated for in the United Kingdom. The United Kingdom might, e.g. restrict a certain Royal prerogative by statute. The Oireachtas (the Irish Free State legislature) might abolish the same prerogative so far as the Free State is concerned. There is no doubt whatever about that. But there had, in the nature of things, to be some arrangement to prevent the whole association (of the Commonwealth) from being confused within itself by con-flicting legislation as to such a matter as the Succession (to the Throne). The (Commonwealth) association is a free association. Freely, therefore, the members of it undertook this arrangement relating to the Crown, which is the symbol of the free association of them all.'

Mr. McGilligan elaborated this argument at length. All that the succession recital did, he said, was to state that the members of the Commonwealth, 'in the exercise of (their) sovereign legislative powers' which 'are supreme, paramount, and uncontrolled', would 'have regard to the desirability of avoiding confusion about the succession to the Crown'. That was 'the extent of the meaning of the recital', which assumed 'the absolute inherent right of each of the Parliaments to legislate for the Crown without regard to these considerations' (as to the succession). When he sat down, he was attacked violently by the de Valera party, which said that the best way available to the British Parliament, if it genuinely wanted to prove to all the States of the Commonwealth that it had abandoned its old supremacy over the Empire, was to 'destroy the legal principle of the unity of the Crown, by dividing the King into six Kings and making each of the Dominions a separate kingdom'. That, the de Valera party contended, the Statute of Westminster did not do.

But that, Mr. McGilligan retorted, was to all intents and purposes what the Statute of Westminster, read in conjunction with the Imperial Conference resolutions and decisions which had preceded it, did do:

'There is the single person of the King. We might say that there is a single physical Crown upon his head, but outside these two items there is no question of unity as between members of the Commonwealth. The King moves and acts in relation to (Southern) Irish affairs as Irish Ministers tell him to move and act, and nobody else can tell him what to do in relation to (Southern) Irish affairs; while Irish Ministers cannot tell him anything of what he is to do except in relation to (Southern) Irish affairs. The difference between that and the six kingdoms specially and clearly announced (by the British Parliament, as the de Valera party had suggested) is very slight indeed. That is where we have progressed since the 1921 point.'

Whatever may be the mature judgement which time will bring on the constitutional effect of the Abdication crisis, the first impression left by the action taken in two of the Dominions is that it has shown that Mr. McGilligan is right in this argument.

South Africa, which had adopted the Statute of Westminster by passing the Status of the Union Act, passed its own Abdication Act. The necessity of this is self-evident, for the Status of the Union Act barred the operation within the Union of South Africa of any Act passed by the Parliament at Westminster. It would have been inconsistent with this provision for the South African Parliament to endorse the British Declaration of Abdication Act by resolution, as the Parliaments of Canada, Australia, and New Zealand did.

But South Africa went farther than merely passing its own Abdication Act. It dated the operation of the Act back to 10 December. 10 December was the day on which King Edward VIII signed the Instrument of Abdication. The Parliament at Westminster passed its Declaration of Abdication Act on the following day, 11 December; and the accession of King George VI in Great Britain and in the Dominions which have endorsed the British Act by resolution of their Parliaments, dates from 11 December. In South Africa the accession of King George VI has been dated 10 December, so that King George VI was King of South Africa a day before he became King of Great Britain, Canada, Australia, New Zealand, and the rest of the Empire, as well as Emperor of India.

The South African Government held that the demise of the Crown caused by the abdication of King Edward took place on the day when he signed the Instrument of Abdication (10 December), not on the day when the Parliament at Westminster passed the Declaration of Abdication Act. As there can be no break in the succession to the Crown, the South African Government, holding this view, had no choice but to date the South African Abdication Act back to the day when the Instrument of Abdication was signed.

The Government of the Irish Free State also held that the demise of the Crown did not occur on the day on which the Parliament at Westminster passed the Declaration of Abdication Act. But it differed from the South African Government about the date when the demise of the Crown did take place. In the view of the Irish Free State Government, the demise took place on the day when the Irish Free State Parliament passed the Act recognizing the abdication of King Edward VIII and the succession of King George VI. That date was 12 December.

It appears therefore that the accession of King George VI to the throne of his various Kingdoms took place on three different days. He became King of South Africa on 10 December. He became King of Great Britain and Northern Ireland, of Australia, Canada, New Zealand, and the rest of the Empire, except India, of which he became Emperor, on 11 December. He became King of the Irish Free State on 12 December.

If the equal status of the member-States of the Commonwealth is accepted as 'the root principle governing our inter-Imperial relations'—and to deny it is to deny the reality of Dominion autonomy—there can be no doubt that each State of the Commonwealth has the right to its own view about the date when the accession of a new Sovereign to its throne takes place. To assert that each Commonwealth State must accept the date which in the view of the Government and Parliament at Westminster is the correct date would be to imply that the right of decision for the whole Commonwealth in such matters rests with the Government and Parliament at Westminster—a wholly untenable and potentially mischief-making proposition.

Just as the body of innovations in the interrelation of the member-States of the Commonwealth constitutes an unprecedented experiment in the association of free communities, so the change in the relation of the Crown to each member-State, which flows necessarily from the practice of Dominionhood, is an almost inconceivably bold experiment in extending the flexibility of monarchical government.

The Crown is one and single as the Crown of the Commonwealth and in the personality of the King; but it is at the same time as many Crowns as there are States of the Commonwealth. It is one as the Commonwealth—of whose structure it is the apex—is one. But because the oneness of the Commonwealth is a oneness of associated equals, the Crown also divides itself, for the practical purpose of the exercise of its several functions in each equal community, into as many Crowns as are required. This Crown, one yet multiple, may seem an impossibly mystical thing: on the contrary, it is the acme of practicality; and without this single yet multiple nature of the Commonwealth Crown, the evolution of the Commonwealth would have been hampered repeatedly.

How much the Commonwealth owed to King George V during the years after the War history will testify. His knowledge of the Dominion point of view was extensive and his sympathy with Dominion aspirations unbounded. He never lost an opportunity of sounding the mind of a Dominion leader and his talks with each of them were frank, eliciting a frankness from them which responded to his own. His breadth of mind, in assenting to each successive stage of Dominion development, even though it touched the Crown, because he realized that it was necessary and fitted into the legitimate fabric of Dominion status, matched the wisdom of Lord Balfour when he inspired the Imperial Conference report in 1926.

This then is the free practice of the Commonwealth, based on a body of convention accepted, without reservation or limitation, by the United Kingdom and all the Dominions. Attempts to fetter it by reservations do not strengthen—they shake and weaken—the Empire through the Commonwealth, whose incalculable vigour is in the elastic and indefinable freedom of all its member-communities. It is no hyperbole to say that the divisibility of the Crown, which can thus adapt itself to the wishes of each member, in every conceivable contingency in which any member may find itself, or be placed by its own volition, is the supreme proof that 'equality of status—the root principle governing our Inter-Imperial relations'—is a living and potent reality.

IX

EMPIRE EFFICIENCY

SUPERFICIALLY at least, the Empire in its present state seems unlikely to be particularly efficient at moments of world crisis. The preceding chapters have described the Commonwealth as lacking in any formal cohesion, with the Dominions shying like startled horses at any hint of unified control, political, military, or judicial. But this devotion to autonomy is the negative side of the Commonwealth partnership. It does not prevent the Dominions from realizing that the Empire is a force in world affairs and may be compelled to act as a unit at any moment. Action, however, is the post-diplomatic last resort of any nation. Because it is so remarkable that all its parts should say the same thing, the Empire, when all its parts do say the same thing, is more likely than any other Power to command that attention which is the best safeguard against being driven to take action. For unanimity, either in pronouncements on world problems or in reluctant deeds in the last resort, consultation on policy is incessantly imperative, however circumspectly obligations are limited as between members of the Commonwealth. Contingencies must be anticipated and policy formulated; otherwise the admitted advantages of the Commonwealth partnership will be forfeited.

The partnership is thus developing on lines of compromise, which are designed to reconcile the dilemma between Dominion autonomy and the repeated need for agreed policy, particularly in external affairs. The positive side of this compromise runs in three channels—improvement of communications between Governments, more effective means of consultation, greater efficiency in common action, if and when the need for it occurs.

Communications improve rapidly as time goes on. Wireless telegraphy is the main channel nowadays and the limits to its development are not yet in sight. Air mails have reduced the time which written dispatches take to go from one capital of the Empire to another. Human channels are more numerous and more organized than just after the War. The Dominions Department in London was created in 1925 and was subsequently put under a separate minister of the British Government. It has its own representatives in the capitals of Canada, Australia, and South Africa, where they are in touch with the Dominion Governments and fill positions hardly distinguishable from that of a British ambassador in a foreign capital. The Dominions have their High Commissioners in London, who meet from time to time and are in communication with British ministers. Dominion ministers in foreign capitals keep in contact with the British ambassadors and with each other. The Foreign Office in London and the Departments of External Affairs in the Dominions are in closer touch than before with the consular services.

This list does not look very imposing, as summing up the methods of the Commonwealth partnership in keeping its various States in contact with each other; but the work that the list represents is considerable and the whole field fairly efficiently covered. The Dominions Department in London, for example, condescends to no great publicity about its activities; nor do the Departments of External Affairs in the Dominions. For all the attention that the respective Parliaments devote to them, by way of set debates, they might be semi-moribund. But communication between them is incessant in its operation and its network is far wider spread than its surface unpretentiousness tempts inquirers to conclude.

Consultation, or at least effective consultation, is much more difficult than communications. The Governments of the Commonwealth are all burdened with their internal work. Prime Ministers spare a few weeks for Imperial Conferences held at infrequent intervals and cut as short as possible. Yet the Imperial Conference, as the sole occasion of these gatherings, has established for itself the highest authority in the Commonwealth. Its meetings recur normally at four-yearly intervals and are always held in London, because London is on the whole the most convenient centre for the Dominion Prime Ministers, because the United Kingdom towers in world stature over its equals in status, because the threads of world policy lead necessarily, for the Empire, to London. The decisions of the Imperial Conference are invariably unanimous. Its members are addressed by British ministers in charge of foreign affairs, the army, the navy, and the air force; they inspect the latest developments, military, naval, and in the air. They have available for them in London trade and other statistics for the whole world, obtainable nowhere else. Their deliberations range over the field of world policy, of internal tendencies within the Empire, of migration, economics, shipping, and so on.

No Prime Minister attending an Imperial Conference can bind his own country to endorse the resolutions for which he votes. They must go before his Parliament and be approved or rejected. But approval is normally a matter of course, for, though rejection is possible, it would be followed by the resignation of the Prime Minister if the rejected resolution of the Imperial Conference was important enough to involve the existence of the Government; and Imperial Conference resolutions are not passed unless they reach that standard of gravity.

The Prime Ministers, or their deputies, who attend Imperial Conferences are the creatures of democratic government. Between conferences, any of them may fall and be succeeded by the Opposition. On the face of it the system seems certain to work badly, for in any of the Commonwealth countries, decisions of the last Imperial Conference might be repudiated because the party in power had changed. In fact, the system works better than that. Repudiation of Commonwealth decisions, made by an Imperial Conference, is rare; and when a new Government takes office it usually prefers to wait for the next Imperial Conference, when it may be able to get the last decision altered, rather than to go against the accepted policy on its own initiative. The Labour decision to stop work on the Singapore base was an exception; but, unwelcome as that exception was, it proved the rule.

In matters of foreign policy, again, the quick changes of modern times make decisions taken by the Imperial

Conference at four-yearly intervals almost certain to be out of date. The relative convention approved by the Imperial Conference authorizes the British Government to make the new decisions necessitated by such changes, but prescribes that they should be made only after consultation with the Dominion Governments. It is a very proper condition to impose, but it is often extremely inconvenient, sometimes an utter impossibility. The chancelleries of Europe are not always willing to be patient while Downing Street communicates with five capitals—four of them at the distance of continents—its views on an international crisis and its plans for handling it; while the Dominion Governments deliberate, ask for more information from Downing Street possibly, and make up their minds; while the process of reconciling incompatibilities in their replies is proceeding laboriously in London; while the necessary suggestions are again communicated to the Dominion capitals and again deliberated over and decided upon. Crises nowadays cannot be coped with in that leisurely fashion, persistently as Dominion susceptibilities require that they should be.

As long ago as 1925, when Sir Austen Chamberlain had made the Locarno Treaty and was replying in the House of Commons to the criticism that he had failed to carry the Dominions and India with him, he defended himself on this ground, with less than his customary suavity. The Foreign Secretary, he protested, could not sit at his desk in Downing Street doing nothing till he had collected and collated views from the Dominions. He had to act. Which was true then and is as true now. The dilemma is inherent in the Commonwealth system; it leads to risks which, again, have to be taken; it can be made the best of by patience and tolerance as between the British and the Dominion Governments. In practice, agreement between Commonwealth members on the principles of foreign policy guides the British Government in aim and method and prevents subsequent repudiation by any Commonwealth State of what the British Government has done in international relations. When agreement is impossible in retrospect, the Locarno principle exempts a Dominion from obligations which it has not expressly accepted.

In minor matters, consultation between the Dominions and the United Kingdom, or between the Dominions themselves, works with less encumbrance. Organs for consultation, permanent or framed for limited purposes, multiply. Chief among them is the Committee for Imperial Defence, which is an offshoot of the British Cabinet, but includes from time to time Dominion representatives. In economics, in shipping, in legislation, in medicine, in education, there is constant inter-Dominion committee work going on. To catalogue it all would be pointless.

X

THE REST OF THE EMPIRE

IT will not be necessary to pay so much attention to the rest of the Empire as has been given to the Dominions, because the United Kingdom speaks for it in all its external affairs. Any respectably comprehensive review of the present stages of government in all parts of the Empire would take far more space than can be spared here. Such reviews are to be found elsewhere.

The Indian Empire, the self-governing colonies, the Crown colonies, and all the other communities which are part of the Empire, are part of the world as well; and British policy is constantly and deeply affected by them. Through them, much more than through the Dominions in their modern stage, Great Britain stands before the world as the great trustee and champion of democratic liberty. In all of them the aim of British policy is constant—to bring them to the point in their development where they will be fit to govern themselves and then to devolve on them the utmost possible degree of self-government consistent with efficiency, public order, and security for all classes of the community. Southern Rhodesia, India, Ceylon, Burma, are already high on this ladder of autonomy. Newfoundland, before its Constitution was suspended, was sometimes reckoned a Dominion, but lacked some of the full rights of Dominion status. It never, apparently, exercised the treaty-making power, possibly because there was no occasion for it. Malta also before its Constitution was suspended had a self-governing status.

From these approximations to full autonomy, the range of Empire communities widens downwards through almost every conceivable stage of what is known as representative government—forms in which there is an elected element in the legislature, more or less strong, but counterbalanced and most frequently outnumbered by nominated official or un-official members. The Governor has the last word. The roll-call of Empire communities is completed by the protectorates, mandated territories, and outlying posts, such as St. Helena, Aden, Hong Kong, the Falkland Islands.

By far the greater number of the peoples of the Empire are not European. British India has three hundred million inhabitants; Indian India, about eighty-five millions; the rest of the Empire, outside the Dominions, some fifty millions. These nearly four hundred and fifty millions of people are of every race, colour, and religion. They inhabit all but four million square miles of the earth's surface and are scattered over two great continents and among the islands of a dozen oceans and seas. A single axiom underlies this diversity— that democratic self-government is the best form of government not only for white peoples, but for peoples of every race and colour, whatever their traditions, customs, or habits. If the disposition of any people in the British Empire is undemocratic; if in its traditions it has been wedded to autocracy since it has been known to modern civilization: no matter. The British Empire doctrine is that it must be converted to believe in democracy, that whatever in its institutions or habits or beliefs is inconsistent with democracy must be gradually reformed, and that it must be led, by successive educational steps, to become democratically self-conscious and progressively fit for full democratic rights. The Empire is thus a continuously progressive challenge to rival theories of government. In the long run democracy can justify itself only if, through the Empire, it proves itself adapted to all peoples, irrespective of race, colour, or traditions.

That is why the new Government of India Act is so important. The use that India makes of it will show whether the British assumption that democracy is best for all the other peoples of the Empire is justified, superficially at least. It would not be outrageous to argue that if democracy can succeed in India it can succeed anywhere; for in India democratic self-government has to get the better of an alarming array of obstacles. India is a sub-continent of many races. It has no single indigenous language and is compelled to use English. Its religious gulfs are wide and there is intense hostility between beliefs. Its caste system is the negation of democracy. It has no tradition of public service, with very limited exceptions; and in its public life it has still to aspire to a consistently high standard. Many of its races have no military qualities, and they might easily be dominated by their militaristic neighbours. It lies on the track of the main sea-route between the Pacific and Europe, a priceless prey for a strong sea-Power. It is bounded on the north by inhospitable mountains inhabited by lawless tribes, behind which lurks the threat of a Russia doubtfully less menacing under the Soviets than under the Tsars. To crown all these obstacles to successful democratic self-government, India has in its States a still powerful tradition of autocracy and everywhere a very high population-incidence of illiteracy and indigency.

If India succeeds in governing itself under the Government of India Act, the British faith that there is a virtue in democracy which makes it a talisman for all peoples will have gone far to justify itself; and that may alter the current of human development in all the continents. In Europe, for example, it would be a severe blow to Dictatorship or Communism. In Africa, it would encourage persistence with the training of the native for democratic institutions; and that, at the present stage, seems an Empire enterprise even less superficially promising than its counterpart in India seemed half a century ago. India is at least a unit under British sovereignty. In Africa, the native population is parcelled out in territory held by half a dozen Powers, of whom Britain is one. Even in British parts of Africa, there are numerous varieties of governmental methods. The Union of South Africa believes in stern control of its native population. Southern Rhodesia has the same theory, less drastically applied. The east-central British colonies, with their settlements of British immigrants, hesitate, unofficially at least, between imitation of the South African method and that paramountcy of native interests which the Colonial Office favours. In the West African colonies, where the climate has prevented white settlement, British government exists entirely in the native interest.

All these varieties are democratic in ultimate aim; the difference between them lies in the value which they assign to native individual rights. In British West Africa, the Colonial Governments are true trustees for native democracy, waiting till it is ready to take control and meanwhile administering the country for the benefit of the native population. In British East-Central Africa the presence of white settler communities prevents any idea of native self-government for years to come, and even the most pro-native official hardly dares to look forward to a time when the white settlers may be under native democratic rule. In South Africa and Southern Rhodesia, the rule of the white community is predominant, and the notion of natives having the franchise on equal terms with white citizens is repudiated. Enlightened opinion in both countries insists that a place will have to be found for the native population as part of the machinery of government; but no one has yet been able to suggest what that place should be, and meanwhile the native draws water and hews wood for the white man.

Democracy, irrespective of race or colour, in India is an immediate challenge to dictatorship; democracy in British-ruled Africa is by no means so immediate a challenge, for it is much less advanced. The African, too, is far behind the Indian in his capacity for self-rule. He has no civilized background; and that sensitive and subtle intellectual quality which, in many Indians, marks them as inheritors of an old civilization, is not found in the African native, however advanced in education and naturally endowed mentally. The African lives in the moment, happy in the sun, childishly amused by trifles. To be fit for even the crudest form of self-government he has to stride, in one generation, over leagues of self-development that other peoples have taken centuries to travel. Yet a perceptible though small minority of African natives have made that tremendous journey of the mind in the last half-century. Their tragedy is that they have outstripped the other 90 per cent. of their kin so far.

In Africa, too, there is a minor complication of democracy in any practical form. Indian labourers and traders, settling in Kenya, in the Union of South Africa and elsewhere, bringing up families and never intending to return to India, begin to demand political rights. British African Governments, having already quite enough hay on their fork in the perplexing riddle of how to give the native some share in government, without swamping it in a tide of native votes, resent the agitation of the Indian intruder and try vainly to invent some expedient for putting off his demands. British rule in India has suffered under the reaction to Indian grievances in Africa; for the Indian is a British citizen and his outcry when he is denied rights in Africa that his compatriot in India is now being given is plausible. No tolerable solution of this dilemma in British Africa has ever been suggested; and probably it will continue to defy solution, even in those Colonial-Office-ruled countries where in the long run a step towards native democracy is inevitable. When the time comes for that advance, the Indian will have a strong claim to share in it; but then he will in all probability be met by the hostility of the African native, denouncing him as an alien and an intruder and asking why the hard-won franchise should be shared with him. In the Union of South Africa, an official Agent of the Government of India acts, fairly successfully, as a buffer between the Government of the Union and the Indian population; but there is very little possibility that South African resistance to granting the Indian political rights will relax.

It is early yet, however, to talk about ultimate forms of democratic government in any part of British Africa. They are far off. Before they are in sight, the rival theories of the South African Union and British West Africa, about the share of the native in the government of his own country, will have to find some means of accommodation. Meanwhile, the other Powers in Africa have their own theories and methods of administration; and the African future is complicated by German claims for the restoration of her colonies. On any realistic view, prospects in Africa are serious. British rule, in all its shapes, recognizes two fundamental principles. There must be no mixture of white and black blood; and the white ruler must not arm, drill, and discipline the native, except for police work in his own country. But both these fundamentals are ignored—except in territories under mandate—by other European Powers in Africa, where the white man is everywhere in a tiny minority among the black masses. If dictatorship takes hold in Africa and proceeds to arm the natives in its territory for use as mercenaries, the British African colonies, and even the Union in the far south, will be hard put to it to hold the passes against it. Even this, too, is not the most appalling possibility that Africa presents. If the natives of Africa are armed and drilled as the mercenaries of a white dictatorship, it is long odds that a leader will rise among them and they will turn on their white masters. That fear, which seems remote but may be not far distant—given development of the European use of black mercenaries—already keeps the statesmen of South Africa awake at nights, as Mr. Pirow, Minister of Defence in the Union, hinted very plainly when he was in London lately. If British policy is less touched by it, British statesmen do not live in Africa and have less cause for alarm. It should not, because of that, be ignored by those who have charge of British colonies in any part of the Continent.

India and Africa, though they have the largest masses of non-Europeans in the Empire, have no monopoly of them; and everywhere the deep problem is the same. How to mould these hives of human varieties—different in race, colour, traditions, religion, and often mixed up with each other in the same country—into communities fit for the privilege of democratic self-government; that is the question which British administration in the Empire always has to answer. The Empire is thus a venture in democracy on a colossal scale; and the fact that Great Britain is committed to it weighs constantly and heavily on British world policy. The intermediate task of governing these masses; of keeping order among them; of seeing that each element in them, each individual as well, gets justice; of reconciling their differences, of educating them, of protecting them from outside aggression; is an immense task, which, if it was the only burden that Great Britain had to carry, would be heavy enough. Yet the people of the United Kingdom shoulder it in a completely light-hearted spirit, even when they understand—which most of them do not—that it has to be borne. They live their self-absorbed lives sublimely unconscious of the

L

human destinies that they control indirectly. If they happen to spare a thought for the Empire, it is with indifference or faint derision. Every now and then they find themselves listening, with hardly concealed resentment, to speeches about it; and when they refer to its peoples they mostly speak of them, with indulgent disdain, as 'niggers'.

Yet this grossly paradoxical dependent Empire lasts. It lasts not meanly or cruelly, either. If some sudden calamity wiped the United Kingdom, and all its power, off the face of the earth, it would not be a shout of triumph that the millions of Asia and Africa would raise at the news, but a wail of despair. The cynicism which nowadays fashionably condescends to the Empire as an anachronism, misguided if not invariably blood-stained in its origins, and oppressive or pompously contemptible in its operation, ignorantly fails to discern the fate of its dependent millions if it perished.

XI

ACCENT ON STATURE

IS the Empire in 1937 worse or better fitted than in 1914 to co-operate with the United Kingdom in planning and executing world policy? Politically, much better. The Dominions have found themselves. Their liberty within the Commonwealth has been justified of its children. Few doubts remain about their complete autonomy; and when these have been removed, they will be less reluctant to turn their minds to the great issues. The Coronation Imperial Conference of 1937 will have the chance of removing the last vestiges of Dominion doubt about their unrestricted right to say for themselves what their future is to be. Even the most irreconcilable Republican is now compelled to acknowledge that the threat to freedom is not from within the Empire but from outside it.

Dominion leaders now have all the knowledge necessary for decisions on international problems. None of them retains any illusions about the possibility of detaching his country from the world current. Each knows that events in Europe must have unpredictable reactions in every corner of the globe. The League of Nations, which some for a time after the War thought a basis for world co-operation in peace and progress even more attractive than that offered by the British Empire, is now palpably dependent on the Empire as the most indispensable of its foundations. Dissension within the Empire on the larger and more vital issues of world policy would clearly drive the last nail into the League's coffin.

The Dominions recognize, too, even more vividly than in 1914, the predominance of the United Kingdom in stature among the member-States of the Empire. The United Kingdom is the only World Power among them. Its leadership is necessary, if the Empire is to make its influence felt and not to disappoint the expectations of the lesser nations. There is no resentment among the Dominions at this natural leadership of the United Kingdom. They accept it, on one or two conditions. It must be based on principles which they share; it must be explained and must justify itself to them; it must not be selfish or narrow-minded or dictated by limited objectives in which they feel that they have no common purpose.

The Empire is a far more powerful influence for freedom in the world in 1937 than it was in 1914. The development of the Dominions, for one thing, is the clearest revelation of the benefits of freedom that has ever been given to humanity. Democracy would be in much less reputable standing if the Commonwealth experiment had not been made, or, having been made, had failed. Neither dictatorship nor sovietism can show anything comparable to it in the period since the Peace of Versailles; for neither has anything to show but internal victories, stained in Germany and Russia by violent extermination of opponents and disfigured everywhere by rigid suppression of criticism. Both, too, are ringed by the hostility of their neighbours and both exist in an atmosphere of world apprehension and foreboding. The Empire, free internally, is looked up to by every people that cherishes its own freedom; and its relations with other nations are relations of confirmed friendliness. It threatens none, and has neglected its own defences to the point of danger in the hope that its example might encourage all the Powers to reduce armaments. Its own armaments are recognized universally as the reluctant insurance of peoples forced to ignore no longer threats against their own survival and compelled to recognize that its destruction would bring the whole fabric of international liberty down with a crash.

In 1914 there were still numbers of politically sophisticated people in the United Kingdom who were certain that when the colonies freed themselves from control in the last resort by the Parliament at Westminster, they would proceed to make their own careers in the world, apart from the Empire. In 1937, though the doctrine that the ultimate legislative authority in the Commonwealth is still latent in the Parliament at Westminster has its adherents, they admit that the authority will never be exercised against the will of any Dominion; and no one dreams of suggesting that a Dominion

is more likely to want to depart from the Commonwealth
because it has its unlimited autonomy. The only Dominion
which does show any inclination to kick over the theoretical
Commonwealth traces is the Irish Free State, and that not
because the traces are too theoretical but because in Southern
Ireland they are believed to be still too substantial.

Yet the looseness of the Commonwealth structure, so surprisingly beneficial politically, has its drawbacks. The Dominions, entirely at liberty to go each its own way in the
world, do want a lead. There is now coming into sight a
new risk to Empire concert in foreign affairs—that the
Dominions may not get the lead from the United Kingdom
which they expect and that the United Kingdom, on its side,
may fail to live up to her function as head of the Commonwealth and Empire.

Equality of status between the United Kingdom and each
of the Dominions is, as the Imperial Conference of 1926 said,
'the root-principle' of 'inter-Imperial relations'. There is
some reason for thinking that the work of this great principle
is done, now that it is recognized everywhere in the Commonwealth and is set up as an ideal for other parts of the Empire,
such as India. But the other principle which the 1926 Conference put its finger on—the inequality of the Commonwealth
States in stature—is as active now as it was in 1926. More
active, in fact, it might be argued; for in 1926 there were hopes
that the world might settle down into secure peace, and in
peace the power or stature of nations matters much less than
when all are armed to the teeth. Now, in 1937, with the
world quivering under the tremors of what may prove to be
another vast upheaval, Great Britain should be thinking, not
only of her stature as a great European Power, but of her
far more responsible stature as the head of the Commonwealth and Empire.

The leadership that the Empire should get from the United
Kingdom is not limited to the spheres of policy and economics.
It should be a leadership that gathers up all the threads of the
life of a modern community. The Empire is formed from
dozens of communities. It stands for a way of life in which
authority derives from those who subject themselves to it;

opinion, conscience, and action are free; conduct, within the limits of the rights of other free persons, is unfettered. But Great Britain shows little sign of having realized that the peoples of the Empire, including the Commonwealth, are looking to her for that type of leadership, all the more because she has recognized their right to control their own destinies politically and in economic matters.

If these communities are to continue in harmonious association—in their way of life and in the aims towards which they direct themselves, as well as politically—there must be real sympathy among them. Sympathy is dependent on mutual knowledge and understanding. The difficulty of both, in the conditions of the Empire, is evident; and the absence of any concerted effort among the peoples of the Empire, under British leadership, to promote both is disturbing. Political freedom, flowing out as a gift from Great Britain to the communities of the Commonwealth and the Empire, has proved a magic talisman, politically. But to assume that it is as magical in the other spheres of life would be a delusion; and a lazy confidence that these other spheres of life can look after themselves, so long as there is no obstruction to the development of freedom in any Empire community, is likely to be calamitous.

The Dominion peoples, to limit ourselves to them for the moment, live under conditions which are radically different from those of life in the British Isles. In two Dominions, Canada and South Africa, a considerable element of the population is not descended from British stock. In South Africa the Dutch stock outnumbers the British about five to three. In all the Dominions, too, there is an underlying similarity between the conditions of life which tends towards a Dominion point of view on domestic and international affairs. Far from Europe, they adapt European traditions, conventions, habits to their own needs; and these adaptations, similar to each other, resemble less and less the way of life in the British Isles. The divergence is the inevitable divergence between age and youth. The Dominion peoples are all young, but they have grown up. They are vigorous, hopeful, irreverent. They have the crudities of youth, which feels its inferiority to age in civilized knowledge of the world and yet cannot help being impatient of the hesitations and indecisions of its elders.

This Dominion tendency to be critical and intolerant of British ways is unavoidable and need do no harm; but there are risks in it. British prestige does not maintain itself automatically now with the Dominion peoples. In 1914, it did. In 1914 Great Britain still led the industrial world. The excellence of British products, their honest workmanship, their lasting qualities, were acknowledged universally, and every one in the Empire was proud of it. Now, in many fields of industrial production, Britain is not in advance of her competitors. If a Dominion air-traffic company wants to buy machines its first impulse usually is still to order them from a British manufacturer; but it is likely to find that machines to meet its requirements cannot be bought in the United Kingdom, have to be specially designed, and cannot be delivered within a reasonable set time. Along comes an American or Belgian or even a German competitor, offering exactly what the company wants and promising delivery on a definite date not many months ahead. Reluctantly the company places the order outside the Empire. Motor-car wholesalers in the Empire find that the low-priced cars which are in almost sole demand can be supplied from America much cheaper than from the United Kingdom and are definitely more efficient for their purpose. The individual buyer would prefer a British car and often insists on having one, for patriotic reasons; but when he finds that he has got something which cannot compare with its American competitor, in efficiency or lasting quality, and that he has had to pay almost double for it, he is apt to reflect that patriotism is an expensive luxury. Buyers of wireless sets have similar experiences all over the Empire. The fact is, of course, that Empire areas vastly exceed the pocket-handkerchief dimensions of the United Kingdom and that Empire buyers want motor-cars and wireless sets designed to work in large areas and in rough conditions. America produces them for her own needs. Empire buyers understand this. But it is trying them rather high to expect them to refrain from profanity when British producers tell them that their products are as good for Empire use as the American and no more costly— which common sense and experience contradict—and to respond submissively to British propaganda, inevitable and time-worn, in which the single substantial argument is an appeal to pro-British sentiment.

There are other instances of British inferiority nowadays, as compared with 1914, to foreign competitors—many others. Here is one: A Canadian, Australian, or South African, inquiring into British electrical services, into efficiency of equipment, cost of current, and so on, is provoked to derisive comment. In everything electrical the United Kingdom is an antediluvian joke compared with any up-to-date Dominion, or even Empire, city. And again, Dominion criticism is torn between ridicule and lamentation when British complacency discredits or resents frank comment.

The too-frequent combination of antiquated methods and self-satisfied belief in British supremacy has lamentable effects on British prestige. All the more because Dominion people in their own countries have been forced to form none too favourable an opinion of the calibre of immigrants from the British Isles. In Canada, British applicants for jobs on farms in the wheat belt are far from being able to rely any longer on being taken on merely because they are from the Old Country. They are more likely to be shown the door, firmly though politely. In Australia, the nickname 'Pommy' expresses with precise irony the local view of the immigrant from 'home'; and in the other Dominions the verdict of Canada and Australia on the British immigrant as a class is not in the least likely to go unconfirmed.

The impatience of the Empire peoples with the United Kingdom produced by all this is mostly underground and can easily be exaggerated. Very possibly it has been exaggerated here, in anxiety to make people in the United Kingdom understand that it does exist and is an ominous phenomenon that should not be ignored or explained away. It is all the more insidious because normally Dominion and Empire people either cannot put it into words or prefer not to.

There is still immense affection and respect for Great

Britain in every Empire country, among those who are not
white in colour or are not of British stock, as well as among
those whose ancestors came from the British Isles. Anti-
monarchists are singular everywhere. Belief in British institutions is fervent, especially perhaps among non-European
peoples who have had no disillusioning experience of their
working in practice when they are exported and put to trial
in countries lacking the British tradition. That is why the
experiment of Federal self-government for India is so vital.

But it would be misleading to mince words about the growing feeling that much more might be done by the people
of the British Isles to help and encourage the Empire and
Commonwealth communities. The leadership which they
look for they are not getting; and there filter through to them,
from time to time, exasperating echoes of the curiously
derogatory tone which some intellectuals use about the
Empire. The Empire is not Imperialistic because it includes
many subordinate non-European peoples, or dubious merely
because it is an Empire, or detestable because it is big; and
to talk about it as though it was all these things is ignorant
and arrogant. Indifference to, or impatience with, Dominion
ways of thinking; the preoccupation of the British public with
sport; its entire ignorance about the Empire; the ingrained
official belief that a dog-fight in the Balkans is infinitely more
significant from the United Kingdom point of view than the
most important event in any Dominion, still more in any
other part of the Empire; and innumerable other signs; all
have the same meaning for Empire observers. They suggest
that Great Britain is incapable, unless she pulls herself together
very sharply, of giving the Commonwealth and the Empire
the lead that they want. The freedom-guaranteeing *laisser-
faire* policy, in fact, which has been so good for the Empire
politically, may quite well be disastrous in the field of Empire
citizenship and culture.

Current British administrative methods and intellectual
approaches to Empire peoples will be altered with difficulty,
no doubt. They are traditional; and have paid so well in the
political sphere that official circles in London resist attempts
to persuade them to experiment with modifications. Some

initiative is actually being taken by numerous unofficial bodies. Chambers of commerce; legal, medical, scientific, newspaper associations; universities; employers' organizations; and many similar bodies have their Commonwealth and Empire extensions. They hold conferences in, and make tours of Commonwealth and Empire countries, sometimes annually. But these activities, valuable as they are, are a drop in the ocean of a great and immediate need. Government backing in authority and money is indispensable. Again, a small beginning has been made; but how small and how grudging. Actually, while this was being written, a letter on the subject appeared in *The Times* from Lord Eustace Percy, as chairman of the British Council, a body, as he explained, 'charged with the general care of "cultural" relations between the United Kingdom and oversea countries, both inside and outside the British Commonwealth'. Though, wrote Lord Eustace, the Council 'has the whole world for its province, it has at present only £15,000 a year from the Government for its sustentation'. Generous private gifts, with which it started its work, Lord Eustace said, were now nearly exhausted. It had subsidized schools for English residents in foreign countries, had made grants to university chairs and readerships in English abroad, helped libraries and established bursaries at English university colleges tenable by student teachers of English from oversea countries, most of them not within the Empire. It had promoted European tours of British orchestras, broadcasts of British music from foreign stations, exhibitions of British art in foreign and Dominion capitals, and had engaged in a number of other activities too detailed to be enumerated. But, Lord Eustace insisted, the money available was quite inadequate. 'The first thing which the public in this country needs to realize is the extent to which Great Britain has neglected her moral and intellectual responsibilities in her own Colonies and Dependencies.'

Almost at the same moment, the *Daily Telegraph* published a letter from Malta, the writer of which described 'the desirability, or, I should say, the absolute necessity, of extending English education and culture in Mediterranean countries under British rule and influence—Gibraltar, Malta, Cyprus, Palestine, Egypt'. These countries, he explained, were mentioned because 'they are inhabited by races, not of British stock, possessing an ancient civilization, high intelligence and remarkable gifts for intellectual development'. British policy in the Mediterranean had limited itself to bringing to these peoples 'traditions of liberty, order and good government'. But 'education has been left to look after itself. The consequence is that Gibraltar is to-day more Spanish and Italian than English; Malta, but for its Phoenician population and its love of England, would have been more Italian than English; Cyprus is more Greek than English; and Palestine and Egypt are entirely under the influence of French, Italian, and Greek culture.' These foreign cultures, the writer went on to say, do not limit their influence to 'mere linguistic attainments'. They 'permeate the lives of these peoples, so as to make them in all but name the subjects, not of England, but of the country whose culture they have absorbed'. Italian culture especially, under the Fascist régime, 'bids fair to become the dominating culture of the whole Mediterranean littoral'. Italy, in the last few years, had been 'spending millions of lire in opening and subsidizing schools and sending the best of her professors to British Mediterranean countries for the purpose of disseminating her language and culture and creating . . . an atmosphere favourable to her trade and the furtherance of her Imperialistic policy. England's subjects in the same latitudes . . . are being slowly but surely won from their allegiance by foreign cultural propaganda. Why should not England bring her people into closer spiritual contact with the Mother Country?'

The anti-Fascist bias of this letter should not obscure its knowledge and sound sense. On a small scale, it describes the need of the Empire. Lord Eustace Percy describes it too:

'In a Europe increasingly split between two contending Dictatorships, of the Right and the Left, Britain claims to represent an alternative social philosophy in which lies the only hope of peace. But she is still only half able to explain that philosophy or to demonstrate its practical results in the life and thought of her people. With the finest education in the world, with the freest and most vivid intellectual life, with the most comprehensive programme of social reform, she remains relatively inarticulate, or articulate only about her shortcomings. Her very freedom militates against an organized effort to make herself known.'

(The quotation has taken the words out of the mouth of an imaginary future historian and has changed its past into present tenses.)

Here is a task of the highest importance. It is not enough that freedom, national and individual, should be guaranteed by the existence of the Empire. Imperial Conferences since the War have given most of their attention to the development of national freedom in the Dominions. They have registered as principles the conventions in which the development is embodied; and these principles guarantee liberty for the individual as much as for nationalities.

Little, in that field, remains for the Imperial Conference of 1937 to do. A stroke or two of the pen will complete it. World politics and economic policy will make great claims on the time of the conference. But just as necessary is the work of initiating an organization to mobilize public opinion everywhere in the Empire in support of the 'social philosophy' which its peoples share; to 'explain' it; to 'demonstrate its practical results' in every-day life; to break down ignorance among the Empire nations, each of the other; to teach them that, in the world of to-day, the benefits they have under the British system cannot be taken for granted as secure, but must be valued and will have to be preserved by an instructed and convinced will not to let them be destroyed.

Pre-eminently, this task is part of the stature or function of the United Kingdom; but it is part of Dominion function, too. The Imperial Conference of 1937 will fall short of its duty if it neglects the task. At the least, it should appoint a Special Committee, as it did in 1926 in connexion with the operation of Dominion legislation, to investigate the Empire need to which Lord Eustace Percy has pointed and to frame plans for taking the task in hand.

PART III

ECONOMICS OF THE EMPIRE

I
INTRODUCTION

THOUGH 'wait and see' is often an excuse for drift, it may sometimes be a slogan for leadership. *Solvitur ambulando* can never be that. In the mouths of the Imperial optimists, whose favourite motto it is, it means: 'we muddle along very well in matters of British Commonwealth relations, so why worry?' This view of Commonwealth affairs is popular, partly because it spares us the painful duty of thought and effort, partly because it shows up well beside what is conceived as the opposite attitude, to imprison fluid facts in a cage of documents and formulae and treaties. To behave thus is regarded as repugnant to the British political genius, and unsuited to the nations of the Commonwealth as a free association of democracies. But this is not the true antithesis. On the contrary, if the peoples of the Commonwealth think out their purposes, make known their ideals, and realize clearly the hard facts with which they have to contend, they will stand in the less need of documents, formulae, and treaties among themselves.

Nowhere is this plainer than in the field of economic relations. 'Muddling along' served its turn here well enough for many years. But we deliberately discarded it, and at Ottawa hammered out our documentary compromises, invented our formulae, and signed our treaties. Yet the long-term principles and purpose of Commonwealth economic policy have not yet been thought out. Ottawa did little more than substitute a joint muddle for a set of individual muddles. When the Ottawa Agreements expire, there will be fresh compromises, formulae, and treaties; but without a recognized purpose we shall still be only muddling along, the only change being that we shall have so much the more to worry about.

Merely to say, as the popular slogan has it, 'the home producer first, the Empire producer next, and the foreigner third', is not in the least to propound a policy of Empire economic co-operation. For it combines two essentially non-co-operative propositions: that the home producer should be protected against all comers, and that foreign imports should be taxed higher than imports from the Empire. National protectionism and a vague Imperialism are both served, but the purpose remains obscure and the practical policy itself may vary almost indefinitely within the broad limits thus laid down.

The problem of finding a real economic policy for the Commonwealth as a whole, based on a common purpose, is parallel, in its essentials, to the problem of Commonwealth relations in international affairs. Six or seven different foreign policies, even though modified by the Commonwealth membership of the countries that conduct them, are very different from a single foreign policy for the whole community of British nations. In the present phase of the Commonwealth's evolution, such a joint foreign policy is out of the question; no machinery exists either to decide upon it or to carry it out, even if there were everywhere the will to support it. But separatism and centralism are only the extremes; between them lies the possibility of a common principle to which the policies of the member-nations of the Commonwealth may be subordinated. In economic affairs the problem is similar. There is no chance, as things are, of establishing a single joint policy for the economic relations of the Commonwealth with the rest of the world, together with those between its different parts. But there is a chance of finding a common principle by which the economic policies of its member-nations may be tested, in order that they may conform to a mutual purpose grounded in the welfare of all.

The problem is complex—more complex, perhaps, than the similar problem of political relations. Migration, money, capital and interest movements, as well as the ramifications of trade and industry, complicate the tangle. There are many more independent fiscal policies in the Empire than there are independent foreign policies. The history of Dominion fiscal independence, moreover, is far longer than that of Dominion independence in foreign affairs, and in the absence of a guiding purpose it has left to posterity a correspondingly large deposit of conflicts and vested interests. It is well to begin, therefore, with a brief résumé of the history of Imperial economic relations, in so far as it bears on the problems of the present. The first step towards undoing a muddle (whether it be a twisted piece of string or a complex international problem) is to recall how the tangling came about.

II

IMPERIAL PREFERENCE BEFORE OTTAWA

SO rapid has been the development of the Dominions and colonies that economically they have changed almost out of recognition within our own lifetimes. Here is an illustration. To-day the State of Western Australia protests vigorously against the economic policies pursued by the Australian Commonwealth Government, because, in its view, they artificially stimulate and favour an urban and industrial development in which it has been left behind. Yet when the Commonwealth was formed in 1901 Australia as a whole was scarcely more urbanized and industrialized, on the average, than the State of Western Australia is to-day. There have been other great changes besides the rising tide of industrialization in the Dominions; within the political memory of many living people the agricultural progress of the Empire has been influenced by such mighty forces as the development of the Canadian prairies, the building of great railways, the introduction of refrigerated transport, the mechanization of farming operations. The next few years may see further great changes as a result of new scientific and mechanical inventions—for instance, the entry of the Dominions of the southern hemisphere into the world market for chilled beef, or the intensive cultivation of land now only lightly tilled.

The 'old colonial system', which ruled in the days before the Dominions became greater exporters of foodstuffs to the world, was a system of Empire protection. It was not, however, an Empire policy as we should recognize the term to-day, but a British policy imposed on subordinate colonies whether they liked it or not. Even if the policy was or had remained sound from the point of view of Great Britain, or of the whole Empire, it must inevitably have been laid aside as the colonies gradually won political and fiscal independence, and chose their economic policies for themselves. The old colonial system was a broom against the political as well as the economic Atlantic.

The next phase, which lasted roughly through the nineteenth century, was characterized by the gradual adoption of free trade by Great Britain and by the use of revenue tariffs in the colonies. Whatever might be said for or against such an Imperial system at the present time, in that period it had great advantages for both parties. The countries that are now the self-governing Dominions were leaving the pioneer stage and achieving surpluses of primary products for sale to the Old World. An open market where they could be sure of selling their products was vitally important to them. Great Britain, on the other hand, dominated the world industrially, and in the overseas Empire she could usually undersell her European competitors. Her interest lay in the rapid development of colonial primary production, since she was the chief supplier of the manufactured goods, both capital and consumable, that the colonies required as they expanded. In turn, their cheap produce was one of the most essential bases of the low industrial costs on which her commercial supremacy was founded.

The end of this phase was brought about by two forces, which so reacted upon each other that it is hard to tell which was cause and which effect. One was the rising industrial protectionism of the Dominions, and the other was the rising agricultural protectionism of the older countries. It must be carefully noted that although one may legitimately slice the story into longish phases the trends were continually deflected by changing circumstances, and each phase merged gradually into the next. Thus when, in the 'eighties, the Dominions really became for the first time world suppliers of grain and other raw products on a large scale (thanks chiefly to the swift improvement of ocean and rail transport), the reaction towards agricultural protectionism in Europe had already begun, and their own industrial ambitions were already simmering.

The rise of agricultural tariffs in Europe was largely a by-product of the great agricultural depression of 1875-95, which was itself the outcome of a complex of forces—cheap supplies from the New World, the increasing productivity of farming everywhere through the use of machinery and chemicals, the general monetary deflation before the great gold discoveries of the 'nineties. The comparison with the period from 1928 to 1933 is obvious. Germany under Bismarck was the most conspicuous example of the new protectionism of the 'eighties and 'nineties, but the movement was shared by many other countries of Europe. Although Great Britain kept her free-trade system, the Tariff Reform movement showed that the same ideas were affecting her as had destroyed free trade in continental Europe. She was influenced also by the new obstacles that her own industrial products had to meet; for it was not only on the products of the oversea agricultural countries that the European countries raised their tariffs.

The British Dominions were likewise stirred by more than one motive. The erection of tariffs against their products in former European markets provoked them to retaliation; at the same time they were seized with industrial ambitions of their own, and demanded a more 'balanced economy' than they had possessed during the previous phase of their development. As generations grew up on their soil whose home had never been the British Isles, they were seized also with a spirit of national patriotism of their own, a sentiment which has so often, though not always reasonably, been expressed in economic nationalism. Thus the first protective tariff of Canada, adopted in 1879, was known as 'The National Policy'—a direct forebear of the 'Canada First' slogan used by Mr. R. B. Bennett in his successful 1930 electoral campaign. The first markedly protective tariff in New Zealand was adopted in 1895. In Australia the different colonies, before the establishment of the Australian Commonwealth, maintained different degrees of protection, and one of the most important reasons advanced for federation was the need for unifying tariffs and for establishing free trade between the different States. In South Africa a customs union preceded the political union of the four colonies (indeed, as early as 1889 there had been a customs union between Cape Colony and the Orange Free State, joined by Natal nine years later), but it was nearly wrecked by differences over protective policy, and was only saved by the political union of 1910.

The United States adopted protectionism even more vigorously than the Dominions. The MacKinley tariff of 1890 and the Dingley tariff of 1897 were the foundations of the economic system of the United States as we know it to-day. Not only were manufacturing industries protected, but the home market was reserved also for those primary industries in which the United States was not a world supplier (flax, for instance). This policy turned her into a great economic island with higher costs of production in many industries (both urban and rural) than in the rest of the world; the inevitable result has been that the United States has steadily eaten into her margin of natural advantage, and shows signs of losing her position in certain world markets that she once dominated, such as the market for wheat and in some measure even for cotton. To the extent that British countries have stepped into her shoes as world suppliers of such commodities, American protectionism may prove in the long run to have been of competitive advantage to the new countries of the British Empire.

The re-emergence of Imperial preference in the Dominions is an instructive piece of history. Preference almost wholly disappeared in the free-trade period of the middle and late nineteenth century. In Cape Colony, for instance, there was a preference on British goods from 1821 to 1855, but it was then abolished, and it did not reappear until 1903. The pioneer of Imperial preference in the later period was Canada. The Canadian tariff of 1897 included a 'reciprocal tariff' one-eighth lower than the general tariff, applicable primarily to goods from the United Kingdom, and secondarily to goods from New South Wales and India, and from foreign countries that had most-favoured-nation treaties with the United Kingdom. But in 1898, following the latter's denunciation of her commercial treaties with Germany and Belgium, the preference became purely Imperial, and its amount was raised first to one-quarter and later to one-third of the general rate of duty. New Zealand followed Canada's lead in introducing Imperial preference in 1903, but the preferential duties related only to a few products until the tariff of 1907. Also in 1903 the new customs union between Cape

Colony, Natal, the Orange Free State, the Transvaal, and Southern Rhodesia adopted the principle of preference on all goods imported either from the United Kingdom or from British colonies that accorded reciprocal treatment to the countries of the union. The Australian Commonwealth did not embody preference for United Kingdom goods in its tariff until 1908, but it already had a reciprocal preferential agreement with the South African colonies.

In all the Dominions the idea of reciprocity was to the fore when they adopted Imperial preference. But it is significant that whereas they usually required reciprocal preferences from other parts of the Empire before according them a preference, they made no such condition for the United Kingdom. Not only were they inspired by a sense of loyalty and kinship; they recognized that, although the Mother Country granted them no equivalent preference against their foreign competitors, the free and open market that she maintained for their products was nevertheless of immense value to them. They gave her a preference while she gave them none, but they imposed duties (sometimes very high ones) on her products while she imposed none on theirs. Thus it was not by any means a one-sided bargain.

There were forces at work, however, that were bound before long to bring it to an end. The War did not create those forces, but it very much intensified them. It stimulated in Europe, in the Far East, and elsewhere the development of industries in which England had previously dominated the world—iron and steel, shipbuilding, textiles. Thus it created in Great Britain an industrial and social situation that offered powerful popular (if unscientific) arguments for the abandonment of free trade. The troubles were later intensified by the over-valuation of the pound. The War also stimulated the production of primary products in oversea countries, and so (when the immediate boom was over) weakened the position of British agriculture. The damage was masked before 1928, but as soon as agricultural values slumped the difficulties of British farmers in competing at world prices began to be acute. The War and its aftermath also promoted the protectionism of the Dominions, making it more and more

difficult to sell British goods there as well as in foreign countries. In these circumstances the demand for protection in
Great Britain and the demand for Imperial preference went
together. Apart from the political and patriotic motive, both
measures were conceived as aids for hard-pressed British
industry. The Dominions, for their part, finding increasing
difficulty in selling their primary products at remunerative
prices, wished for preference in Great Britain as a means of
safeguarding their greatest market against under-selling by
foreign countries.

III

OTTAWA AND AFTER

SO the British Government went to Ottawa in August
1932 with a ravelled tangle of motives behind its intention of negotiating preferential agreements with the Dominions. There was the feeling that because the Empire was
good in itself—or good, at least, for many other reasons than
economic ones—trade within the Empire was better in itself
than trade with foreign countries. There was the protectionist purpose of 'projecting the tariff' beyond the national
borders, in order to secure for export trades an advantage
that would balance the favour of import duties for home
trades. There was the free-trade purpose of obtaining within
the Empire that liberation of trade which it seemed impossible to obtain in the world at large.

On the whole, the last motive seems to have been upper-
most in the mind of Mr. Baldwin, who led the United Kingdom delegation to Ottawa; for, although echoes of the other
motives can be found in his speeches and statements at
Ottawa, his chief emphasis was unmistakably upon the desirability of seeking additional preferences by way of lower
tariffs within the Empire, rather than by way of higher tariffs
against the products of foreign countries.

'What then (he asked in his opening speech) should be the first
aim of this Conference? It should be to clear out the channels of
trade among ourselves. . . .

'There are two ways in which increased preference can be given
—either by lowering barriers among ourselves or by raising them
against others. The choice between these two must be governed
largely by local considerations, but, subject to that, it seems to us
that we should endeavour to follow the first rather than the second
course. For however great our resources, we cannot isolate ourselves from the world.' . . .

Earlier in his speech Mr. Baldwin had referred to the
advantages that had been 'provisionally' granted to the
Dominions through the free admission of their products

under the Import Duties Act, as well as through earlier preferences, and he described such free entry as 'the greatest
privilege that can be extended to sister nations'. These
remarks seemed to imply that Great Britain was seeking from
the Dominions further preferences for her exports, through
a reduction of their tariffs, as a condition of retaining the
privileges granted to them under the Import Duties Act.
That was certainly the view of some British people. Mr.
Bruce, in a supplementary statement, hotly repudiated such
a suggestion.

'The unanimous view of the Australian people (he said) is that
while for a quarter of a century they have given preferences to
Great Britain freely and unconditionally, they regard the British
preferences under the Import Duties Act as a somewhat tardy
response for the benefits from Australia long enjoyed by British
industry.'

Mr. Bruce went on to indicate the form of assistance that
Australia desired in the British market. She recognized that
for economic reasons Great Britain could do little to assist
her in wool and perhaps in wheat, 'but the exclusion of meat
would create a position which would be somewhat similar to
Australia excluding from the benefits of preference the whole
of Great Britain's great staple industries and restricting preferential assistance to a series of relatively minor forms of
manufacturing'. Australia also wanted additional preferences on dairy products and fruits. It was possible, said Mr.
Bruce, that the Conference might be forced to the conclusion
that preferential duties alone would not prove effective, and
that the only way in which the Empire markets could be
secured for certain important commodities, such as meat and
butter, was by the adoption of a scheme of restrictions upon
imports from outside the Empire.

It must be recalled at this point that the second National
Government in Great Britain, formed after the election of
1931, had 'agreed to differ' over the Import Duties Act, the
Liberal element under Sir Herbert Samuel retaining their
free-trade faith. Moreover, not only the 'Samuelites' but
others also, including Mr. Runciman, one of the members of
the delegation to Ottawa, were pledged against taxes on

primary foodstuffs, and Mr. Runciman had explicitly mentioned meat as included in this pledge. It was, perhaps, this political complication more than any other factor that made the policy of quota restriction attractive to the Government.

But there was, besides, another motive almost as weighty. Low prices for primary products formed one of the most injurious symptoms of the world depression. Hence, through the association of effect with cause, the idea took root that prices should be raised by any available means, not just as a measure of relief to the producers of the commodities in question, but as part of the effort towards general recovery. Thus, in the Monetary and Financial Committee of the Ottawa Conference, Mr. Neville Chamberlain criticized the view that the raising of the price-level could be secured by monetary measures alone, urging that these should be reinforced by the adjustment of supplies to demand. This was really a very odd argument; for the expansion of money and the contraction of supply were not complementary but contrasting policies, the latter being indeed potentially deflationary in effect.

Mr. Chamberlain's suggestion was very different in character from that put forward by Mr. Bruce. The latter was asking that Empire preference should be made effective, if necessary, by the quantitative restriction of *foreign* imports. Mr. Chamberlain, on the other hand, explicitly stated that 'all the main sources of supply—*home, Empire, and foreign*— must be brought into the plan'. Thus the compromise on quotas that emerged at Ottawa reflected a fundamental conflict of motives and theories. Mr. Coates, in his opening speech for New Zealand, accepted the principle of import quotas 'as an emergency measure designed to tide us over this abnormal period', but 'in no case do we think the quota, or quantitative restrictions, should apply to products of the Empire'.

The practical points at issue at the Conference thus took shape. The chief of them were: whether Great Britain could be induced to give extra preferences beyond those provisionally granted in the Import Duties Act; whether and to what extent quota restrictions would be used as a supplement or a substitute for tariffs; whether quotas must apply to Dominion as well as foreign products; whether the Dominions would bring down their preferential tariffs or merely add another row of bricks to the barrier against foreign goods.

As far as the United Kingdom delegation was concerned another vital question arose: whether the preferences granted should apply to all the Dominions equally, or whether better results could not be obtained by negotiating separate bargains with each Dominion, giving wider preferences to those who were prepared to offer the more favourable terms for British products. The delegation had set its face against discrimination between the different Dominions, except the Irish Free State, but it was nearly forced to change its mind by the reluctance of the Canadian Government to grant preferences comparable with those already promised by other Dominions in return for uniform advantages in the British market. The question cannot even now be said to have been settled for all time. Not only may similar practical problems arise at future Imperial Economic Conferences; the question of discrimination or no discrimination is fundamental in the economics of the Commonwealth. It bears closely on the question whether economic or political reasons are invoked to justify Imperial preference—as the incident of the Anglo-Irish 'tariff war' vividly shows. For if the preferential system is to be regarded as grounded primarily on mutual economic interest there was possibly even more reason for securing a trade agreement with the Irish Free State than with any oversea Dominion. It was obviously on political grounds that both the discrimination against the Irish Free State and the refusal to discriminate between the other Dominions were based at Ottawa.

The results of the hard bargaining that unfortunately proved necessary at Ottawa need not be related in detail here. As far as tariff preferences were concerned, the United Kingdom undertakings involved a certain increase of duties on foreign products beyond those already embodied in the Import Duties Act; the proportion of foreign imports taxed at more than 10 per cent. *ad valorem* rose from 19·9 per cent. to 29·5 per cent. This was a definite setback to the free-trade purpose that was mingled with other objectives of Imperial policy before Ottawa.

What of the counter-concessions by the Dominions? An extremely detailed analysis would be required to ascertain just how far they involved higher barriers to foreign goods and how far lower barriers to British goods. The specific concessions granted by New Zealand were all by way of reduction of the British preferential duty, but those granted by other Dominions were to be effected partly by increases of general tariff rates. In Canada, for instance, the preferential tariff was to be reduced to zero in categories of which total imports in 1931–2 had been £31 millions; the preferential tariff would be lowered in categories of which total imports had been £59 millions; and the foreign tariff was to be raised in categories totalling £35 millions. The Australian promise of a regular minimum scale of preferential margins also implied a considerable number of increases in the general tariff. On the other hand, both Canada and Australia undertook to abolish as soon as possible the surcharges, prohibitions, and other abnormal hindrances to British goods which had been imposed during the crisis. In default of detailed statistical research, it is impossible to make a balance-sheet of these various undertakings; but at least it is clear that the arrangements made on either side at Ottawa involved an appreciable increase of barriers between the Empire and the rest of the world.

It is equally difficult to tell, on the basis of unquestionable facts and figures, what has been the net effect of the Ottawa Agreements, in practice, on the trade of the United Kingdom and the Dominions. A scrutiny of the figures of our own overseas trade during the past five or six years shows that since Ottawa there has been a rise in the proportion of both exports and imports accounted for by Empire countries. Leaving out the highly abnormal year 1931, the Empire share of United Kingdom imports rose from 29·1 per cent. in 1930 to 37·8 per cent. in 1935, and of United Kingdom exports from 43·8 per cent. to 48·2 per cent. in the same period.[1] Experience in the different Dominions varied some-

[1] This rise is more striking still if we omit the Irish Free State, which was

what. In the same interval Canada's imports from British countries rose from 20·2 per cent. to 30·0 per cent. of total imports, and her exports to British countries from 33·8 per cent. to 51·8 per cent. of total exports. For Australia the figures were:[1] imports, 53·3 per cent. to 57·5 per cent.; exports, 56·4 per cent. to 62·5 per cent. For New Zealand: imports, 68·6 per cent. to 73·4 per cent.; exports, 91·4 per cent. to 89·7 per cent. For the Union of South Africa: imports, 57·8 per cent. to 58·4 per cent.; exports, 59·7 per cent. to 54·2 per cent. In spite of the South African figures (which must be viewed against the fact that the total volume of the Union's external trade increased considerably after the abandonment of the gold standard), the general picture is one of a steady increase of the proportion of intra-Empire trade to trade with foreign countries. This summing-up is reinforced by the figures for Newfoundland, Southern Rhodesia, and the dependent Empire.

But many other forces than the Ottawa Agreements may have contributed to this result. For instance, there was the effect of the abandonment of the gold standard. After Ottawa, sterling fell further against gold, South Africa went off the gold standard, New Zealand increased the depreciation of her exchange. Hence the change in trade ratios may have been partly due to an intensification of 'sterling-bloc' ties. Great Britain (possibly, in turn, aided by the Ottawa Agreements) experienced a considerable measure of internal recovery, and so did most of the countries of the Empire. The improvement in the Dominions was due partly to the rise in the price of certain primary commodities, which would automatically raise the proportion (by value) of Empire to foreign imports in Great Britain's trade, quite apart from any influence of tariffs. Even if we could isolate the residuum of effect of Ottawa, the bare statistics would not tell us how far the result represented simply a diversion of trade from foreign countries and how far it represented, in Mr. Baldwin's

---

fiscally at war with the United Kingdom during this period. The figures then become: imports, 24·9 per cent. in 1930 and 35·3 per cent. in 1935; exports, 37·8 per cent. in 1930 and 43·5 per cent. in 1935.

[1] Years ending 30 June 1930 and 1935 respectively.

words, 'a clearing out of the channels of trade between ourselves'.

Prima facie, the mutual concessions granted at Ottawa
did not represent, on balance, any large clearing-out of the
channels of trade. The continued optimism of those who had
hoped for this outcome was largely based on the general
undertakings given by Canada, Australia, and New Zealand;
namely, to give tariff protection only to industries that were
reasonably assured of sound opportunities of success, and
not to raise tariff duties above a level that would give United
Kingdom producers full opportunity of reasonable competition on the basis of the relative costs of economical and efficient production (provided that special consideration might
be given to industries not yet fully established).

There were cynics unkind enough to point out that if these
undertakings were literally observed (in the sense that the
maximum height of tariff thus indicated became also the
minimum height) trade would be stopped altogether, because
the motive for trade would be precisely counterpoised. Setting aside the effect of patents, brands, cartels, and exclusive
rights generally, international trade proceeds only because,
quality for quality, relative costs are different, and derives
from this *raison d'être* its whole economic worth. Besides this
arm-chair argument there was the practical example of the
United States, which had employed a similar general principle to justify an unsurpassed policy of high protectionism.
But the optimists laid less emphasis upon logic than upon
'common sense', and less emphasis on the experience of
foreign countries than upon the saving readiness for compromise and for 'entering into the spirit of the thing' that is
traditionally inherent in the British character.

Whatever else may be laid at the door of British illogicality,
the notorious anomalies in British Commonwealth relations
are fully matched by the variety of interpretation subsequently put upon those Ottawa clauses. The Australian
Tariff Board frankly refused to apply the clauses strictly. A
fine adjustment of duties, they declared, so as to place efficient manufacturers of the United Kingdom and of Australia
on exactly the same price-level in the Australian market,

would seriously dislocate industries which had been established in Australia for years, and the subversive consequences of such an employment-destroying policy could not fail to engender opposition to the Ottawa Agreement.

'There is no hard and fast formula (they wrote) which can be used with any degree of satisfaction, and the problem of reasonably interpreting the agreement involves much more than an arithmetical calculation of the difference between the costs in the United Kingdom and in Australia. Each case must be considered on its merits and judgment given after a close examination of all available relevant facts.'

Another report of the Board made it clear that their method of applying the Ottawa clauses could be not unfairly described as rough rule-of-thumb. Investigations under the agreement had shown that in a number of industries labour costs in Australia, expressed in Australian currency, were approximately half as much again as those in the United Kingdom, expressed in sterling. In some industries the ratio was higher and in some lower.

The New Zealand Tariff Commission likewise refused to be bound by legal or logical pedantry in its interpretation of the Ottawa Agreements. The undertaking to limit tariffs to the level required to give United Kingdom producers full opportunity of competition on the basis of relative production costs was intended, in their view, to give the United Kingdom manufacturer a 'fair deal' in the New Zealand market, 'in the sense in which that popular though vague expression would be understood by a reasonable and fair-minded man'. A high degree of mathematical accuracy could not be expected or attained in the actual calculations of tariff rates based on comparisons of costs; the application of the principle depended on applying common sense to the data available.

The Australian Tariff Board, it must be noted, was a permanent body already experienced in the adjustment of tariffs, while the New Zealand Tariff Commission, though formed *ad hoc*, was under the chairmanship of the permanent head of the Customs Department. This helps to explain the unjuridical but not ineffective methods used by these bodies in applying the Ottawa clauses. Canada presents a contrast both in procedure and in results. The interpretation of the Ottawa Agreements was entrusted to a semi-judicial tribunal, presided over by a High Court judge, which examined with meticulous care masses of evidence in individual industries, and in what was regarded as virtually a test case (the application for a reduction of duty on woollens) came to the conclusion that no recommendation was possible in default of a thorough study of the records and costing methods of each firm that had been represented in the inquiry. This, of course, was not the sum total of their labours, which on occasion resulted in appreciable advantage to United Kingdom exporters; but the incident shows the difficulty of entrusting practical policies to the mercies of treaty formulas in general terms, or of finding a scientific principle of tariff-making that is genuinely capable of scientific interpretation.

The want of an accepted science in this field cannot be better illustrated than by the contrast between the decisions of the Australian Tariff Board and those of the New Zealand Tariff Commission regarding the relation between tariff levels and exchange rates. Each of the two countries, whose general economic circumstances were very much alike, had depreciated its currency to a level 20 per cent. below English sterling. In each of them, it must also be remembered, the local pound was habitually regarded as inherently the same article as the English pound, despite the fact that the latter might temporarily command a premium of five shillings in local money. The Australian Board noted that the cost of imported goods had been materially increased by the depreciation of the exchange, while over the same period Australian costs had fallen substantially. Protection to local industry had thus been increased well above the level that had been considered reasonable when adopted by Parliament. In another report they declared that the continuance of excess protection under the depreciated exchange 'must leave room to question the proper implementing of the Ottawa agreement'. They therefore planned to present their recommendations thenceforward in the form of a schedule allowing for the adjustment of tariff rates in accordance with movements of the exchange rate between its existing position and par.

The New Zealand Tariff Commission, whose good faith in interpreting the Ottawa Agreements with fairness to the United Kingdom manufacturer could not be impugned, took precisely the contrary line. They were opposed to making variations in tariff rates for the purpose of offsetting the protective effect of a depreciating or depreciated currency. This seemed to them to be unsound in principle and based on a misunderstanding of the effect of currency depreciation upon prices. The major effects of depreciation, they thought, were soon worked out.

Economic students, faced with this remarkable conflict of judgement, may observe that much depends on the question whether the depreciation was deliberately undertaken in order to procure a rise of export prices, or was forced upon the country by the appearance of a debit balance of payments. This consideration, however, sound as it may be, would have indicated a precisely opposite result. For it was New Zealand that depreciated deliberately as a matter of policy, and might therefore have taken the opportunity to reduce tariff barriers; whereas Australia was forced into depreciation by the weakness of her overseas balance, and might therefore have been excused for keeping up her defences against excessive imports. Nor does the confusion of thought end there. While United Kingdom interests were naturally pleased by the Australian view, which facilitated the lowering of tariffs on their goods, they would have been vastly perturbed, and would probably have protested vigorously, if a converse view had been accepted in the gold-standard countries when sterling itself depreciated, that is to say, if tariffs against British exports had been raised proportionately to the fall of the pound.

IV

MEAT AND MILK

ON one side the Ottawa agreements, and the experience under their general clauses, formed a test of the readiness of the Dominions to lower tariffs on British goods in return for preferences in the United Kingdom market. On the other side they formed a test of the readiness of a protectionist United Kingdom Government to forgo protection on Dominion products that might compete with British agriculture, in return for preferences in the Dominions. It cannot be said that in either case the test proved the overwhelming strength of the Empire connexion in combating national protectionism. Hesitations in the Dominions gave rise to some acrimonious feeling in the United Kingdom, expressing itself in charges of bad faith in carrying out the 'spirit of the Ottawa agreements'. Similar feelings and similar charges were engendered in the Dominions by the British Government's agricultural policy. The Ottawa agreements had precluded the Government from imposing duties on Dominion meat during their currency, and from imposing any quantitative restriction on meat from Australia or New Zealand until June 1934. The United Kingdom also undertook not to restrict the import of Dominion butter and cheese until November 1935. Before these undertakings expired they were proving irksome to a Government whose policy included the specially favourable treatment of home agriculture.

It must be noted, however, that the Dominions chiefly concerned accepted at Ottawa the principle of raising the price of primary products by restricting the supply to the United Kingdom market. Their attitude, of course, was that only the foreign supply should be restricted. In support of the view that all sources of supply should be in some measure controlled, the United Kingdom Government could advance two very powerful arguments. First, British trade connexions with some of the foreign countries competing with

the Dominions were very strong—so strong, indeed, that the
degree of restriction necessary if Dominion supplies were to
be unchecked might seriously injure our export business,
with eventual reactions on our purchasing power for Dominion goods. Secondly, if the price were raised while Dominion
supplies were entirely unrestricted, the latter might thereupon expand to an uneconomic degree, and the problem
would be renewed in an even more acute form than before.
Alternatively, the pressure on remaining world markets,
exerted by the surplus of foreign products that had been
lopped off the supply to the United Kingdom, would prevent
the desired rise of world prices.

The opposition of the Dominions to the quota restriction
of their exports of primary products was equally firmly
founded in principle. Public and private capital, they could
claim, had been invested in their rural development on the
assumption that a continuously expanding volume of production would take care of the heavy overhead expenses.
Mechanical and scientific improvements (often subsidized
by the Government or by Imperial bodies) had enabled an
increasing quantity of produce to be won from a given area
of land, and presumably would continue to do so. Hence
even the stabilization of the volume of output at its existing
level implied the eventual abandonment of cultivation on
some land—land that carried mortgages or on which, perhaps, settlers had been placed with Government aid and
encouragement. A still more urgent aspect of the problem
for the Dominions was its relation to unemployment.
Other things being equal, a reduction of primary output,
whatever the price received, meant a reduction in the volume
of employment offering in primary industry and ancillary
trades; and the problem of unemployment was just as
serious in the Dominions as the problem of low prices.

These arguments, which Dominion spokesmen put forward
both at the Imperial Economic Conference and at the World
Conference of the following year, may be regarded as victors
so far in the long-drawn-out campaign of controversy that
began at Ottawa and is still being waged, the *casus belli* being
British protection for agriculture. The Ottawa Agreements

recorded only certain voluntary measures of regulation to be effected by Australia and New Zealand in the meat trade; indeed, they explicitly guaranteed those Dominions, for the time being, against any compulsory curtailment of their meat exports to the United Kingdom. It is true that in November 1932, when Argentina contracted to cut down her beef exports to Great Britain by 10 per cent. and her exports of mutton and lamb by 20 per cent., Australia and New Zealand agreed for their part to reduce their mutton and lamb exports by 10 per cent. But they would not promise any curtailment of their exports of frozen or chilled beef, and their bargaining strength *vis-à-vis* the United Kingdom was clearly displayed in the negotiations of 1935 for a temporary pact on meat exports, and in those of 1936 for a permanent arrangement to follow the expiry of the Anglo-Argentine trade agreement.

As a result of these discussions, not only is there to be no compulsory restriction of Dominion meat exports; no import duty (or 'levy') is to be payable on them, whereas Argentine and other foreign beef is to be taxed at a rate equivalent to about 20 per cent. *ad valorem*. The objections of political expediency, or principle, to 'food taxes' seem to have diminished with time, which makes it easier for the British Government to give up quotas in favour of the straight tariff for the protection of home agriculture. They have, however, made a neat attempt to serve both God and Mammon by appropriating (indirectly but explicitly) the proceeds of the duty on foreign meat for the payment of a subsidy on home-killed meat, thus seeking by the self-same act to make food dearer and to make it cheaper. This device appears to have been incorporated as a permanent element in British policy of agricultural protection.

In reality it is a matter of some doubt how closely the prices and consumption of imported chilled and frozen meat are linked with those of the home-killed product. Generally speaking, the two things appeal to different classes of consumers, though there must certainly be some border-line households that would switch from one to the other according to the variations in the price-margin between them. If cake becomes cheap relative to bread, some former bread-eaters will eat cake. But that is not to say that if bread becomes dear more cake will be eaten; what happens then is that the bread-eaters eat less.

What happens to the ordinary housewife's marketing if the price of some article of daily consumption rises? Suppose she has ten shillings to spend, and the price of bacon, of which she usually buys two pounds, has gone up from 1s. 2d. to 1s. 4d. She may say: 'I can't afford so much bacon at that price. I'll buy a pound of bacon and spend the extra shilling on something else.' Or she may still buy two pounds of bacon, in which case she has only 7s. 4d. left instead of 7s. 8d., and she must manage to economize on some other purchase. Hence the problem of meat or bacon prices cannot be separated from the problem of marketing milk and other necessaries. If meat becomes dearer, either expenditure will be diverted to other things or there will be less room in the family budget for supplementary or alternative articles of food (or possibly for boots or clothing).

This train of thought was started by consideration of the Ottawa and post-Ottawa efforts to regulate the trade in mutton and beef; but the principles involved are generally valid, and point important lessons for the future of Empire trade. Nowhere have the swirling waters of depression created a more vicious vortex than in the trade in primary foodstuffs. With rising production and falling demand, prices dropped to unremunerative levels, and each fall in prices led to ever more stringent tariffs, quotas, and prohibitions in importing countries, which had their own farmers to consider. These restrictions, in turn, by limiting the area of demand, drove world prices still lower, with the result that tariffs were further raised, quotas were narrowed, and prohibitions multiplied, till in some high-protectionist countries the agricultural price-level stood twice or three times as high as the level ruling in free markets. No wonder consumption could not revive. To escape from this evil spiral is still among the leading problems that face world statesmen.

One of the most likely clues to a solution is the question of public health. We are just beginning to realize the immense importance, for the health and vitality of the population, of an ample consumption of the protective foods. It so happens that certain of the most valuable foodstuffs in this sense—milk, eggs, fresh vegetables, and fruit—are those that can be grown only, or most economically, near to consuming centres, that is to say in countries like Great Britain, where they enjoy a strong natural protection without the interference of Governments. The problem of increasing the consumption of them is not merely a problem of making them cheap, relative to the incomes of consumers; it is equally a problem of making other necessities cheap, in order to raise the proportion of narrow incomes left over for the purchase of such alimentary 'luxuries', which ought to be treated as necessaries for every household. This suggests that as between Great Britain on the one hand and its main suppliers of foodstuffs, like Argentina and the Dominions, on the other there should be a pact of specialization, the exporting countries producing and selling as cheaply as possible such products as wheat and meat, the importing country concentrating on milk and eggs and fresh vegetables and fruit.

This sounds simple when expressed in these general terms, but in practice it encounters great difficulties, of which a notorious example is furnished by the problem of dairy products. The average wholesale price of milk in Great Britain is bound to be governed in some degree by the price of butter and cheese; for in the most favourable circumstances there will be at some seasons a surplus of milk over liquid requirements, and this surplus must be sold for manufacture at a price dependent on the price of the final product. Hence, on the face of things, the fortunes of British dairy farmers are threatened by imports of cheap butter and cheese from the Dominions, Scandinavia, and elsewhere. Yet these are products which those countries are eminently suited to produce for export. Moreover, if British families are to have enough money to spare for an ample consumption of liquid milk, it is important that other articles of diet, including butter and cheese, should be as cheap as possible. It is equally important, in the same cause, that liquid milk should be as cheap as possible, and should not have to be kept dear in order to

compensate British farmers for the loss on that portion of
their output which must be sold for manufacture.

What is the conclusion for British policy? Obviously that
farmers should be discouraged from producing milk surplus
to liquid requirements, and that every effort should be
directed towards expanding the consumption of liquid milk
by lowering its price, rather than towards increasing the total
output of milk by raising the price of the surplus.

The argument may be reinforced by an arithmetical
example, which, though deliberately simplified, is sufficiently
near the facts not to be misleading. Suppose that one-
quarter of a total output of, say, a million gallons of milk is
sold for manufacture at 5d. a gallon, the remainder being
sold for liquid consumption at 1s. 3d. a gallon. The total
return in pence is therefore a quarter of 5 millions plus three-
quarters of 15 millions, which equals 12½ millions. Now
suppose that instead of one-quarter only one-eighth of the
milk has to be sold for manufacture. At what price must the
remaining seven-eighths be sold in order to give the farmers
the same total return? (Shades of the school-room). The
answer is given by subtracting the new return from milk for
manufacture (five-eighths of a million pence) from the old
total return of 12½ million pence, and dividing the difference
by seven-eighths of a million (the new amount sold for liquid
consumption). This works out at roughly 13½d. In other
words, the price of liquid milk may be lowered by 1½d. a
gallon, and still the total return to dairy farmers will not be
diminished.

Clearly, therefore, British policy has hitherto been on
wrong lines. By guaranteeing a minimum price for milk for
manufacture, it has subsidized sales in the very direction that
should have been discouraged, and has thus promoted a
further expansion of output. The enlarged surplus can find
a market only in manufacture, with the result that it has
become more difficult rather than less difficult to lower the
price of milk for liquid consumption. Meanwhile, expansion
of output and lowering of prices of butter and cheese in the
Dominions and other countries best fitted to supply them
have been correspondingly discouraged. Such a policy is

a denial of international specialization, and it is equally a denial of the aim of bringing as much wholesome food as possible, at the lowest prices, to the people of Great Britain.

The above paragraphs were drafted before the publication of the report of the Milk Marketing Reorganization Commission in November 1936. That unanimous report followed closely the lines of the argument here set out, and reached conclusions fully consonant with the policy suggested. To concentrate on making liquid milk cheap, and to discourage through the price system the production of a surplus that can be sold only for butter and cheese making, these were the two main principles recommended by the Commission. They were not invited to deal with the Empire-trade aspect of the milk problem, but their proposals in fact fit excellently into a scheme of international specialization within the Commonwealth.

The difficulties in Empire trade over dairy produce and meat are sufficient proof that Ottawa, whatever it may have done in the field of manufacturing industry, provided no permanent or reliable principle for trade in agricultural produce. Why was this? The first reason was that British agricultural protectionism, instead of having reached maturity like the industrial protectionism of the Dominions, was still in adolescence and had scarcely begun to test its strength. The second reason was that the principle of restriction, which was tentatively applied at Ottawa to agricultural production and trade, was wrongly conceived. It was regarded, not simply as a powerful instrument of national protection, nor simply as a means of rationalizing a depressed industry in its own interest (subject to due regard for the interests of consumers), but rather—indeed even primarily—as a specific for curing general economic depression. This, of course, it decidedly was not. Hence the theoretical background of United Kingdom and Empire policy was confused and even at times self-contradictory.

The third and much the most fundamental reason was that no principle (apart from the spurious one of restriction) was sought or appealed to in this field of the Ottawa discussions. There was merely a bargain, an exchange of advantages—at the expense, inevitably, of foreign suppliers and consequently of exporters to foreign markets. Fair though the bargain may have been at the time, its balance must inevitably have been disturbed by any sharp changes in price levels or in relative conditions of production—changes that are always much more likely to take place in agriculture than in manufacturing industry. Hence the moral of the whole story is the need for a clear intellectual conception of the principles and purpose of Commonwealth economic policy.

V

POSSIBLE POLICIES

WHY are we entitled to assume the need for a special
economic policy for the Commonwealth? That is the
kind of question that we hardly ever ask ourselves in
these days, though a generation ago few British politicians
would have treated it as axiomatic. The question may be
answered by two different arguments, either of which, if
sound, serves to justify a special economic policy for the
Commonwealth, in which a large practical part is bound to
be played by mutual tariff preferences. Hence both arguments have been indiscriminately used by those who approved the conclusion first and sought the vindication of it
afterwards. They are, however, contrary in their trend, and
may indicate different policies in practice.

On the one hand, we may take the following line. World
trade is dammed and distorted by nationalistic efforts based
on the apparent self-interest of sovereign States. The units
are too small, prosperity is hindered, depression exaggerated.
In the group of nations forming the British Commonwealth,
however, we have a much larger unit, to a great extent complementary in its mutual trade, and able to promote prosperity by 'clearing out the channels of trade' within itself. It
is in a position to do that because its internal economic ties
are complementary as well as extremely strong. Moreover,
by good fortune, economic motives are reinforced by political
and sentimental attachments that predispose its members
towards mutual co-operation. In this respect it starts with
an enormous advantage by comparison with the jealousies
that have hitherto frustrated every attempt to tackle the
problem on a world-wide scale. In this first argument the
emphasis is first and foremost on the *economic* suitability of
the Commonwealth for serving an *economic* purpose. Let us
therefore call it the economic argument for Imperial preference.

On the other hand we may start from the *political* facts,

arguing that the strength and integrity of the Commonwealth must be preserved if the ideals and institutions of freedom for which it stands, as well as its own safety, are to be defended in a dangerous world. To strengthen the Commonwealth in trade and finance, and to draw its economic ties closer, helps (so the argument runs) in securing its general strength and integrity. By good fortune, the present close and complementary character of those ties predisposes its members towards such economic co-operation, and checks the economic antagonisms that elsewhere hinder a relaxation of political tension. This we will call the political argument.

The contrast between those two lines of thought—both of which have been freely expressed by Commonwealth statesmen before and after Ottawa—is almost complete. It would seem at first sight that mutually hostile conclusions for practical policy might be drawn from them. Thus a highly protective tariff on foreign goods, imposed for the sake of promoting Empire trade, while damaging world trade as a whole, might be justified by the political argument for Imperial preference, but must equally be condemned on appeal to the economic argument. In practice, however, the conflict is less violent, partly because each argument must to some extent respect the virtue in the other, partly because the political argument leaps a dangerous logical gap, and on retracing its steps more cautiously finds its conclusions distinctly modified. The gap is the assumption that to strengthen the economic ties between the Commonwealth nations, at the expense of their trade and financial exchanges with foreign countries, adds political and general strength to the Commonwealth as a whole.

This chapter is no place to dilate on world politics or the causes of war, but no one can doubt that existing economic barriers have helped to bring about that state of fear, distrust, and jealousy between nations which fosters war, and that any significant increase of those barriers must add to the almost universal sense of national strangulation and danger.[1] Since the most vital interest of the British Commonwealth is world peace based on justice, it is for us a far greater risk to

[1] See Part I, Chapter V.

increase the chances of world war than to forgo certain mutual privileges we might grant ourselves in trade and finance.

What would be the use, for instance, of our enlarging the volume of trade between Great Britain and Australia, if the price to be paid were a greater chance, not merely that the trade might be interrupted by war, but even possibly that the Empire might be destroyed? (Of course this example is exaggerated, as any isolated example must be; it is the accumulation of small actions that counts.) If, indeed, power politics and war are the prime considerations governing economic policy—if, that is to say, war is inevitable and we must subordinate Imperial economics to Imperial strategy —it may well be that the proper policy for us to adopt is the reverse of that ostensibly adopted at Ottawa; in brief, that instead of clearing out the channels of Empire trade we should consider which of those channels we could conveniently dam and drain, so as to lessen our strategic risks and liabilities.

In short, the political argument must be qualified by the premiss of the economic argument, that the promotion of Empire trade is secondary to the promotion of world trade. For this wider purpose is just as important politically to the British Commonwealth as it is economically. Naturally the force of this reference to the problem of world trade varies between the different parts of the Commonwealth, according to their strategic position on the one hand and their dependence on foreign trade on the other. It is thus most persuasive for Great Britain, who besides being more closely involved than any single Dominion in the risks of general war is also peculiarly dependent for economic life on her trade with the foreign world. The remainder of this chapter is concerned primarily with the national policy of Great Britain towards Empire trade relations, regarded as one of the key elements in formulating a Commonwealth-wide economic purpose or plan.

In 1935 her imports from foreign countries exceeded £472 millions, and her exports to them £221 millions (not counting re-exports); while her imports from Empire countries were

£284 millions, and her exports to them £204 millions. If she were to cut down her imports from foreign countries, she could not expect them to buy so much from her. She would run the risk of seeing her exports to them fall by as great an absolute amount as her imports from them; the least she could expect would be an equal proportionate fall, the difference being made up by a drop in her invisible receipts from abroad. Her experience in the depression, and as a result of her tariffs, justifies such a calculation, since between 1929 and 1935 her imports from foreign countries and her exports to them fell in value by almost exactly the same percentage. A reduction of a quarter in her imports from foreign countries, we may therefore estimate, might mean a reduction of a quarter, or £55 millions, in her exports to them; if, then, her aggregate exports were not to decline, her exports to British countries would have to increase by the same amount. It is doubtful whether it is a practical proposition to ask the rest of the Empire to increase its imports of United Kingdom goods by 27 per cent., except by virtue of a general revival of world trade. Even if, in such a case, the total exports of the United Kingdom were not to suffer, she would have lost over £60 millions in investment and service income from foreign sources, unless this were somehow made up by a triangular process.

Hence all schools of fiscal thought in Great Britain, except the extreme protectionists, agree that Britain's Imperial economic policy should not be such as to prevent her from negotiating a more liberal system of trade relations with foreign countries. It follows that part of her aim must be to make trade within the Empire as free as possible, since the lower her Imperial tariff is the lower her general tariff may be, given a prescribed margin of Imperial preference. Indeed, *any* system of fixed margins of Imperial preference is liable to check the grant of preferences to a group of foreign countries that might be willing to offer special concessions in exchange. Such a policy, the policy of the 'multi-decker' tariff, may or may not be a good thing; at present it is ruled out, as far as Great Britain is concerned, by treaties containing the most-favoured-nation clause. And the most-favoured-nation clause remains an integral part of her official commercial policy.

That policy, however, is self-contradictory. If, in the words of the Ottawa Conference, by means of Imperial preferential agreements 'the trade of the world will be stimulated and increased', then it is *prima facie* illogical to argue that preferential agreements with certain foreign countries would check and diminish the trade of the world. Both systems equally transcend the most-favoured-nation principle—which, by a stroke of hypocrisy which it is charitable to call confusion of thought, the Governments of the Commonwealth vigorously deny as between the Empire and foreign countries, while in the same breath upholding it for foreign trade by itself.[1] There is nothing peculiar about trade relations in the Empire that prevents the following Ottawa phrases from being equally honestly used of a low-tariff group including foreign countries, or of a group pledged to progressive reduction of mutual barriers to trade: 'that by the lowering or removal of barriers among themselves the flow of trade between the various participating countries will be facilitated, and that by the consequent increase of the purchasing power of their peoples the trade of the world will also be stimulated and increased.'

In brief, a two-decker tariff, regarded as an economic rather than a political instrument, implies the possibility of a three-decker tariff. Hence it must be accounted a weakness of the multiple-decker policy if the lowest deck (Imperial

---

[1] Contrast the two following excerpts from the report of the Committee of the Ottawa Conference on Commercial Relations with Foreign Countries. (a) 'The representatives of the various Governments on the Committee stated that it was their policy that no treaty obligations into which they might enter in the future should be allowed to interfere with any mutual preferences which the Governments of the Commonwealth might decide to accord to each other, and that they would free themselves from existing treaties, if any, which might so interfere.' (b) 'Attention was drawn to recent tendencies in foreign countries to conclude regional agreements between themselves for the mutual accord of preferences which were designed as being exclusive, and not to be extended to countries which were not parties to, or did not adhere to the agreements. On this point, there was general agreement that foreign countries which had existing treaty obligations to grant most-favoured-nation treatment to the products of the particular parts of the Commonwealth could not be allowed to override such obligations by regional agreements of the character in question.'

preference) is so high, or the promised margin between it
and any other deck is so great, that no middle-deck can
be low enough to gain any advantage in foreign trade
relations.

There are political as well as economic objections to Great
Britain's adoption of too protectionist or too rigid a tariff
policy for Empire trade. It would be a disaster if Imperial
preference as such became an internal political issue, or if the
principle of a special commercial policy for the Empire were
to be associated with one party or parliamentary group. It
was not altogether the fault of the Ottawa Agreements that
they provoked at Westminster a final split between the free-
trade Liberals and the rest of the National Government
forces; for the real split had come earlier with the Import
Duties Act, and the Ottawa Agreements were a much less
serious concession to protectionism than the Act itself under
which they were negotiated. Nevertheless, the incident was
a warning of the dangerous possibilities of the future.

A democracy lives by compromises, and nowhere has
political compromise been more successful than in the field
of British Commonwealth relations. So long as free trade
was the secular economic policy of the United Kingdom, the
compromise on Empire trade relations was effected by the
free-traders' acceptance of the principle that if a tariff were
to be imposed for any reason it would if possible carry an
Imperial preference. To-day, none but the most rabid Cob-
denite would deny that protection has become the United
Kingdom's secular policy, in the sense that the former free-
trade parties (Liberal and Labour), if returned to power,
would not think of trying to overthrow it completely or at
once, however much they might adjust the tariff or proclaim
the eventual goal to be a return to free trade. In these circumstances a new compromise on Empire trade relations is
necessary in British politics. It can be established only if the
protectionists accept the principle that Imperial preference
must not be allowed to stand in the way of a general move
towards freer trade in the world at large. This, indeed,
would be, not a reversal, but a natural corollary of United
Kingdom policy as expressed at Ottawa.

This consideration for the interests of world commerce as a whole lends special merit to the 'free-trade' as contrasted with the 'protectionist' attitude towards Empire trade by itself, as the proper attitude for the British Government to adopt. A free-trade attitude towards Empire economic relations does not here mean what has been popularly advertised as 'Empire free trade'; for genuine free trade within the Empire, however desirable, is frankly and completely out of the picture of practical possibilities, and the phrase has been merely used by unscrupulous propagandists as a stalking-horse for a policy of high protection in the United Kingdom, especially for agricultural products. Here the free-trade attitude means the genuine pursuit of as free terms of trade as possible within the Empire, as the deliberate objective of Imperial economic policy; it implies the virtual absence of restrictions on Empire goods entering the United Kingdom. A protectionist attitude towards Empire trade, on the other hand, means deliberately regarding the Imperial tariff system as a dilute form of the general protective tariff—dilute, partly because the goods concerned are for the most part different from those entering into British trade with foreign countries, and will not bear as high a rate of protection as is afforded, for instance, to the iron and steel industry against foreign imports; partly because 'sacrifices' of protectionist purpose have to be made for the sake of profitable tariff bargains, and also for the sake of the wider, political purposes of Imperial preference.

The British Government and people do not seem yet to have made up their minds between these two choices. The system of quota restriction was in effect an attempt to evade the issue, by imposing protection against imports from the Dominions while keeping alive the principle of no tariffs on Empire goods. But it was a fruitless attempt; for the 1936 meat agreement, following other signs of redirection of British policy, showed that the resistance of the Dominions had banished restriction as an effective general principle for Empire trade in primary produce. Great Britain has therefore still to decide whether within the Commonwealth, as in the world at large, she is going to answer protection with protection, or whether she is going to allow the Dominions to continue to enjoy the free entry into her market that they had up to 1932, trusting to secure in return some liberation of her own trade in their markets.

If she chooses the first alternative, then various alternative lines of Imperial economic policy are open to her. The general clauses of the Ottawa Agreements indicate one possibility. Their theoretical defects have been admitted, but a 'common-sense' interpretation of them gives a clue to a practical plan, of which the gist might be this. No primary or secondary industry, first of all, shall be protected that has no chance of standing on its own feet. Standing on its own feet cannot be understood to mean surviving without protection while having its costs increased and its markets restricted by protection for other industries; rather it must mean surviving with a degree of protection no higher than the rate applied for reasons of national policy to the bulk of other protected industries. Secondly, no industry shall be given a degree of protection that does not allow other Empire producers a fair chance of competing on equal terms; they should never be forced, by the height of the tariff, to sell below their production costs. These principles were to be applied, under the Ottawa Agreements, to United Kingdom trade with three Dominions. Can they be applied to Empire trade as a whole, and in particular to the import of Dominion primary produce into the United Kingdom?

In practical terms, this would mean that the United Kingdom should not protect any agricultural industry that had no chance of standing on its own feet, in the sense of requiring no greater degree of protection than is given to the general average of industries. Thus she would have to ask herself what would be the chances of survival of wheat and sugar-beet, for instance, if they were given no higher degree of protection than would correspond to, say, a $33\frac{1}{3}$ per cent. tariff with a preferential rate of 20 per cent. Secondly, she would have to allow Empire producers a fair chance of competing on equal terms with her own producers of foodstuffs, after compensating through the tariff for different costs of production. In a concrete case, if the cost of growing wheat in

o

Australia and sending it to the British markets were, say, 30s. a cwt., and the home cost were 40s. a cwt., then the maximum preferential duty on wheat would be 10s. a cwt.—or, if wheat from the Dominions continued to enter duty free, the rate of subsidy to home wheat farmers would not exceed 10s. per cwt.

When we come down to cases like this we perceive at once a grave theoretical defect in this principle of tariff-making and a practical obstacle to its being carried out. The theoretical trouble is that the higher the home cost of production, and therefore the less deserving the industry is of protection on any economic grounds, the higher would be the permissible rate of duty; conversely, any economy in production costs in the Dominions, instead of benefiting the consumer, would be countered by an equivalent increase in the rate of protection that could be granted to the home industry. In other words, the principle of the 'scientific' tariff contradicts the principle of economic specialization. Specialization, on the other hand, has been rightly extolled as one of the guides to tariff policy in the Empire. It would allow both the Dominions and the United Kingdom to concentrate their efforts on those industries, primary and manufacturing, for which they are relatively best fitted, within the limits of national policies designed to afford strategic security or to promote a more even balance between industry and agriculture.

Now let us turn to the practical obstacle which lies in the way of a planned specialization as well as in that of a compensatory tariff. Both must be based, though in inverse senses, upon a consideration of relative costs of production; yet we have only the haziest knowledge of costs of production in actual fact. Economists will tell us, indeed, that there is no such thing as a single cost of production in any industry; for some factories or farms or mines will be producing more cheaply than others, so that the limiting cost of production will vary according to the number of production-units taken into consideration, as well as with the total volume of production. Even if we leave aside these paper difficulties, in agricultural industries there are two special obstacles to an ascertainment of national costs of production. There is, first, the variation of average costs with the quality and volume of the crops, which fluctuate more with meteorological than with any economic forces. Secondly, for very few agricultural products can the cost of production be separated from costs and prices in other branches of agriculture. Thus the cost of producing wool may be said to fall when the price of mutton rises, since the two commodities derive from the same beast; and the price of raising fat cattle, to take another example, depends on the cost of growing or buying grain and other animal foodstuffs.

Vital as these objections are, they do not prevent our finding some nucleus of practical worth in the idea of a 'scientific' tariff for agricultural goods entering the United Kingdom, to match the scientific tariff on manufactured goods entering the Dominions that was implied in the Ottawa Agreements. We can at least keep at the back of our minds the two negative tests—no protection for uneconomic industries, no protection so high that Dominion producers are forced to sell below their costs of production in order to reach the United Kingdom market while British farmers are making profits.

For more positive guides to Great Britain's policy—still assuming that protection is to be the foundation of her Imperial economic policy, as it now is of her world economic policy—we must look to the idea of specialization. This idea was tentatively applied to certain classes of goods in the so-called 'Montreal Pact' between British and Canadian steel-masters, and in isolated items of the Ottawa Agreements. If we want to know how far it is applicable to Empire trade in primary products, we must first ask ourselves what agricultural goods the United Kingdom, as the main importing market, is relatively best fitted to produce. Climate, and the necessity of near markets for perishable foodstuffs, point obviously to liquid milk, eggs, fresh-killed meat, green vegetables, and fruit; secondarily, to grains and grasses used as fodder for live-stock.

As we have noted in the previous chapter, to expand the home production and consumption of those foods, while allowing the fullest possible freedom of trade in such products as cheap cheese and butter, frozen and chilled meat, and bread-cereals, is to adopt a far-seeing policy for raising the national standard of health. But to defend the home production of essential foodstuffs by methods that involved raising their price above the world economic level would, on the contrary, be an attack on the national health. In this lies the attraction of the plan to use the proceeds of a levy on imported products to promote the consumption of the most nutritive foods. It may be noted, however, that there is no particular virtue in allotting the proceeds of an import tax on any given article for the promotion of the home production of that same article. It might be best to tax one article and subsidize another—to tax imported butter, for instance, in order to cheapen liquid milk or fresh eggs.

It is clear that restriction of supply has no place in an economic policy based either on international specialization or on the furtherance of public health. Restriction as a means, deliberately adopted, of bringing order out of chaos in an individual industry ruined by over-production has much to recommend it. Under the disguise of 'rationalization' it has enjoyed a certain vogue as a cure for depression in secondary industry. But if this is the motive then the restriction should be so designed as to eliminate as far as possible the high-cost producers, rather than allowing them to continue in production at the expense of their low-cost competitors. Therefore restriction applied to the products of low-cost areas, while high-cost areas maintain or even expand their output, can be treated only as a sheer protectionist policy.

Judged thus as an instrument of protection, the restriction of imports of primary products can never figure satisfactorily in the United Kingdom's Imperial economic policy. It is opposed to the long-term interests of the Dominions, and it conflicts with the standards of specialization and nutrition, as well as the principle that fair chances of competing on equal terms shall be allowed to producers in all parts of the Empire.

We can thus sum up the possible outlines of an Imperial economic policy for the United Kingdom, based on the assumption that within the Commonwealth national protection is to be the starting-point of policy. No encouragement shall be given to the introduction or expansion of industries unlikely to be able to survive without an abnormal degree of protection. Protection shall not be so high that producers elsewhere in the Empire can only reach the market by dint of selling below costs of production. No policy of restriction of output or sales shall be applied that does not apply equally to producers in all parts of the Empire, including importing as well as exporting countries. As far as possible, policy shall be directed towards stimulating those industries upon which each country is best fitted to concentrate. For this purpose, as far as agricultural products are concerned, the handiest instrument (though by no means without faults of its own) is a series of import duties the proceeds of which are used to promote the consumption of the articles on which the importing country intends to concentrate, special attention being paid to the need for expanding the consumption of foodstuffs rich in nutritive value.

What, then, are the possibilities for an Imperial economic policy based on free trade? Such free trade, in existing circumstances, cannot be mutual. The Dominions and India have built up industrial systems under shelter of protection which they are certainly not going to abandon; both they and the colonies rely for a great part of their revenue on import duties on British as well as on foreign goods, and the protective and fiscal aspects of their import tariffs cannot be separated. The essence of a 'free-trade' Imperial system, from Great Britain's point of view, would be that she would afford free entry to goods from the Dominions in return for a downward revision (which she would hope would be progressive) in their tariffs on her goods. This was, generally speaking, the Baldwin view of the purpose of Ottawa.

Neither the quantitative restriction of imports nor the continued dumping of Dominion primary products in the United Kingdom market would be consistent with such a system. Free trade is not fair trade if it is countered by dumping (that is to say, by the persistent sale of any product at a lower price in external markets than in the home market). Free entry for Empire primary products would have to be made contingent on there being no dumping on the British market. This applies particularly to Australia and South Africa, both of whom seem to have adopted the 'home consumption price'—a pseudonym for organized dumping—as an integral part of their policy towards their agricultural and pastoral industries.

The abolition of dumping would be a negative response that the United Kingdom could properly demand from the Dominions in return for her contribution of free trade in primary products. A positive return for which she ought certainly to press would be free entry for her primary products into their markets. This mainly means, in practice, free entry for British coal, though a few other items would be affected—fish, for instance, and pedigree stock. Some of the industries concerned are just as highly protected in the Dominions as any manufactures, and this protection would be most reluctantly abandoned or curtailed. Nevertheless, as a matter of principle the United Kingdom should press for all-round free trade in primary products as the foundation-stone of Imperial economic policy. We are seeking, after all, not just a course of action for to-day or this year or within the life of a Government in office. We require a standard to which at all times we may repair, a lodestone to guide (though not, of course, alone to determine) the policies of successive Governments and even successive generations.

For this reason it need not be considered a final obstacle to a free-trade basis for Imperial economic policy that the return in the shape of liberation of British export trade with the Dominions is likely to be slow in coming. The ability of the Dominions to buy is conditioned by their ability to sell, and the more freely they can sell to Great Britain the better able they will be, and therefore the more willing, to buy from her. It may well be the wiser plan, rather than to seek a progressive all-over shrinkage of Dominion tariffs, to proceed from either end of the scale—that is to say, to urge them to abolish prohibitions and to lop off the heads of tariffs exceeding a fairly high maximum, and gradually to extend the list of duty-free or revenue-tariff items. The latter process would be furthered by continuous exploration of the possibilities of specialization—the Dominions to manufacture, without under-cutting by United Kingdom makers, those things on which their situation and economic development fit them to specialize, while buying from the United Kingdom, without hindrance from protective tariffs, those things in whose production the latter has the overwhelming advantage.

Nevertheless it is well to beware of an insidious danger inherent in this programme. If the United Kingdom, as a matter of principle, grants free entry to the main products of the Dominions and colonies, she has then no further concession to offer them that involves any liberation of trade; thus she is all too likely to be tempted into progressively raising her tariff on foreign goods, as the price of any fresh mitigation of Dominion tariffs on her exports. This was certainly her experience at Ottawa. We are therefore brought back to the problem of the relations between Imperial economic policy and world trade. It cannot be too often repeated that if a measure of increased preference in the Empire, or any other step for the tightening of Imperial economic ties, entails on balance a raising of aggregate barriers to world trade as a whole, it is unlikely to be of permanent advantage to the Empire. There is no reason to suppose, once the fundamental principles of British policy have been stabilized, that this need be the result; nevertheless, the danger is real, and should be a constant warning to over-zealous imperialists.

VI
THE COLONIAL EMPIRE

IT is impossible to leave the subject of the relation between Imperial economic policy and world trade without turning to the problem of tariffs in the colonial Empire. The problem is different in character from that of tariffs in the self-governing parts of the Commonwealth, not only for economic reasons—the tropical character of most colonial exports, the absence of industrial development in the colonies, their dependence on revenue tariffs rather than protection— but also because the administrative and political issues are quite different. The United Kingdom may seek to persuade the governments and peoples of the Dominions, but they must ultimately be the judges of what is in their own interest. If they consent to an Imperial policy, or subscribe to an Imperial agreement, they do so of their own free will and for their own reasons. The governments of the colonies, on the other hand, are not the responsible representatives of their peoples. It is the duty of the British Government, as trustees, to weigh the interests of these peoples and to uphold them as tenaciously as they would be upheld by a responsible government on behalf of a self-governing country. Inevitably there is a danger that the Imperial Government's bias towards its own accepted policies may deceive it in the performance of this duty. It may too easily be tempted into assuming that policies profitable to the mother country must be profitable to the colonies also.

Trusteeship in the government of native peoples is an international as well as an Imperial duty. It found its first international expression in the Berlin Act of 1885, concerning the territories of the Congo basin, and its most striking expression in the Covenant of the League of Nations and the terms of the League mandates. Our undertakings in these instruments relate only to a limited field, but we cannot claim—nor have we sought to claim—that a principle of trusteeship applicable to Tanganyika is not applicable to

Nigeria or Kenya, or that a principle applicable to Africa is not applicable to the East or West Indies; though, of course, the application of the principle must be varied to suit local circumstances, including the type of native population and the degree of white settlement. It is significant that both under the Berlin Act and under the League Covenant the economic counterpart of trusteeship was the principle of the Open Door. As trustees for the development of colonial territories, in the interests at once of the natives themselves and of civilization at large (the 'dual mandate'), Great Britain denied herself the right of economic exploitation in her own national interest.

The maintenance of the principle of the Open Door was facilitated by Great Britain's adherence to free trade. The Open Door was her own national policy; hence she felt no pressure to seek any other for the tropical colonies. The adoption of the twin policies of protection and preference in 1932 radically altered the situation. A protectionist imperialism was held to be a wise policy for Great Britain, in association with the Dominions; why not for the dependent empire also?

The colonies and protectorates were included in the Imperial economic system that was constructed at Ottawa. The United Kingdom Government, in its agreements with the Dominions, undertook to invite the governments of the non-self-governing colonies and protectorates to accord to the Dominions any preferences that might be accorded to any other part of the British Empire (save as provided in the customs agreement of 1930 between Southern Rhodesia and the Union), and to accord also certain specified new or additional Imperial preferences. Some of the preferences promised by the Dominions related, in return, to the products of the colonies and protectorates. Whether, in detail, these mutual undertakings were well devised or not cannot be discussed here. The important thing is that they initiated a new phase in the economic relations of the colonies to the rest of the Empire. Henceforward the non-self-governing colonies must be regarded—save as provided in international treaties—as part of the Imperial economic system based on preferences and on a varying measure of protection against the products of the rest of the world.

The latent danger of this new principle has already been stressed—the danger of forgetting that Great Britain, and such Dominions as are colonial Powers, are trustees for the natives and for the world. It is the danger of letting the Secretary of State for the Colonies become, not the spokesman for the colonial peoples in criticism or endorsement of policies planned primarily in British interests, but the instrument for imposing British policies on unwilling or uncomprehending colonial peoples.

This danger became all too apparent when, in 1934, quotas restricting the import of Japanese cotton and rayon goods were applied in those colonies where such a policy was feasible. Objections were raised in some of the colonies affected, and were overruled, but the United Kingdom Government made little attempt to justify their action as having been devised in the interests of the native populations for whom they were trustees. The announcement of the Government's decision by the President of the Board of Trade referred to the continuous expansion of Japanese exports 'in *our* markets to the detriment of Lancashire'; the Government were thus 'obliged to resume their liberty to take such action as they deemed necessary to safeguard *our* commercial interests'.[1] And in authorizing the Governor of Ceylon to regulate textile imports by quota the Secretary of State declared: 'It would be impossible that Ceylon should be excluded from a broad imperial policy of this kind, which is regarded as essential in the economic interests of *the Empire as a whole*.' In the Government's eyes, therefore, the colonies and protectorates were to be regarded as Great Britain's private markets, and their economic interests as subservient to those of the Empire as a whole.

The moral justification for this theory of exclusiveness in our economic relations with the colonial Empire is dubious —but that is no part of our concern for the moment. Its economic expediency, even from a United Kingdom point of view, depends on the relative value of two-way over

[1] Italics in these quotations are mine (H. V. H.).

triangular or multilateral trade. If we are to be gainers in the long run from colonial preference, the expected increase in our direct trade with the colonies must be large enough to compensate for two things. It must compensate for intensified foreign competition elsewhere, or for the curtailment of the buying power of foreign countries, and it must compensate for the injury to the economic welfare of the colonies themselves through the denial of their opportunity to buy in the cheapest market; this injury to their economic welfare is likely to show itself eventually in the shape of reduced external trade.

The political expediency of the exclusive theory of colonial economic relations is as doubtful as its moral authority. Three highly armed and determined Powers, Germany, Italy, and Japan, are urging upon the world their claims to colonial expansion. Even if these claims were not directed towards our own Empire, we could not afford to ignore them, since they might one day provoke a war into which we would inevitably be drawn. Our moral strength in proposing or assenting to solutions at other people's expense would be gravely undermined if we regarded our own colonies as an exclusive economic preserve.

But, as it happens, those claims are already developing into a direct challenge to the British Empire itself. We shall need all our moral as well as material strength successfully to meet that challenge. The moment for the final yea or nay, with its possibly fearful consequences, is brought all the nearer by a policy of economic exclusion. It is postponed by the policy of the Open Door, which relaxes the pressure on the dissatisfied Powers, diminishes their envy, and undermines their ambition to establish an exclusive colonial empire for themselves. In other words, even if the Open Door were injurious to Great Britain economically—which in the long run is most unlikely—it is the best contribution she can make to the maintenance of world justice and peace.

Many of these considerations, though lent a peculiar force by the principle of trusteeship for native peoples, apply also to Imperial trade as a whole. Thus a method of expanding trade within the Empire by raising higher tariff walls against foreign goods, rather than by reducing our own mutual barriers, exalts two-way trade at the expense of multilateral trade—a dangerous doctrine indeed for a country like Great Britain, with its intricately ramified system of foreign trade and its world-wide interests in finance and shipping. We must remember that foreign goods, by being excluded from our own or Dominion markets, are not thereby destroyed. The foreign producers are bound to intensify their efforts to find markets elsewhere, and thus not only is the world price level depressed, but British goods have also to meet with more damaging competition in neutral markets. At the same time, whether or not the foreign countries affected retort by raising retaliatory tariffs, their purchasing power is impaired and our exports to them are likely to suffer.

Moral standards appropriate to our relations with colonial peoples may not apply where it is a matter of trade agreements freely negotiated between self-governing countries; but the political reactions must not be lost sight of. The pressure to obtain sources of raw material and opportunities for emigration is greatly intensified, if it is not actually caused, by a world régime of protection. If a country like Japan can provide for its population by selling its industrial products, it need not seek an outlet for colonization in the enviable vacant spaces of the world. And if it can sell it can also buy all that it needs; for there is no present shortage of raw materials and foodstuffs in the world—on the contrary, the complaint is still of excessive capacity to produce and of the narrowness of markets. Strategic and other non-economic motives for desiring control of raw-material-producing areas are undoubtedly most important, but they are irrelevant to the present issue.

The practice of organized restriction of primary production however, does add a certain complication. So long as the restriction is not preferential or discriminatory (and there has yet been no substantial instance to the contrary) all countries alike are forced to pay the higher prices, whether they are colonial Powers or not. In this regard, therefore, the question remains one of securing the necessary additional foreign exchange. Especially it is a question of ability to sell more to the restricting countries themselves, whose international purchasing power is increased by the higher prices obtained for their products. On the other hand, a disproportionate advantage is secured by countries having colonial investments—not necessarily colonial possessions in the political sense. For they are likely to obtain all the extra means of payment needed through the higher dividends on their capital invested in the restricting industries. It is as an investor that Great Britain finds her chief interest in the restriction of output of rubber, tin, copper, tea, and so on.

The transfer of Germany's colonies to other Powers was much less important to her, economically, than the loss of her oversea investments. Investment is a function that a non-imperialist country can perform as well as an imperialist country, provided it has the available resources. Conversely, if Germany were handed back her former colonies to-morrow she would gain nothing on this score unless she could find the capital to buy out existing investors in their industries. Once again, therefore, the problem is reduced to that of markets and foreign exchange, and the political terms fall into the background.

Nevertheless, a country's ability to procure the means of paying for imports and investing abroad may have some relation to the extent of its colonial dominions. By compelling or inducing its colonies to buy from itself rather than from foreign countries, it may obtain more means of payment than it otherwise could in face of a world-wide protectionist system. Hence an Empire organized on an exclusive basis, with high tariff barriers against the rest of the world, is far more susceptible to the jealousy and eventually the attack of less fortunate countries than is an Empire organized for a co-operative effort to reduce barriers to world trade, beginning with the barriers between its constituent members.

Exclusiveness in the economic field marches with isolationism in the political field, and isolationism must be paid for in a cost of armaments that may well prove beyond our capacity, or beyond the consent of public opinion, both in the United Kingdom and in the Dominions. It is not only professed socialists who refuse to participate in 'imperialist' or 'capitalist' wars; this feeling is widespread throughout the Commonwealth, and whether praiseworthy or not, it stands across the path of those political policies, including great armaments, which are required by an exclusive economic imperialism. To raise tariffs is not indeed a *casus belli*, but it gives rise to a situation in which war grows steadily more likely.

VII

INDIA

NOWHERE in the Empire are political and economic relations more closely entwined than between the United Kingdom and India. The extreme Conservative opposition to the Indian constitutional reforms was given much of its driving power by the fear that self-government would mean prohibitive tariffs on British goods entering India, especially cotton goods; while the agitation in India for immediate complete self-government drew much of its popular strength from allegations that India had been exploited in the interests of British commerce and industry. A complete examination of this charge would require an investigation of general economic theories of free trade and protection; for exploitation must imply not only that external interests are served but also that internal interests are injured. It must be remembered that the free-trade doctrine, which was applied to India (modified only by a 'revenue tariff') virtually until the Great War, was almost unanimously accepted as gospel in Great Britain, and that the statesmen responsible for policy probably believed quite sincerely that what was sauce for the British goose was sauce for the Indian gander. It must also be remembered that the ruling British caste in India was recruited almost exclusively from the aristocratic and professional elements, and that industrial and commercial progress was as foreign to their public purposes as to their private ambitions.

Whatever the reasons, and whatever the rights and wrongs, it is undoubtedly true that India's industrial development was handicapped, up to the War, by the unimpeded competition of European and particularly British factory products. The increase of the revenue tariff under pressure of war-time financial necessity automatically created a certain measure of protection, and since the Indian Fiscal Commission reported in 1922 India has acquired a 'selective' or 'discriminating' tariff, that is to say, one of considerable height on selected products considered suitable for manufacture in India, but moderate on the generality of imports.

The first thing to keep clear in our minds is that full fiscal autonomy is inherent in Dominion status. Historically, the colonies asserted the right to levy what taxes they choose while they were still politically and administratively dependent on Whitehall, and they imposed protective tariffs against British and foreign goods alike long before their constitutional independence was recognized in the post-war era. The Canadian protective tariff—the 'National Policy'—antedated by two generations the Statute of Westminster. It is therefore idle to talk of Dominion status for India unless she is to be granted full fiscal liberty.

Under the Government of India Act, 1935, the Governor-General is charged, as a 'special responsibility', with

'the prevention of action which would subject goods of United Kingdom or Burmese origin imported into India to discriminatory or penal treatment.'

'Discriminatory' clearly does not mean 'more favourable to Indian than British or Burmese products', for this would stultify the whole existing tariff system in India. It means, therefore, 'less favourable to British or Burmese products than to those of other countries outside India', and a safeguard barring this form of discrimination plainly does not imply any practical derogation from Dominion status.

It may, however, be claimed that as far as status goes, the Dominions have the *right* to impose discriminatory tariffs, though they may not exercise it; the kind and degree of things that the Dominions have the right to do (while still remaining in the Commonwealth), but do not in fact do, is a matter for endless, almost metaphysical argument. Two questions therefore must be kept separate: does India want to discriminate in her tariff against the United Kingdom or Burma? and does India want the right so to discriminate? If the answer to the second question is Yes, then it seems hard to deny that the refusal of that right is a qualification of theoretical Dominion status. The issue is then transferred to a purely pragmatic plane: in view of the answer (whatever it may be) to the first of the two questions, is it wise or unwise to give India full Dominion status?

What of the ban on 'penal' treatment of United Kingdom or Burmese goods? This is a phrase which Governors-General may well find difficulty in interpreting. Does a tariff so high as to be actually or almost prohibitive, which is imposed in time of emergency in order to defend a precarious exchange, constitute penal treatment? The answer must surely be 'no'. If a Governor-General were to seek to interpret his special responsibility in that sense, he would, it seems, be immediately faced with such opposition as would make the continuance of good government under the new Constitution extremely difficult, and he would certainly be derogating from the Dominion status of India; for prohibitively high tariffs have been common in the Dominions since 1929, and in some instances earlier. If, on the other hand, penal treatment is interpreted as meaning treatment inspired by vindictive nationalism—designed, that is to say, to injure British trade because it is British, not because it interferes with the development of India's industries—then the safeguard places India on no different practical footing from the Dominions, none of whom has claimed the right to act in such a fashion.

What, in these circumstances, are we to expect under the new régime? Although India is accorded a permanent seat on the Governing Body of the International Labour Office by reason of the numbers of her population engaged in factory industry, she is industrially under-developed and industrially ambitious. In her case, moreover, the economic argument for protection has been powerfully reinforced by racial and nationalistic feeling, which has rallied to the protectionist banner many elements whose true economic interests would appear to lie rather in the direction of freedom of trade. Hence Dominion status is likely to reveal itself, in the fiscal field, in the shape of protectionism as ardent as that practised to-day in Dominions like Canada or Australia.

At the same time the non-industrial consumer interest is immense in India—far greater, proportionately, than in either of those two countries—and if only it is organized it ought to act as a constant and powerful check on excessive protectionism. Already there are signs that this consumer interest is making itself felt, and the relaxation of anti-British feeling upon the establishment of the new constitution should give it a clearer field. The conflict between the different economic elements hitherto united under the Congress standard is becoming more open, and a party cleavage along economic lines is a natural line of development in political India.

Nevertheless, the persistence of fairly high protectionism is quite certain, and the establishment of new industries in India, or the extension of the scope of those already established, will assuredly enlarge the 'selection' of protected commodities. This is not, however, a prospect to be regarded with unmixed dread by Great Britain. The economic capacity of the Indian market depends on its wealth, and nothing is more certain than that the wealth of India cannot expand while the increase of the population is forced to parcel out a limited area of primitively tilled and often unfertile land. The development and improvement of money crops—wheat, cotton, sugar, indigo, flax, &c.—mean very often that a given area of land, while yielding much more in value, directly supports fewer people; thus the pressure of population on the land under subsistence cultivation is actually increased. The general improvement of cultivation, both of subsistence crops and of products for sale, may stave off the malthusian check; but in the long run there can be no substantial relief save in an increase in the numbers engaged in industry and commerce.

This will have to be secured, no doubt, by means of protection, but it does not follow that the total quantity of British goods sold to India will therefore decline; on the contrary, since it is in the cheapest qualities of goods that British industry competes least favourably in the Indian market, a rise of India's standard of wealth, even if unaccompanied by an increase in her total volume of imports, might well result in a greater share for Great Britain by comparison with other suppliers.

By various devices British industry may possibly be able

to hold its ground in the markets of India at her present stage of economic progress. But there can be no security, and no permanent expansion, for British trade in India until her wealth is increased. That will happen only if she becomes more industrialized, which inevitably means an injury to certain present British exports. It is a grave misfortune that so high a proportion of United Kingdom exports to India are products of a single industry, which was in the grip of depression even before the world slump and even apart from its difficulties in the Indian market. The fact that Lancashire's exports to India are unlikely ever to recover their former level is a bitter pill to swallow, no doubt; the consoling jam is the expectation that with rising industrialism in India, her demand for other British goods—machinery, electrical appliances, hardware, and so on—will steadily expand.

What, then, of the future of Imperial preference in India? As a principle, obviously, it has a history of racial and nationalistic prejudice to live down. A self-governing India will not readily take her part in an exclusive Imperial system. But the Ottawa Agreement and the Clare Lees–Mody Cotton Pact indicated that some elements at least in India are shrewdly prepared to conclude preferential agreements on the basis of *quid pro quo*. The nationalistic opposition that has since flared up, causing the Ottawa Agreement to be terminated, has been fed largely with political fuel; if a delegation composed of Congressmen had gone to Ottawa the Agreement might not have been much different. The sense of membership in a Commonwealth of Nations has yet to be tested in India under the new constitutional régime. But, in spite of all the frictions that have been generated latterly, India has powerful ties of interest that bind her to the rest of the Empire, and these ties are fully recognized by the more responsible of her political and industrial leaders. She may well be ready, on the same footing as the settled Dominions, to adopt a Commonwealth-wide objective for her trade policy, consistently with her own pressing interests.

It is true that her agreement with the United Kingdom Government at Ottawa did not contain those general clauses which were repeated in the Canadian, Australian, and New Zealand treaties and which were regarded by many as the nucleus of a long-term policy for Empire trade as a whole. But it is significant that when, in September 1935, a special tariff board was set up to consider the future of duties on British cottons and rayons, after the expiry of the Clare Lees–Mody agreement, the term 'adequate protection' was defined as 'duties which will equate the prices of imported goods to the fair selling prices for similar goods produced in India'. This comes to almost exactly the same thing as the 'equalization of costs' formula in the Ottawa Agreements.

In brief, there is no reason to suppose that India presents any greater basic problems than other Dominions in the task of building up an economic policy for the whole British Commonwealth. If she is protectionist and nationalist, so are they. If she is on the road to further industrialization, at the expense of some British industries, so are they. She is, indeed, an emigrant rather than an immigrant country (a fact that itself creates economic as well as social problems in Commonwealth relations); but, like the immigrant Dominions, she is in need of imported capital for her proper development. And as far as political reasons for a special imperial economic policy are concerned, India's ties to the Commonwealth, and her interest in its strength, though different from those of the settled Dominions, are no less real.

VIII

MONEY AND CAPITAL

THE world economic depression has revolutionized the monetary organization of the nations of the British Commonwealth. Not only has the gold standard given place to managed currencies throughout the Empire; the Dominions and India, who previously had no regular central banking institutions (with the exception of the Irish Free State, and the partial exception of Australia) are now all furnished with full-blown central banks.[1] The two developments are not independent but closely related. In the régime of the gold standard, central banking in a country without a large independent money-market of its own is a semi-automatic function which may be quite well performed by a Government department or by trading banks co-operating in a conventional way under statute. But when exchanges are unstable, and when public opinion is liable to demand monetary experiment, a separate, specialized central bank becomes essential.

The future of the new monetary system is of great moment for Empire trade. Experience since 1931, especially the development of special trade relations within the 'sterling area', has taught us the importance of monetary connexions in the furtherance of trade. It has already been suggested above that the increase in the Empire's share in Great Britain's external trade, over the past few years, may be due as much to monetary factors as to tariff preferences.

It is important to note, however, that 'sterling-area stability', even within the Empire, has in practice been only

[1] The Reserve Bank of New Zealand commenced operations in August 1934, the Reserve Bank of Canada in March 1935, and the Indian Reserve Bank in April 1935. The statutory basis of the Commonwealth Bank of Australia has been little amended, but since 1931 the Bank has assumed control of the exchange rate, the most critical monetary factor in a country like Australia, and has taken a more active lead in adjusting the structure of interest rates; while in the greatly enlarged volume of treasury bills it has been furnished with a powerful instrument of monetary policy that was not previously available.

comparative. In gold standard days (though Australia and Canada were early forsakers of the strict international standard) the degree of stability in Empire exchanges was actually greater than it is to-day. Tremendous and embittered controversy formerly raged (and now shows signs of revival) over the question whether the value of the rupee should be 1s. 4d. or 1s. 6d.—a difference of 12½ per cent.; yet in 1933 the New Zealand exchange—to take only one example —moved from £NZ110 to £NZ125 for £100 English sterling without our being sensible that any grave impairment of sterling-area stability had occurred. That movement happened after the Ottawa Conference; so did the lapse of South Africa from the gold standard, and so also did the return of the Canadian dollar close to parity with the United States dollar after the latter went off gold in 1933.

When they were on the gold standard, the currencies of the Dominions, being rigidly attached to gold, were rigidly attached to the English pound also. To-day, while India and the Irish Free State are on a definite sterling standard, and the South African pound is for the time being pegged at par with sterling, in Canada, Australia, and New Zealand the rate of exchange is statutorily flexible. The Governments and central banks of those Dominions, presumably, co-operate to maintain whatever rate of exchange is regarded as suited to the national interest for the time being.

Thus it is entirely false to imagine that a sterling standard exists generally throughout the Empire. The future of Empire monetary co-operation is in the melting-pot. A Commonwealth sterling standard may possibly be the eventual outcome, but its value and durability will have to be proved to the countries that are expected to belong to it, and machinery for conducting it has yet to be devised. Monetary affairs cannot be detached from trade and tariffs. One of the lessons of the slump has been that exchange stability is not enough; it is but a means to an end—the betterment of trade as a whole—and if that end can be more successfully served by other means, for instance by internal inflation behind a falling exchange, then exchange stability will almost certainly be jettisoned.

That this has been the view of the Governments of the Commonwealth is apparent from the two joint declarations on monetary policy to which they have subscribed since 1931. The Ottawa Conference, on the recommendation of its Monetary and Financial Committee, recognized the value of maintaining stability of exchange rates between the countries of the Commonwealth whose currencies were linked to sterling, and 'looked to a rise in the general level of wholesale prices as the most desirable means of facilitating this result'. The British delegations to the World Economic Conference of 1933 (except the Irish Free State delegation) issued a joint statement urging that the Governments of the Commonwealth should persist by all means in their power, within the limits of sound finance, in the policy of furthering the rise in wholesale prices until equilibrium had been re-established. The ultimate aim of monetary policy should be the restoration of a satisfactory international gold standard, but in the meantime the signatories recognized the importance of stability of exchange rates between the countries of the Commonwealth, in the interests of trade. That objective would be constantly borne in mind in determining their monetary policies. The adherence of non-British countries to a price-raising policy would make possible the maintenance of exchange stability over a still wider area. The signatories would recommend their Governments to consult with one another from time to time on monetary policy, with a view to establishing their common purpose and to furthering such measures as might conduce towards its achievement.

The underlying theme of these pronouncements was that, while stability was a desirable goal, it could be achieved only if there were a substantial rise of prices; otherwise, each country must resume its liberty to choose whatever means it could safely employ to maintain its local price-level. Developments since 1933 may have partly relieved the Dominions of this particular preoccupation; for the prices of some of their most important products have risen considerably, and their economies have become more completely adjusted to the prevailing level of world prices. The problem of monetary policy seems now to be one not so much of raising the price-level as of maintaining and expanding the volume of business and employment.

This objective, of course, has a direct connexion with the external balance of trade, both because of the employment afforded by production for export and because of the limit set to a policy of internal monetary ease by the need for keeping the country's external accounts in a state of balance. For some at least of the Empire countries the monetary objective may soon be to prevent or check those boom conditions which hold in store a fresh economic slump, and to further the expansion, not of industry in general, but of subnormal industries and subnormal areas, while checking that of industries and areas that are already short of labour. Here again the connexion between internal monetary problems and external trade is obvious.

In any case, monetary policy for the Empire is necessarily subordinate to policy for Empire trade and production. If any particular monetary policy is held desirable then the trade policy necessary to secure it is rendered thereby the more attractive. If all goes well with trade there is every reason why a special monetary relation should subsist between the different parts of the Commonwealth, since they are so closely linked financially and commercially. The Commonwealth presents a grand field for experiment in monetary co-operation, from whose results all the world may profit. If, indeed, co-operation with the interlocking purposes of exchange stability and defence against business fluctuations is impossible within the British Commonwealth, how can one hope for similar co-operation to be successful between foreign countries with no such close economic and political ties?

The Dominions were not parties to the monetary agreement of 26 September 1936 between Great Britain, the United States, and France, nor in the circumstances could they have been. How far their monetary authorities were consulted in the negotiations that led up to the agreement is a secret. But at least it is certain that the Dominions and India were and remain deeply interested. This, indeed, the Treasury statement acknowledged in the following terms:

'His Majesty's Government must, of course, in its policy towards international monetary relations, take into full account the requirements of internal prosperity of the countries of the Empire.'

But that was not the only way in which the interests of the rest of the Empire were involved. In the first place, both directly and indirectly the Dominions and India and the colonies were concerned with the declared aim of developing international trade (with which the success of the new monetary policy was said to be bound up), and, in particular, of relaxing progressively 'the present system of quotas and exchange controls with a view to their abolition'. In the second place, in a certain measure the agreement restricted the monetary liberty of the United Kingdom, and therefore reacted on the understanding among the Commonwealth countries to consult and act together in pursuing their common monetary aim. The aim of the tripartite agreement, however, was in essence identical with that acknowledged by the members of the Commonwealth, so that the new episode meant for the problem of Empire monetary co-operation a complication rather than a conflict.

That problem is not simple in itself. There are many different currencies in the British Empire, though their names do not always differ. Thus the Australian pound is just as different a currency from the English pound as if it were called a dollar or a zloty; it is worth a different sum in gold or any foreign currency, and it is capable of fluctuating independently in the future. The use of the same denominations of coinage obscures the fact that the root problem involved in stabilizing the Australian pound against the English pound is exactly the same as that involved in stabilizing the Canadian dollar against sterling, or even, say, the Argentine peso against the dollar. The task is a dual one—to link the two currencies together, and to co-operate in conducting a monetary policy that will suit the internal economic needs of both countries.

For the first part of this task, as far as the countries of the Commonwealth are concerned, three possibilities are open. The first is their adherence to a common international monetary base, of which the only example open in practice is the gold standard in its various forms; the second is the adoption of a sterling standard throughout the Empire; the third is the creation of a series of reciprocal 'exchange equalization funds'. These possibilities are quite distinct. The first would subject all the participants to the fortunes of the common international standard. The second would subject all the other countries of the Commonwealth to the monetary fortunes of Great Britain. The third would subject the several pairs of contracting countries to each other's monetary fortunes.

Whether Great Britain or the Dominions ought to return to the gold standard is a question it is unnecessary to discuss here; for while they have jointly declared such a return to be their ultimate aim, there is no sign of their intending to bring it to fulfilment in the near future. The problem of Commonwealth co-operation comes first.

What does the sterling standard mean? If it were adopted, say, by New Zealand, the New Zealand Reserve Bank would hold sterling as part of its legal reserves against currency, valued at a fixed rate in terms of the New Zealand pound; and it would be obliged by law to convert New Zealand currency into sterling, or vice versa, at roughly the same rate (allowing a small margin, between buying and selling prices, for costs and profit). To-day the Reserve Bank is not legally obliged to maintain an open buying-and-selling counter for sterling at permanently fixed rates; the exchange rate may be varied from time to time in accordance with national policy. It was open for New Zealand to adopt a sterling standard when the Reserve Bank Bill was passed in 1934. Her omission to do so was at least partly due to a belief that a sterling standard was a one-sided affair, which would subordinate her currency system to a monetary policy into which consideration of her needs would enter only as a side-issue. If the sterling standard solution is rejected by New Zealand, who does more than three-quarters of her whole trade with Great Britain, it is hardly likely to be acceptable to other self-governing members of the Commonwealth.

Reciprocal machinery for maintaining exchange stability

would mean, in the same instance, that the Bank of England would hold New Zealand currency as part of its 'buffer fund', with which it controlled exchange fluctuations. Any policy injurious to New Zealand's economic interest would to that extent weaken the assets of the Bank of England. And similarly the other way about. It might be retorted that Threadneedle Street could still afford to neglect considerations of vital importance to the Dominion; for 10 per cent., say, of the assets of the Reserve Bank of New Zealand would represent less than one-half of 1 per cent. of the assets of the Bank of England. But over the Commonwealth as a whole the balance would be more equal, for the combined assets of the central banks of Canada, Australia, New Zealand, South Africa, and India exceed the total assets of the Bank of England.

The scheme of reciprocal exchange funds is inherently complicated, and if exchange stability can be maintained without it so much the better. Whether or not stability is systematically secured, it must be founded on a parallelism of monetary and financial policies in the different countries of the Commonwealth. That is the crux of the matter. Policy is much more important than machinery. Consistent co-operation between the different central banks is essential in order that a common objective may be visualized, and mutually helpful methods employed in pursuing it. Such co-operation already exists, happily, in the shape of informal and personal connexions. But as the Dominion reserve banks grow to maturity, and expand in strength and will, more organized co-operation will become necessary, and an Empire financial council must be envisaged, to perform those co-operative functions within the Commonwealth which the board-meetings of the Bank for International Settlements perform in the wider world field.

An Empire financial council is needed for more than purely monetary purposes. One of the most vital economic facts about the Empire is the interchange of capital. Of Great Britain's total investments abroad, roughly one-half, or about £2,000 millions, has been invested in the countries of the Empire. A complete cessation of lending, following upon a period of unregulated and possibly excessive outpouring of capital, has been succeeded in turn by a slight revival of lending from Great Britain to the Dominions, and by the gradual conversion of old loans to lower rates of interest. The slump has increased the relative importance of the Empire in Britain's overseas investments, and the experiences that it has brought are certain to extend that movement into the future. Save for a brief period in Australia, none of the Dominions or colonies has imposed exchange restrictions, and none except Newfoundland has defaulted even partially on its public obligations.

While the experience of the depression has been favourable to the investment of capital in the Dominions, it has taught us that even in their case uncontrolled lending, although perhaps not unsoundly conceived in detail, may have, in the mass, disastrous results both for creditors and for debtors. The private parties to a loan cannot take fully into account the wider economic repercussions of their own and similar activities. The British embargo on oversea lending, now partially modified in favour of the Empire and other portions of the sterling bloc, is one of the fruits of this salutary lesson, but for the future something more than a coarse filter at the lender's end is needed. The Dominions know their requirements of capital; the authorities here can estimate the capacity of the United Kingdom to fulfil them. There is no need for new executive machinery, since the control of the Bank of England is sufficiently powerful and can be exercised with a loose rein. But there is need for machinery of consultation and co-operation between the Governments and financial authorities of the lending and borrowing countries of the Empire for the purpose of deciding upon a Commonwealth policy for capital movements.

Such a policy ought not to be merely a negative censorship. Capital investment is a constructive economic function, and a constructive policy for Empire trade must include a positive policy for using the investable surplus of the Empire in the best service of the whole community of nations. It should be associated, not only with plans for the development of trade, but also with plans for guiding migration, if, indeed, a movement of population is held to be desirable. It should be linked particularly with the project of specialization in Dominion industry, which, as we have seen, is one of the most hopeful ways of tackling the problem of Empire trade. It should be conceived as part of a general *mise-en-valeur* of the opportunities and the human and material resources of the Empire.

Unfortunately, the instruments available for promoting investment are much feebler than those for checking it. They are also much more dangerous to handle. The investor is essentially a risk-taker, and to relieve him of that risk—even to encourage him to believe that the Government has assumed any part of the responsibility that properly belongs to the entrepreneur—is a very hazardous policy. There is little difficulty with regard to Dominion Government loans, provided they pass the censorship of the market control of the Treasury and the Bank of England. Otherwise, it must be sufficient that a loan or a share issue is permitted and encouraged by the authorities; they cannot be expected to assume responsibility for its eventual success.

A word in passing, however, is necessary about the Colonial Stock Act, since its implication with regard to United Kingdom responsibility is liable to misunderstanding. The United Kingdom Government, in admitting certain classes of Dominion and Colonial Government loans to trustee status, has not guaranteed those loans. It has undertaken, however, to see that the Empire Governments concerned do not pass legislation endangering the sanctity of the loan contracts; in accordance with the new constitutional status of the Dominions, under which their projected laws can no longer be 'reserved for His Majesty's consideration', the undertaking is being replaced by voluntary agreements between the United Kingdom and Dominion Governments to the effect that no such legislation will be passed.

When Newfoundland became insolvent in 1933, her trustee obligations received preferential treatment under the scheme of financial reconstruction carried out by the Imperial Government. On the face of it, this would seem to be a precedent for regarding the imprimatur of trustee status under

the Colonial Stock Act as constituting a United Kingdom
Government guarantee. In fact, however, the United Kingdom Government assumed financial responsibility on that
occasion only as part of a comprehensive scheme of Commission government under the Crown as advised by United
Kingdom Ministers. It provided the funds, not merely for
the interest on trustee loans as such, but for the balancing
of the whole budget of the Island until equilibrium could be
restored; it was entitled to do what it would with its own, and
not unnaturally it chose to avoid the trouble consequent upon
a default on trustee securities. The affair is a precedent only
if we envisage the possibility of a suspension of responsible
government in some other Dominion, and this is surely out of
the picture.

There can be no question of our guaranteeing loans to
the Dominion Governments, though a joint Dominion and
United Kingdom guarantee on a private issue of public.
importance is a possibility that need not be entirely ruled out.
The problem of United Kingdom responsibility for loans to
the colonies, protectorates, and mandated territories is in
another category altogether. It is fundamentally a political
problem, not an economic one; for it turns on the conflict
between local responsibility for paying the service of the
loans and imperial responsibility for the conduct of colonial
finances. When times are bad and the interest burden grows
heavy, the cry is raised that he who calls the tune should pay
the piper. The political issue cannot be tackled here. The
economic issue is, in brief: ought not a planned programme
of capital development of the colonies to be considered by an
imperial body with a wider economic vision than any single
colony or purely technical department can possess? Even so,
the political problem cannot be altogether extruded, for in
the absence of colonial financial autonomy such a programme
would have to involve some measure of Imperial responsibility for the service of loans, if it were to have any claim
to being equitable for the colonial taxpayers.

IX

SHIPS AND AEROPLANES

PERHAPS the most striking feature of the old mercantile system was the reservation of colonial cargoes for British shipping. In the later nineteenth century, by contrast, complete freedom of shipping business from national or imperial discrimination matched the policy of commercial free trade; and just as the free-trade period was associated with Great Britain's commercial domination of the world, so the policy of shipping freedom was associated with the rise of the British mercantile marine to the foremost place in the world's ocean carrying trade. It was associated as both cause and effect. Shipping discrimination would have encouraged a similar retort from foreign countries, and the very supremacy of Great Britain in world shipping business made her the most vulnerable of all countries to retaliation against any protective or preferential policies for her vessels.

That vulnerability remains, but the situation has fundamentally altered since the heyday of free trade. Just as Great Britain is no longer the workshop of the world, so her domination in the ocean carrying business has been challenged by the same forces of economic nationalism, expressing themselves in reservation of coastal or inter-territory trade, and in subsidies on shipbuilding or the running of ships. The right to reserve coastal trade for ships flying the national flag has long been recognized as a legitimate exception to pledges of non-discrimination; but the United States, the leader in maritime protectionism, has extended the principle to cover trade between ports as far distant from each other as the continental United States and Hawaii or Alaska. The amount spent each year by various foreign Governments in subsidies to their ships must now be in the neighbourhood of £50 millions. Partly as a result of these subsidies, the proportion of world ocean-going tonnage flying the British flag has fallen from over 40 per cent. before the War to a little over one-quarter to-day.

What means we would be best advised to employ in meeting this menace it is not the purpose of this chapter to debate. As a national policy the United Kingdom has already adopted the principle of a subsidy for tramp shipping, together with a scrap-and-build programme. The problem is mooted here because it is of vital Imperial as well as national importance. It is important for the Empire, first, for strategic reasons. The mercantile marine is the indispensable ally of the navy in time of war, and despite the growing importance of air power the security of the shores and trade of the scattered countries of the Empire still rests primarily on naval strength. Even if this were not so, and the security of our ocean routes came to depend chiefly on air power, a strong mercantile marine with ample reserves of tonnage and of shipbuilding capacity would still be vital if the United Kingdom were not to be starved into submission in the event of war.

The shipping problem is an imperial issue for economic reasons also. Any decline in the United Kingdom's shipping earnings must have a serious effect on her national purchasing power, with prompt reactions on the Dominions' export trade. Furthermore, the Dominions themselves are maritime Powers, faced with the same threats to their shipping as the United Kingdom has to withstand; indeed, one of the most injurious instances of subsidized shipping, the American line from San Francisco to New Zealand and Australia, is primarily the concern of New Zealand, under whose ensign the competing British ships have sailed, and secondarily of Canada and Australia, who have contributed to their mail subsidy. A policy adopted by the whole Commonwealth to meet the menace of subsidies and discrimination would have far more weight than one adopted by its several members on purely national grounds. Already there is a dangerous tendency for the Commonwealth to be divided by protectionism in shipping, just as it is in trade. Finally, we must consider the fundamental question, whether imperial preference in shipping is not inherently as desirable as Imperial preference in customs tariffs.

The arguments against Imperial shipping preference are

formidable. There would be grave risk of provoking retaliation from foreign countries, and thus of having to sacrifice much of our shipping business with them. It would be particularly disastrous if our relations with great shipping countries like Norway and Sweden, who have not joined in the subsidy ramp, were jeopardized, or if the potential 'united front' against subsidies were broken. Exporters in the United Kingdom and the Dominions, furthermore, might complain against any action that tended to enlarge the costs of shipping their goods to oversea markets. Nevertheless, we ought at least to consider the possibility of Imperial shipping preference in two alternative directions: first, discriminatory dues in all Commonwealth ports to be levied upon the vessels of countries that subsidize their shipping in competition with our own; or, second, reservation of ocean-borne trade between different countries of the Commonwealth for ships under a British flag. What is certain is that a joint, co-operative shipping policy for the whole Commonwealth is urgently required.

The Imperial War Conference of 1918 passed a resolution declaring that in order to maintain satisfactorily the connexion, and encourage commercial and industrial relations, between the different countries of the British Empire, an Imperial board should be set up, with power to inquire into and report on all matters connected with ocean freights and facilities, or with the development and improvement of sea communications in the Empire, with special reference to the size and type of ships and the capacity of harbours. In accordance with this resolution, the Imperial Shipping Committee was set up in 1920, and continues to act. It consists of representatives of the Commonwealth Governments, who form a majority, together with representatives of shipping, commerce, and aviation.

The mixture of breadth and narrowness in the Committee's original instructions is remarkable. The 1930 Imperial Conference revised its terms of reference with greater emphasis on its narrow technical functions, and as at present constituted it certainly cannot be considered a satisfactory body for dealing with the larger questions that affect the mercantile

Q

marine of the Commonwealth nations. A committee of this kind should properly be a permanent technical sub-committee of a Commonwealth Communications Conference, which would be subordinate in turn to the Imperial Conference itself, but would be capable, on its own initiative, of advising the Governments of the United Kingdom and the Dominions on the general policy to be adopted for the shipping of the Empire as a whole.

The Imperial Conference of 1930 added as a rider to the new terms of reference of the Imperial Shipping Committee that it should take into account facilities for air transport on the Empire trade routes; and a representative of civil aviation was added to the personnel of the Committee. This implied a recognition both of the Imperial importance of the new means of transport and of the essential unity of the whole communications problem. But on so vital a matter it was a very meagre contribution to Commonwealth co-operation.

The potentialities of air transport are immense, both in the civil and in the strategic fields, and nowhere are they greater than within the British Commonwealth. The effective distance between the different countries under the British Crown is to be measured not in miles but in the time necessary to make postal, personal, and commercial communication between them. The invention of the steamship and the telegraph worked an unseen revolution in Commonwealth relations. In our own time the invention of radio-telegraphy and the aeroplane may work another. To-day, moreover, a country or an empire that is weak in the air cannot be considered a great Power; and air strength, even military air strength, must be founded on civil aviation, just as sea-power in the past has always been founded on the possession of a great mercantile marine.

Indeed, the direct connexion is even closer; for not merely are civilian air-ports and ground organization just as essential for air defence as mercantile ports and fuelling stations are for naval defence, but moreover the actual machines are more readily convertible to martial purposes than are unarmoured merchant vessels.

Here, then, is a great new field of endeavour, in which

the opportunities of Commonwealth co-operation have not yet been fatally encumbered by exclusive national policies or a narrow sectionalism. Two recent examples have shown up the present lack of adequate permanent means of Commonwealth collaboration in this field. The negotiations for the establishment of the flying-boat service between the United Kingdom and Australia and New Zealand required a special *ad hoc* conference in Australia and afterwards arduous discussions by cable and in London between the British Government and Dominion Ministers who happened to be available. Second, with regard to the proposals, originating in the United States, for a trans-Pacific air system linking the southern Dominions with North America, there was an open danger at one time that the Governments of the British Commonwealth concerned might act separately, and with an eye rather to their own national interests and bargaining strength than to those of the Commonwealth as a whole.

The least that is needed is a body equal in status and powers to the Imperial Shipping Committee, to deal with problems of air communications within the Empire, and between Empire countries and the rest of the world, from a wide Commonwealth standpoint. Air mails would, of course, come within its purview. But as in shipping, so in aviation, a semi-technical committee is not really enough. It ought likewise to be a permanent sub-committee of a Commonwealth Communications Conference, which should meet at longer intervals and always before Imperial Conferences, in order to present the latter with proposals for governmental ratification.

The nucleus of still another such permanent sub-commitee exists in the Imperial Communications Advisory Committee, which was established at the time of the Cables and Wireless merger to serve as a link between that corporation and the Governments of the Empire. This Committee, whose members are appointed by the several Governments, is armed with the right of veto on important fields of action by Cables and Wireless, including the sale or disposal of any of the company's assets, the issue of new share capital, the disposal of one-half of any net revenue above £1,865,000, the raising of rates or the discontinuance of any services. Unlike most organs of Imperial co-operation, therefore, it is a body for decision as well as advice. There seems to be no reason why the same principle should not be established for Empire air-mail services, which are heavily subsidized by Governments, and hence under their financial control.

Clearly there is no lack of opportunity for Imperial co-operation in these fields of communication—shipping, aviation, and cables and wireless. To these should be added broadcasting. The British Broadcasting Corporation has made great strides with its short-wave Empire programmes, and the service has reached a stage at which it is becoming increasingly reciprocal in character. While the independence of national broadcasting systems from Government control must be preserved within the British Commonwealth in the cause of democracy and freedom of utterance, the time has surely come for the promotion and regulation of broadcasting exchanges in the Empire by a single representative body.

X

MACHINERY OF CO-OPERATION

THE fate of organs of Imperial economic co-operation has not been altogether happy. The Empire Marketing Board was set up by the Home Government in 1926 to promote the sale of Empire produce in the United Kingdom. Though its design was thus unilateral, its work in the fields of technical research, statistics, market intelligence, and economic investigation was of service to the whole Commonwealth, and a considerable portion of its funds was used in financing research institutions which were themselves on an Imperial co-operative basis, such as the Imperial Institute of Entomology or the Imperial Forestry Institute.

The Board was originally devised as a compensation to the oversea Empire countries for the failure to ratify the promise of preferential duties that had been made by the United Kingdom Government at the Imperial Conference of 1923. When, therefore, the fiscal policy of the United Kingdom was changed in 1932, and far more extensive preferences were granted under the Import Duties Act and the Ottawa Agreements, this *raison d'être* vanished. The Government thereupon indicated that unless the Board could be re-established on a co-operative basis, that is to say, with financial contributions from all the beneficiary countries, it must disappear. The Skelton Committee, set up under a resolution of the Ottawa Conference to examine all the existing permanent organs of Imperial economic co-operation, sounded the tocsin of the Empire Marketing Board; for the representatives of the different Dominion Governments on the Committee, whatever may have been their views on the value of the Board, were unable to offer the necessary finance.

The Skelton Committee, though generally negative in its conclusions, effected a certain valuable tidying-up of the various institutions, placing under the Executive Council of the Imperial Agricultural Bureaux the administration and finances, not only of the eight Imperial agricultural bureaux,

but also of the Imperial Institute of Entomology and the
Imperial Mycological Institute, together with all such research activities in the United Kingdom as the participating
Governments might agree in future should be conducted
on a co-operative basis. This satisfactorily co-ordinated the
scientific branches of co-operation, and separated them from
the more directly economic branches. As far as the latter
were concerned, the work of the Empire Marketing Board
in connexion with periodical market intelligence and world
surveys of production and trade was transferred to the
Imperial Economic Committee; the cost was to be borne
by all the Governments of the Empire according to an agreed
scale of contributions.

The recommendation extending the functions of the Imperial Economic Committee was an important move towards
the co-ordination of all forms of economic co-operation in the
Empire through a central ganglion. The Imperial Economic
Committee itself has had a far more restricted scope than
its title would indicate. It was originally set up in 1925 'to
consider the possibility of improving the methods of prepar-
ing for market and marketing within the United Kingdom
the food products of the overseas parts of the Empire, with a
view to increasing the consumption of such products in the
United Kingdom in preference to imports from foreign
countries and to promote the interests of both producers
and consumers'. The Imperial Conference of 1926 slightly
enlarged the Committee's terms of reference, and the 1930
Conference, besides repeating the instructions to carry out
surveys of trade and marketing, added that the Committee
was to 'facilitate conferences among those engaged in particular industries in various parts of the Commonwealth',
and to 'examine and report on any economic question which
the Governments of the Commonwealth might agree to refer
to the Committee'.

The Imperial Economic Committee was thus beginning to
acquire functions commensurate with its title. The Skelton
Committee went farther, and, besides transferring the above-
mentioned functions of the Empire Marketing Board, proposed that the Imperial Economic Committee be authorized

on its own initiative to make proposals to Governments in regard to other economic services and inquiries that might be conducted on a co-operative basis. It was to be understood that this should not give the Committee any power to initiate proposals regarding consultation in respect of economic policy.

With the amendments proposed by the Skelton Committee, the terms of reference of the Imperial Economic Committee are ample for practical purposes. No committee will be trusted by the Governments of the Commonwealth with the formulation of broad economic policy, or even with advising them on issues that cut deep into politics. The fate of the Economic Advisory Council in the United Kingdom shows that even nationally a Government is not going to refer vital issues of this kind to specialist bodies that cannot take political responsibility for the lines of action proposed. That is truer still of international policy, even within the British Commonwealth. To suggest, therefore, that a permanent secretariat should be set up to pursue the possibilities of Imperial economic co-operation, and to advise the Governments of the Dominions and the United Kingdom on the policies they should adopt, is only to prejudice the issues and to turn Dominion suspicions against the whole conception.

The Imperial Economic Committee is and must remain a semi-technical body for research and for giving advice on limited economic questions that do not involve major questions of policy. It is there to be used: the problem is to get the Governments to use it. The chief reform needed in its constitution is to co-ordinate under it all the specialized co-operative activities in the economic field, including shipping and other communications, migration, and the movement of capital. A central organization should exist to consider more general questions and to provide a secretariat for the series of technical committees; it should be governed, presumably, by a regularly meeting body comprising the High Commissioners with their economic advisers, similar representatives of the United Kingdom Government, and the chairmen of the half-dozen technical committees.

Such an organization, it must be repeated, can in no

way be a substitute for direct co-operation and consultation between the Governments who have to take the decisions. Imperial economic policy is no more capable than national economic policy of being formulated by 'experts'. By continuous contacts, and through the Imperial Conference system, the Governments must find an Imperial economic policy to which their national policies may be adjusted. It was the greatest defect of the Ottawa Conference that instead of concentrating on a policy it lost itself in detailed negotiations which should not have begun until the policy itself had been thrashed out.

But, however well agreed the different Governments of the Commonwealth may be on their general objectives, each of them is faced from day to day with economic issues, inevitably affecting the whole Commonwealth, which must be decided without any opportunity of bringing all the other Governments into consultation. Hence what is needed is a warp as well as a weft of Imperial co-operation, that is to say, in each self-governing Dominion and in the United Kingdom, a purely national co-ordination of different aspects of economic policy that may affect the Commonwealth. In this country there should be a permanent inter-departmental committee, with representatives from the Board of Trade, the Ministry of Agriculture, the Dominions Office, the Colonial Office, the Empire Migration Committee, the Treasury, and any other departments concerned, charged with the duty of collating the different aspects of economic policy into a broad plan for the economic progress of the Empire.

The details of such machinery are of minor moment. The problem of organization is indeed fundamentally unimportant; for it is subordinate to the problem of policy, which itself is subordinate to the problem of will. If there is no Imperial economic policy, or if the will of the peoples and Governments behind that policy is weak, the elaboration of administrative or consultative machinery is a waste of time and money. Committees, boards, secretariats, conferences, councils—these are instruments only, requiring a hand to use them and a purpose for their use.

XI

EMPIRE MIGRATION

ANGELS sometimes intrude where fools are not foolhardy enough to tread, and it is a curious fact that the subject of emigration, an intricate economic problem that deserves but does not receive the most luminous exposition from trained economists, is largely the controversial preserve of Salvationists, church societies, sentimental imperialists, and others to whom its economic factors usually appear so obvious that they can be comfortably left out of account. There is nothing mystic about migration that divorces it from other economic and social phenomena and renders it less subject to the rules that govern them. Like trade or capital movements, it is the mass reflection of individual action, and its springs must be sought, like theirs, in individual motive. Why have so many individuals and families transferred their lives and properties from these islands to the British Dominions, or from any emigrant country to any immigrant country? Often there have been profound social motives— repression of a class, a race, or a religion in the country of the migrant's birth, or the prospect of special political or social opportunities in the country of his settlement. Thus no one would seek to analyse in purely economic terms the scattering of the Huguenots or the colonization of Palestine by the Jews. Nevertheless, reinforcing and often far exceeding the social and other motives, an economic urge has driven every large migration movement of the past, and within the self-governing communities of the British Commonwealth it must be counted the dominating force.

Stated broadly, the economic motive was the migrant's expectation of making a better living in the new country than he could make in the old. Sometimes his expectation took the form of ambitions for his sons and grandsons rather than immediately for himself. Sometimes hopes were falsified, sometimes exceeded; certainly they could not have persisted among whole classes of people for year after year if on the whole they were not fulfilled. Then the next question must be, why could a better living be made in the new country than in the old, in the Dominions than in the Mother Country?

The answer is to be found, not in any simple formula, but in the whole complex of world economic conditions and changes. From the Industrial Revolution to the World War, the population of western Europe was rapidly expanding. Mechanical inventions cheapened the products of industry and drew millions of men into the great urban aggregates of population. The standard of life steadily rose. Discovery—geographical and scientific—and, still more important, the progress of transport and communications, enabled the fruits of distant and previously undeveloped lands to be brought to those urban populations and sold at least as cheaply as local agricultural products. Industry's hunger for raw materials was as insatiable as its servants' hunger for food. This was the economic complex that gave rise to the stream of migration from the Old to the New World. As far, at least, as migration from Great Britain to the Dominions was concerned, the key to it was not the poverty but the wealth of the industrial motherland, which furnished a great and growing market for the products of the daughter countries. Thus whenever world depression ruled, this flow of migration stopped, showing that the impulse was not the negative one of bad times at home (whether or not resulting from 'pressure of the population') but the positive one of better times in the Dominions.

From this historical fact we can learn much that bears on the present-day problem of Empire migration. For it shows, first, how false is the prevalent association in men's minds between unemployment and over-population. Unless prevented by hindrances to free economic movement, relative over-population will manifest itself in a tendency towards an outflow of migrants. Yet so far from such an outflow's having been identified with periods of abnormal unemployment in Great Britain, the contrary has commonly been the case. Theoretically, a country can be relatively over-populated and yet have no unemployment, or can have high unemployment together with under-population; indeed unemployment may possibly be caused by under-population. There are some people who believe, by no means without reason, that one of the contributory causes of the extreme economic depression of 1932–3 in the United States was the check imposed on the influx of migrants from Europe during the previous decade. The fact that there is a considerable volume of unemployment in this country is by itself no proof whatever that the country is relatively over-populated, or that it would be economically better off if a proportion of its people were shipped to the Dominions or other new countries.

In the second place, the history of migration from Great Britain to the Dominions shows that its mainspring was the rising prosperity of the daughter countries, which in turn was founded on their ability to sell their primary produce in ever-increasing quantity. It is true that by this time they have developed also great manufacturing industries of their own, and that in post-war days a large proportion of emigrants from the United Kingdom to the Dominions have found work in the towns and cities and not on the land; even those who went on the land virtually filled places vacated by Dominion-born citizens who preferred to migrate to the urban areas. Thus in Australia the increase of 862,000 in the population of the urban areas between the censuses of 1921 and 1933 appears to have been composed as follows: 563,000 by natural increase of the already urban population, 130,000 by new immigration direct to the towns, and about 170,000 by an influx of people from the country, making room on the land and in ancillary industries for an almost exactly equal number of fresh immigrants.

Hence it might be concluded that the urban and not the rural industries of the Dominions were those whose prosperity now governed the flow of immigration. On the face of it this would be true; but those urban industries themselves are in a large measure dependent for their prosperity on the continued ability of the primary producers to export their products on an expanding scale. For primary industry is still the mainspring of the economic machine in the Dominions.

Not only does it supply purchasing power for the manufactured goods they produce for themselves; it provides them with the international credits necessary to buy industrial raw materials, fuel, and machinery, without which manufacture could not function. It follows that migration will not naturally take place, and that artificially promoted migration will recoil disastrously, unless wide markets can be kept for the primary products of the Dominions, or unless they become far more self-sufficient both in final manufactured products and in the materials of industry.

If this alternative of greater self-sufficiency is secured by dint of higher general protection against British goods, it is unlikely to be palatable to the people who preach migration as a cure for unemployment in Great Britain. In the words of the Malcolm Macdonald Inter-Departmental Committee on Migration Policy:[1]

'the United Kingdom Government can give no greater or more direct stimulus to migration than by assisting to create increased markets in this country or elsewhere for the Dominion producer.'

In past times, it is true, emigrants were often content to live at a subsistence level on their own farms, until they could market a surplus yielding a cash return. They may still be ready to do so, but only if the prospect of obtaining a good living from the marketable surplus is sufficiently rosy to offset the hardships of the earlier period. That, indeed, was always true, even if sometimes the vision of prosperity was cherished by the settler for his children rather than himself; the only difference to-day is that the prospect must be more gilded than before, because the standard of life that the settler forsakes for his new adventure in the Dominion has reached a higher level.

Social services are an integral part of the standard of life of the working population. We ought not to complain that as a result of 'the dole' fewer people are ready to emigrate to the Dominions. We ought rather to congratulate ourselves on having established a standard of life higher in relation to the standard in the Dominions (even allowing for rosier

[1] Cmd. 4689, August 1934.

future chances there) than we possessed when the great streams of migration were flowing. We could certainly promote empire migration by depressing the workers' standard of life in Great Britain, including social services, but what merits has empire migration in itself to justify such a sacrifice?

We must indeed ask ourselves what are the inherent merits of empire emigration that we should spend thousands of pounds upon stimulating what is, in essence, a normal economic phenomenon. One answer might be that we need to relieve the pressure of population upon the area of these crowded islands. The population problem, it must be insisted, is entirely different from that of unemployment; for abnormal unemployment of a cyclical kind is no indicator whatever of over-population, and even a persistently high average of unemployment over good times and bad is more likely to arise from an over-valued national currency than from an over-populated national area. The magnitude of the unemployment problem in the Dominions is alone sufficient answer to those who deduce from the high level of unemployment in Great Britain that people should be despatched in large numbers from this country to the Dominions.

Over-population would presumably manifest itself in a falling standard of life, or in one that lagged falteringly behind the standard in relatively under-populated countries. There is no evidence that this condition is at present satisfied as between Great Britain and the Dominions. On the contrary, taking into account the level of unemployment on the one hand and the level of prices on the other, the average standard of life is to-day higher in the United Kingdom than it was before 1929, a proposition that is probably not true of the oversea Dominions other than South Africa.

Nor do the calculations of the demographers encourage the idea that over-population is likely to be a serious economic factor in the future, if it is not so now. In a very few years, according to present trends, the population of Great Britain will have reached its maximum size, and by 1976 it will have fallen to less than 33 millions, compared with a present total of 45 millions. These forecasts make no allowance for emigration. If we assume that British industry will continue to expand, and that, in the absence of special stimulants, labour-saving inventions will no more than keep pace with that expansion, then the time is not far ahead when British industry will be short of labour. The progress of labour-saving, of course, will be accelerated by that shortage. Since every pair of hands means also a mouth, this prospect will not be fulfilled unless the rise in the average economic demand per head is more than sufficient to counteract the fall in demand through shrinking total numbers. But here, again, we are faced with a problem of economic organization, of distribution in the widest sense, rather than one of over- or under-population.

The ability, on purely economic grounds, to spare emigrants depends as much on the make-up of the population as upon its total size. And in this respect the facts are extremely remarkable. To-day (1936) the population of 45 millions consists of about 10 million children under 15 years of age, 21·4 millions in the younger working-age group from 15 to 45 years, 10 millions of older working-age from 45 to 65, and 3·6 millions of old people, over 65 years of age. Twenty years hence, if the estimates of the experts prove right, the 10 million children will have fallen to under 6 millions; there will be only 18·7 millions in the younger working-age group; the 10 millions in the older working-age group will have become 11·7 millions, and the numbers over 65 will be not far off 5 millions. Twenty years farther on still, the change will have been even more extraordinary. The under-15 group will number scarcely 4 millions, say 40 per cent. of its present numbers; the younger working-age group will have fallen to less than 12 millions, under one-half of the present figure; the older working-age group will still be greater in numbers than it is now, and the number of old people will have risen to some 5·7 millions, well over half as much again as the 3·6 millions of to-day.

These figures are based on certain assumptions which may prove false. But it is well to remember that even if the declining trend of the birth-rate is now reversed the age-structure of the population will not diverge far from these forecasts for a long time to come; for the people who will be

of an age to marry and have children twenty or so years
hence are already born, and their numbers, therefore, cannot
now be increased. Whether the estimates are correct or not
in detail, they are the clearest evidence we have in a field
that is of vital importance in considering the future of Empire
migration.

On purely selfish, economico-demographic grounds, then,
from what age-classes of the population ought Great Britain
to encourage emigrants, if any, to be drawn? The answer is
plain enough. Not from the group of children; for after
about 1946 the people who are now in nurseries and schools
will be badly needed to redress the balance in favour of the
group that is most productive, from 15 to 45 years of age.
The old people must in any case be reckoned outside the
scope of emigration. If the proportion of non-workers to the
rest of the population is to be kept down to more nearly its
present level in future decades, the emigrants of to-day must
come from the age-groups whose survivors will be over 65 in,
say, twenty to thirty years' time. In other words, the people
who should go are the men and women who are now in their
thirties and early forties. Are these likely to be welcome
emigrants in the Dominions? They will obviously not be so
welcome as younger men and women, but if we encourage
the latter to emigrate we shall be losing not only the best of
their working life, but also their value to us as potential
fathers or mothers of the children who will be so few in the
years to come.

One further demographic fact may be mentioned. At
present there is notoriously an excess of females over males
in the British Isles, while in the Dominions the reverse is
true. Thus it would obviously be of social advantage if
women of marriageable age were to emigrate in considerable
numbers. But it must be noted that this discrepancy is only
a temporary one; there is a steady tendency towards an
equalization of the numbers of the sexes in the Dominions,
and it will not be long before their need for more women to
right the balance will have disappeared. The surplus of
women in the United Kingdom is likewise a declining factor.

These, then, are the main economic facts that affect the

course of migration from Great Britain to the Dominions. The dominating force attracting migrants to the new countries in pre-war decades—the rapid exploitation of primary resources for export to Europe and other industrial areas—has practically vanished. For the industrial countries are no longer able or willing to offer ever-expanding markets for primary products, and any foreseeable expansion of demand can in any case be taken care of by mechanical and scientific improvements in methods of production. Indeed, throughout the post-war period it was not the rural but the urban industries of the Dominions that furnished the direct power of economic suction drawing emigrants from Great Britain. If this was true before 1930 it is certain to be still more decisively true in the years to come.

Nevertheless, the further economic expansion of the Dominions, and thus their need for immigrants, are clearly dependent either on the enlargement of overseas markets for their primary produce or on an extension of their manufacturing industries. The latter alternative would have a nugatory or even negative effect upon migration if it were achieved at the cost of depressing the Dominions' standard of life through excessive protection. If, however, it could be accomplished without paying that price, it would create a local demand for labour that would be translated into a demand for immigrants, either directly to work in urban trade and industry or to fill the places of rural inhabitants of the Dominions who would move to the towns. In the words of an Australian writer in the *Round Table*:

'The problem is not to transform the misfits in a predominantly industrial Great Britain into productive units in a predominantly agricultural and pastoral Australia. It is to lift a portion of the British economy and plant it in Australia.

While the attractive forces affecting Empire migration have altered, so also have the projective forces. The rapid increase of the population of Great Britain has come to an end, and the days are near when we shall jealously scrutinize the toll of emigrants lest we lose the young workers that our industry needs. Heavy unemployment is in itself no sure evidence of relative over-population, for it is equally compatible with relative under-population. It is a symptom, partly of world depression (which has also created grievous unemployment problems in the Dominions themselves), partly of industrial disorganization. At the same time, emigration may well be conceived as part of the industrial reorganization that is necessary to set matters right. Certainly, if we think of the youthful population of the specially distressed areas of Great Britain as facing the economic world with a clean slate—without ties to any industry or locality— there are obvious reasons why transference to the Dominions might be preferable to transference to another industrial area at home, or to an artificially maintained subsistence on the land.

Yet even here the purely economic considerations are less decisive than the social considerations. It is not because the Dominions are lands of higher wages or steadier employment that they are so salutary an antidote to the environment of Tyneside or the South Wales coal-fields, but because they are lands of opportunity. The rungs of the ladder of advancement may be less comfortable than in an older community, but they are less encumbered by prejudice and privilege. Most of the muddled thinking in Great Britain about Empire migration results from confusing economic with social factors. The purely economic reasons for desiring a greater flow of migrants from Great Britain to the Dominions are indeed as weak as the social and political reasons are strong. The great urban concentrations of population in a country like Great Britain are economic inevitabilities, but social nuisances. Approaching one-half of the school children of London never see the 'real country' from one year's end to another. A lifetime bounded by bricks means a shrivelled imagination as well as a stunted body. And wholesome as the country-side itself may be, in these days it tends to be socially stagnant in Great Britain. For the favoured few, life in an old, urbanized land is full of sweets. For the multitude, it is probably safer than life in newer, more struggling, and less amply populated countries, and at least as well rewarded in pounds, shillings, and pence. But for many men and women in whom ambition

R

is not dead it is less salty, less complete than the life they might find in the newer countries of the Empire.

While we reflect on this we must remember, nevertheless, that the idea of life in the Dominions as a log-cabin settlement in virgin spaces is utterly false. The best land in the Dominions is to-day almost all intensively farmed, and the frontier of cultivation is receding rather than advancing, as technical improvements enable more and more to be grown on less and less land. Even in New Zealand, the least industrialized of the Dominions, the proportion of the population living in urban areas steadily increases. Four Dominion cities (Melbourne, Montreal, Sydney, Toronto) have roughly a million inhabitants or more, and there are others not far behind. The typical Dominion citizen is a townsman. If the Dominions were to go on expanding in population and wealth as in the past, they would soon come to possess urban concentrations as formidable as those of the Mother Country. Australia now has approaching 7 million inhabitants, and is sometimes said to be capable of holding 20 millions or more. But as the urban population already outnumbers the rural population by 16 to 9, and is increasing nearly twice as fast, we may conclude that, if Australia had 20 million inhabitants, at least 14 or 15 millions of them would dwell in her towns and cities. Thus even the social argument has its limitations.

It may, however, be reinforced by a political argument. The British people are politically minded and politically experienced. They and the Scandinavians boast the oldest and most firmly established democratic constitutions in the world. Not all the races upon whom the Dominions have drawn for immigrants, or might be forced to draw in the future, have proved equally assimilable into the political system that we have inherited and must treat as a trust for civilization. Since these alien races are often far more prolific than the British, immigration from the Mother Country may be necessary to preserve the political balance in the Dominions.

There are also defensive arguments to be considered. Regarded as a whole, the British Commonwealth is strategically unwieldy. Its greatest concentration of wealth, manpower, and industry is also its most vulnerable point. Its

smaller constituents are ill-equipped in those respects to
defend themselves against the aggression of a Great Power.
If there were a more even balance between the United Kingdom and the Dominions, the defensive solidity of the Commonwealth would be improved, and fewer hostages would
be pledged to the danger of widespread war. There is a
broader consideration still to guide migration policy. The
British Commonwealth of Nations not merely depends on
the people who dwell in it; in the last resort, it is those people.
Economic policies are devised, foreign relations are conducted, political institutions are administered, not as moves
in some gigantic game, but ultimately for the benefit of
men and women. Who the people of the British Commonwealth are, how and where they live, are thus the fundamental issues for the Commonwealth's future.

What conclusions, then, must we draw, in the field of practical policy, from the basic fact that while migration from
Great Britain to the Dominions is socially and politically
desirable it is to-day no longer impelled by the powerful
economic forces that held sway in the past? It is futile to
push against stern economic forces—futile, for instance, to
promote migration to the Dominions if their economic systems are not ready to absorb a greater working force; futile
to promote migration to the land so long as existing farmers
in the Dominions find it hard to dispose of their produce
at a fair price; futile to break in virgin bush when better
favoured land is being abandoned because it cannot be pro-
fitably worked in the existing state of world markets. Economic forces have a way of asserting themselves, and if we
defy them in the matter of migration we shall be heading
for trouble.

Political effort should be concentrated on two objects, the
first of which is to remove the obstacles that might hinder the
smooth play of economic attractions. That is to say, without
bribing emigrants we should cheapen emigration through
subsidized ocean passages, and should help to bring the
opportunities and attractions of the Dominions to the notice
of our people, truthfully and without exaggeration. We
should seek every means of eliminating the serious friction

inherent in schemes of social insurance by establishing, in co-operation with the Dominions, a system of transferable rights to benefits under health, unemployment, and pensions schemes; it might be necessary for us to make a financial contribution to the Dominions' social services in order to adjust the matter equitably, but it would be worth while.

The second and more fundamental objective of policy should be to further such an economic development of the Commonwealth as will deflect the economic forces in favour of the migration that we desire. We should therefore do all we can to promote the economic expansion of the Dominions by offering the widest possible market for their products, and by encouraging them in the development of industries and trades, not by means of generally higher protectionism (which, if it favoured migration at all, would do so because it impoverished the United Kingdom, not because it enriched the Dominions), but by means of orderly and planned development on the principle of specialization.

XII

LOOKING FORWARD

IT is tempting to draw together the conclusions that have been reached in the foregoing chapters about Empire trade, finance, and migration into a single catch-phrase, 'planning for the Empire'. Economic planning for the Empire, however, if it is to include the self-governing members of the Commonwealth, must clearly be very different from the 'planning' that has been popularized by the British Left-Centre as the theme of governmental action at home. There is no Government for the whole Empire. There is no co-ordinated machinery for the carrying out of an Empire 'plan', no single electorate to whom the designers and operators of the plan must be responsible for success or failure. What is in question is no more than the co-operation of half a dozen independent Governments, relying on half a dozen Parliaments for the translation of the plan into Acts and Orders, which must then be administered by half a dozen separate public services. In the first place, the gist of the co-operative 'plan' is unlikely to go much beyond the highest common factor of a series of national policies or plans. In the second place, changes of government, or of parliamentary balances, or of national policies, may frequently prevent the parties to the plan from carrying out their share exactly as intended.

We must be more modest in our conceptions. Although 'planning' conveys the right notion of the nature of the task, it misleads when applied to the means of carrying it out. What is needed may rather be described as 'common purpose and co-operative action'. Hitherto, it has been the lack of an agreed purpose, more than anything else, that has limited the scope of co-operative action in Empire economic affairs. In this respect a close parallel may be drawn with Commonwealth co-operation in foreign relations. If the common purpose of the members of the Commonwealth is complete and all-pervading, as in the conduct of a great war, the unity of action is equally complete, and co-operative machinery of government, like the Imperial War Cabinet, springs up to meet the need. But the less clear and certain the common purpose in foreign affairs, the less continuous and reliable is the co-operation in action, and the greater the objections that are raised in this quarter and that to the use or creation of co-operative institutions. The problem is exactly the same in economic affairs. The common purpose must come first, and the co-operative action and institutions will follow.

In seeking a common purpose, we do well to start by considering what state of economic affairs we expect or would like to find, say, twenty years hence. If past trends are projected into the future, we should expect to find, among other things, a fall of costs of production and values of primary commodities, an increased volume of international trade in industrial raw materials, and possibly a diminished volume of international trade in foodstuffs, accompanied by a decline of the relative importance (by value) of heavy staples and semi-manufactures in international trade compared with highly finished commodities, especially 'new' manufactures such as aeroplanes and electrical and radio equipment. We should expect to find, also, a further industrialization of the Dominions and India, and a smaller population in the United Kingdom.

One large speculative element in the future economic picture is the trend of national tariffs and other barriers to trade. Will it be on the whole upward or downward? Those who have read so far will not need to be reminded of the writer's firm opinion that the nations of the Commonwealth stand to gain both politically and economically by freer world trade, and should do all they can to make it possible; and that for that reason their purpose as between themselves should be freer trade rather than national protection.

Unfortunately, we have to face the all too likely chance of still higher protection in foreign countries, contracting the markets for British exports and forcing the countries of the Commonwealth either into greater national self-sufficiency or into greater reliance on each other's markets. To some extent, political questions and questions of strategy may have to determine the choice between those two alternatives; for too great reliance on external trade, even within the Empire, may be a hostage to fortune in war, especially if that trade is in vital foodstuffs on the one hand or in military manufactures on the other. Putting such considerations aside, it is plainly preferable economically that the unit of greater self-sufficiency should be as wide as possible. The British Commonwealth will be better off if the greater self-sufficiency that is forced upon it is Commonwealth-wide than if it is restricted to the borders of each member-nation.

A drift towards higher world tariffs must cause persistent difficulties, both for the United Kingdom in selling her staple manufactures and for the Dominions in selling their staple primary products. They cannot count upon an automatically expanding market in the United Kingdom itself, whatever the latter's policy may be, since its population is almost certain to decline. Greater wealth will not compensate for smaller numbers, as far as the international trade in foodstuffs is concerned. Hence, while the further industrialization of the Dominions is both inevitable and to be desired, it ought to be pursued with the idea rather of maintaining than of contracting the market for United Kingdom goods. This suggests that the principle of the greatest possible freedom of trade within the Commonwealth ought to be associated with the principle of specialization, to apply both to primary and to secondary products. For it is only if the industrial development of the Dominions and India is planned to follow the lines of selective specialization that it will be compatible with an advancing standard of living in those countries, with an extended market there for British goods, and with the maintenance at their maximum size of the markets in Great Britain and elsewhere for Dominion primary products (and, later on, for Dominion manufactures).

In this industrial development of the Dominions and India, capital from the United Kingdom is bound to play a considerable part. At the stage of economic progress now reached by the United Kingdom, the accumulation of capital tends naturally to surpass the opportunities for its investment at a return attractive to capitalists (which is the same as saying that the rate of interest attuned to a condition of full employment tends to be permanently low). The opposite, given non-crisis conditions, tends to be true of the Dominions and India at their respective stages of economic progress.[1] Thus there is a natural suction drawing capital to them from the United Kingdom. This process of international dissemination of capital is profitable and sound in itself, but it is dangerous if unplanned and unregulated. The inflow of capital itself creates conditions of temporary economic expansion (amounting at times to a boom) which in turn attract more capital, until the bubble is pricked and what formerly appeared profitable is found no longer to be so. Even if this danger of wave movements of capital export and import can be avoided, the problem of paying the interest and dividends on a steadily growing volume of borrowed money may not solve itself. Not only the profitability of the borrowing enterprise or the solvency of the borrowing Government must be preserved, but also the borrowing country's ability to maintain a sufficient credit balance of external trade. The problem becomes all the more difficult when the lending country is declining in population, and therefore unable to provide an expanding market for staple commodities.

Two practical conclusions follow: first, that the flow of capital should be supervised by an authority capable of envisaging the future economic conditions under which the service of the debt will be met, and of encouraging the investment of capital in directions that will help rather than hinder the establishment of the necessary trade balance; second, that the trade between the borrowing and lending countries should be as free as possible, in order to ensure the quickest and easiest adjustment of the terms of trade to suit the movement of the capital itself and later of the interest on it. Once more, therefore, we return to the combination of economic specialization with the maintenance of liberal conditions of Empire trade.

[1] Possibly Canada is already able to supply her own needs of capital in normal times without resort to relatively high rates of interest. The Irish Free State has passed the saturation point of capital self-sufficiency, but may fall below it again if her attempt at industrialization proves an economic success.

Both these objectives were perceived and praised by
Empire statesmen at the time of the Ottawa Conference.
If, in the light of actual results, they appear to have been
seen only 'through a glass, darkly', the fault may be held to
lie in the failure of the Conference to discuss and agree upon
objectives before proceeding to adjust policies to them. The
objectives, differently conceived by the various participants
according to their personal and national prejudices, became
little more than a verbal smoke-screen behind which the real
business of striking tariff bargains was conducted. This fault
of the Ottawa Conference is to be blamed partly on the
circumstances of the time. It was the nadir of world depression. Every Government was preoccupied with its immediate
problems of safeguarding its currency and caring for its
unemployed. It was hard to take risks, difficult to forecast
the long-term future, almost impossible to formulate a plan
of positive economic development for the Commonwealth,
involving the movement of capital and migrants. To-day,
being better off, we have an opportunity of fresh and coura-
geous action.

It would, nevertheless, be a mistake to conclude that we
need more comprehensive and more detailed written agreements of the Ottawa type. On the contrary, the more
narrowly we attempt to define our policy in written pledges,
the more likely are we to be distracted from the major
purpose of wrangles over details, over interpretation, over
charges of bad faith in carrying out our undertakings. A
trade treaty will always be regarded as a bargain, as an
exchange of 'concessions', talk about it how you will. The
task of an Imperial Conference should not be to strike bargains and sign contracts, but to agree upon an economic
purpose for the whole Commonwealth.

PART IV
FOREIGN POLICY

I
FRANCE AND GERMANY

WE come now to the foreign policy of the Empire. We have seen that, in their own political and economic relationships, its countries, in spite of the mechanical imperfections of those relationships, have 'muddled through' not unsatisfactorily. In their relations with other countries there has been just as great a lack of precision, together with an even greater tendency than there was, for instance, at the Ottawa Conference, to try to hide the lack behind 'verbal smokescreens'.

'Muddling through' may work as between the members of the Commonwealth with their prevailing sense of fellowship and common origin and with their complete and absolute unreadiness to fight each other, however grave the quarrel might be. But it is a dangerous procedure in regard to the outside world, especially in these days of dictatorships, the rulers of which know their own minds, act according to policy and plan, are not afraid to use force if necessary and can, by pressing the appropriate buttons, make their will the national will almost over-night.

London is the centre of the high politics of the Commonwealth. The Imperial Conference of 1926 recognized 'that in the conduct of foreign affairs generally as in the sphere of defence, the major share of the responsibility . . . must for some time continue to rest with His Majesty's Government in Great Britain'. Various factors compelled that decision and still confirm its validity. Europe, as we have seen, remains the most important theatre of international relations. In London, alone among the capitals of the Empire, exists the equipment for handling the complexities of modern diplomacy; and, where the work is done, there also must centre the responsibility, for the international kaleidoscope moves too quickly for previous consultation with the Dominion Governments always to be possible.

The present discomfiture of our diplomacy is attributed,

especially by the Opposition parties, to the shortcomings of the successive Foreign Ministers of the National Government. None of these Ministers can be held guiltless. But for the real cause of the trouble one must look behind them. One must go back to the Peace Conference and the subsequent years. The discomfiture of Mr. Eden over Abyssinian sanctions followed logically, though at long distance, upon President Wilson's failure to persuade his countrymen to accept membership in the League of Nations and to honour his signature of the Treaty of Versailles.

One of the most important of the problems which confronted the Peace Conference was that of French security. Germany, though beaten and racked by internal troubles, was still potentially powerful. Shorn as she was bound to be of part of her population and of part of her industrial and natural resources, she would remain better off than France in man-power and eventually in material as well. It was a disquieting prospect for France and also for the Peace Conference. France could not forget that Germany was her traditional enemy and had invaded her in three successive wars. The Conference knew that there could be no real peace in Europe unless France could be reassured.

There were three ways in which France could be reassured. She could be given the left bank of the Rhine for all the distance that the French and German frontiers marched together; she could have her safety guaranteed by other countries; or the German Reich could be dissolved into its component parts. The last course was, naturally, never broached before the Conference; the first course was suggested by Marshal Foch and others in a somewhat attenuated form. It was suggested, not that the German territory between France and the Rhine should be annexed, but that it should be taken away from Germany and turned into a buffer State. This the Conference refused to do.

The Conference took the second course, leading to the protection of the eastern frontier by international guarantee. The United States, Great Britain, and the Dominions suggested that this could best be done under the League of

Nations. France on her side was unwilling to rely upon what she regarded as a questionable experiment. It was all very well, she argued, for the English-speaking nations, with no dangerous neighbours across their borders, to rely for the protection of peace upon a plan the efficacy of which remained to be tested, but it was a very different thing for her to do so, living, as she did, cheek by jowl with a country of proved aggressiveness. The United States (or rather President Wilson) and Great Britain saw the justice of that argument and promised to give France treaties which would pledge them, until such time as it had been shown that the League of Nations would really work, to come to her assistance in the event of wanton German aggression. These treaties never materialized. The American Senate refused to ratify the American one as it refused to ratify the rest of the work of the Peace Conference. Great Britain took advantage of a clause in her treaty which allowed her to draw out of it if the United States drew out of hers. That was in 1919. In 1922 we again offered the guarantee but it was then too late for reasons to which we will return. France was engrossed in an effort to gain security by other means. She was busy organizing the encirclement of Germany in the old Balance of Power manner and she was exploiting the penalty clauses of the Treaty of Versailles for all that they were worth in order to keep Germany weak. Hence the ruthless and uneconomic pressure to which she subjected Germany in regard to reparations, culminating in 1923 in the occupation of the Ruhr.

The Treaty of Versailles, as has already been shown, was meant to be improved later. It was hoped that the combined influence of the United States and Great Britain would be sufficient to make France, reassured as to her safety by the Guarantee Treaties, play the part of a generous and constructive victor, when once her very natural passions against Germany had cooled. This hope crumbled into disappointment when the United States deserted the Peace of Versailles. Not only was France forced back to the old diplomacy of alliances, but Great Britain alone was unable to prevent her misusing the penalty clauses of the Treaty of Versailles against Germany. This was particularly true in regard to reparations. We could not secure anything like constructive or conciliatory continence in regard either to demands or to their enforcement, until their failure to exploit economically the occupation of the Ruhr and the general criticism which that occupation had aroused abroad convinced the French that gentler tactics might bring better results, and led to the first step towards the final abandonment of reparations, under the stress of the world depression, at the Lausanne Conference in the summer of 1932. This first step was taken at the so-called Dawes Conference held in London in 1924. Though various European factors helped to bring about the scaling down of reparations at that Conference to what then seemed reasonable proportions, it is significant that much of the necessary motive power came from the reappearance of the United States upon the economic battle-field of Europe. Two years earlier Mr. Hughes, the American Secretary of State, or Foreign Minister, whose force and vision had, with the vision and diplomacy of Lord Balfour, been responsible for the Washington Naval Treaty and for the other Washington Treaties which had liquidated, as it was then hoped, the situation left by the War in the Far East, pointed out in a public speech that economic conditions in Europe were more than a European problem, that they were a world problem in which the United States was intimately concerned. Mr. Hughes suggested the creation by the Governments of Europe of an expert commission to advise as to the amount of reparations which Germany could pay and to suggest a method of effecting the transfer of the money, and so on. He expressed confidence that Americans would be found to serve on such a commission.

This expert commission was finally instituted only after the United States had again thrown her weight into the scales of diplomacy on the side of reason, thus breaking a deadlock between us and the French. We wanted the commission to be empowered to compute on Germany's ultimate capacity to pay and to arrange for a schedule of payments stretching over many years. The French Government, on the other hand, wished the commission to report only on Germany's present capacity to pay, hoping to be able to increase reparations later, if Germany showed signs of becoming too strong. Mr. Hughes announced that no Americans would be found to serve on the commission if the French were allowed to have their way and the British plan prevailed.

Such was the genesis of the Dawes Commission, so called because its chairman was the American business man and administrator, General Dawes, afterwards American Ambassador to the Court of St. James's. It was followed by the London Conference and the Dawes Plan for reparations; and when the Dawes Plan turned out still to have envisaged impossibly heavy payments another plan was drawn up by another commission under the chairmanship of another American, Mr. Young.

But if the return of the United States to the European economic field kept the reparations problem within more or less manageable bounds when once the excesses of the first four years of the Peace were out of the way, there was in the political field no return of American co-operation on anything like the same scale. There Great Britain was forced to fight the battle for moderation unaided by any Great Power. She fought for many years with energy, ingenuity, and pertinacity and there were times when it looked as if she might be not unsuccessful. But in the end she failed, and, except in the case of reparations, Germany had to wait to regain that status of equality among the great Powers which France had been given almost at once after the Napoleonic War until Herr Hitler found himself strong enough and the diplomacy of the other Powers weak enough to enable him to end the inequalities by unilateral and illegal action. For this failure there are two interconnected reasons. France, though at times—especially while her foreign policy was under the guidance of M. Briand—she seemed on the point of doing so, never really relaxed her nervously suspicious hostility towards Germany; and Great Britain, though under Sir Austen Chamberlain's leadership she made a gesture in that direction, was never really ready to sacrifice upon the altar of changed conditions her old posture of semi-isolation from the politics of Europe. She never supported the League of

Nations in the way in which its founders saw that it would have to be supported if it was really to succeed.

This half-heartedness, as will be shown in greater detail in the next chapter, must rank with the fears of France and the discontents of Germany and Italy among the major causes for the present bankruptcy of the League of Nations and for the discomfiture of the democratic Powers.

\

II

WHY THE LEAGUE HAS FAILED

THE chief function of the League of Nations as an agency for the protection of peace was, in the minds of its founders, to give permanency, organization, and status to the machinery which the 'old diplomacy' had used for the settlement of disputes. The essential parts of that machinery were international conferences and arbitration, mediation, and inquiry.

The first modern Arbitration Treaty was signed in 1794 between England and the then new United States. It was successfully used for the liquidation of various questions, such as frontier controversies between the United States and Canada, which had been left outstanding at the end of the Revolutionary War. By the time the Great War broke out, the majority of countries were bound together by a nexus of treaties under which they promised to submit many categories of disputes to arbitration, mediation, or inquiry; and the Permanent Court of Arbitration had been set up at The Hague, the chief duty of which was to provide suitable arbitrators for any countries wishing to have recourse to it.

International conferences had been held in the period just before the War as well as earlier. Sir Edward Grey had successfully used conference diplomacy in 1913 to prevent the Balkan war of that date from dangerously troubling the relations of the Great Powers; and one of the strongest incentives of those who worked in England for the establishment of the League of Nations was his oft-repeated statement that, had there been a standing committee of the Powers, like the Council of the League, which he could have summoned during the crisis, war might have been averted in 1914 also.

The provision of the Covenant for the periodic meetings of the Council of the League in Geneva, for rarer meetings of all its member-nations in the Assembly and for a permanent secretariat, one of whose functions would be to prepare for those meetings and to summon at the instance of members such extra meetings as might be needed, was thus no more than an effort to give the new diplomacy a regular machine for work which the old diplomacy had done spasmodically. The intention to hold special conferences in times of emergency is codified in Article 11 of the Covenant, which says that:

'Any war or threat of war, whether immediately affecting any members of the League or not, is hereby declared a matter of concern to the whole League and the League shall take any action that may be deemed wise and effectual to safeguard the peace of nations. . . .

This article reveals another major objective of the makers of the League. The Great War had been fought as a 'war to end war'. Therefore it was only right that the Peace Settlement should go as far as possible towards the outlawry of war by the nations as (to quote the subsequent Kellogg Pact) 'an instrument of national policy towards each other'.

It was recognized, moreover, not only at the Peace Conference but also in the preparatory work done in France, the United States, England, and other countries, that the new diplomacy would have to rest upon force just as much as the old diplomacy had done. In America, during the War, the League to Enforce Peace, of which the chairman was ex-President Taft, a great jurist and afterwards Chief Justice of the Supreme Court of the United States, came out strongly in favour of sanctions against countries which ignored the new machinery for the peaceful settlement of disputes. The sanctions paragraph of their plan said:

'The signatory Powers shall jointly use forthwith both their economic and military forces against one of the number who goes to war, or commits acts of hostility against another of the signatories before any question arising shall be submitted as provided in the foregoing.'

In England during the War a similar unofficial committee went into the question of the avoidance of war and came equally to the conclusion that the nations must organize a peace-keeping machine and support it by sanctions. The chairman of the committee was the late Lord Bryce, one of

the soundest and best-equipped political thinkers of his day
and a Liberal of anything but bellicose tendencies. Lord
Bryce and his colleagues advised that any Power which
violated the provisions of its plan against the use of war
should be subject to 'economic and forcible' sanctions by all
the other signatory Powers. The committee later appointed
by the British Government to consider the League of Nations
question advocated sanctions with equal emphasis. It suggested that if a signatory of the Covenant broke its terms,
then

'this State shall become *ipso facto* at war with all the other Allied
States and the latter agree to take, and to support each other in
taking jointly and severally all such measures—military, naval,
financial and economic—as will best avail for restraining the
breach of covenant. . . .'

A French committee found that the usefulness of the League
as a guardian of international peace would depend upon the
efficacy of the economic and military sanctions at its disposal.
It suggested that the carrying out of military sanctions should
be entrusted to a permanent international general staff who
would be empowered to demand from different countries
contingents for the forces to be employed against the law-
breaking State.

It is hardly surprising, therefore, that the Covenant should
contain a sanctions clause, the famous Article 16, and that
in submitting the draft of the Covenant to the Conference
President Wilson should have said: 'Armed force is in the
background of this programme, but it is in the background;
and if the moral force of the world will not suffice, the
physical force of the world shall.'

Both Article 10 and Article 16 contemplate the use of force.
With Article 10 must be read Article 19, which was originally drafted to be part of it and was meant to prevent an
undue crystallization of the *status quo* by Article 10.

There are obvious 'gaps' in the Covenant, through which
war could and can creep in. Article 10, for instance, does
not define aggression, and there has been no general agreement upon a definition since. Article 15 which deals with

reference to the League of disputes 'likely to lead to a rupture', obviously and deliberately fails to catch all disputes within its net. Nor are the obligations to go to war against a transgressor watertight.[1]

It was soon evident that Great Britain and other countries of the Empire were inclined to use these and other pretexts to weaken the peace-keeping functions of the League. They were discouraged by the continued political and economic confusions of Europe. They saw the United States returning to the shell of her traditional isolation from Old World Affairs. They wondered whether they could make the new idea work without her. They wondered whether they, also, would not be well advised to return to the traditional British policy of protection, if necessary, for the shores of the North Sea and the Channel from dominance by a dangerous Power, but a 'free hand' and no permanent commitments further afield.

Great Britain was ready to recognize that the Rhine had become her defensive frontier and therefore was ready to offer to renew in 1921 and 1922 the Treaty for the guarantee of the French frontier, but beyond that she would not go. At a meeting of the Council of the League in 1920 Lord Balfour asked whether the League could effectively proceed against an aggressor in the absence not only of Germany and Russia but also of the United States. A committee was appointed to study the question with a special reference to the blockade of a transgressor. In the same year Canada proposed that Article 10 should be struck from the Covenant on the ground that the blank cheque which it asked members of the League to sign might be too dangerously filled in. Nothing came of the Canadian motion, and the report of the Blockade Committee which suggested the weakening of Article 16 by slowing down the action of the League under it was never adopted. But the tendency revealed by these incidents, coupled with other indications of the same nature, were held by France and the other frightened nations of Europe more than ever to justify their distrust of the League

[1] The second sentence of Article 10, for instance, provides a loophole. So does the second clause of Article 16.

as a purveyor of security and their determination to keep Germany down and secure their safety by direct action.

The principal agents for direct action were, it must be repeated, the encircling armies of France, Poland, and the Little Entente. At first they were unnecessary, so weak was Germany on account of war-shock and of economic and political troubles aggravated by pressure from the outside. Then came the better period between 1924 and 1930, brought about, as we have seen, by the reparations settlement and by the happy and statesmanlike co-operation during and after the negotiation of the Pact of Locarno between Sir Austen Chamberlain, M. Briand, and Herr Streseman. It looked in those days as if Europe were on the verge of real appeasement. Germany came into the League of Nations and prospered internally, and Herr Streseman and M. Briand were on terms of confidence very different from any relations that had existed between French and German statesmen in the memory of man or almost of history.

But in retrospect one sees that appeasement was superficial rather than real. One sees that the stability of Europe was still resting upon the armed force of France and her allies and was destined to be disturbed as soon as that superiority was questioned. One of the main reasons for the failure of the effort to revive in 1921 and 1922 the project for a Franco-British Treaty under which Great Britain would guarantee the eastern frontier of France was that France did not believe that such a guarantee would really give her security, were it limited to direct aggression by Germany. Direct aggression, said M. de St. Aulaire, the French Ambassador in London, to our Foreign Office, was altogether improbable:

'Unless Germany is smitten with incurable lunacy, she will not repeat the mistake of 1914 after the lesson of the last war. Her game will be more skilful and incomparably more formidable. She will recollect the Ems Telegram and make every effort to invest the origins of the conflict with a dubious character. Or rather she will seek inspiration in the methods employed by Bismarck in 1866, throw herself first upon her weakest adversary, and, following the line of least resistance, invade Poland as she did in 1772. No doubt France would not tolerate that and would take up arms to defend Poland and the European equilibrium on the Rhine. But France would be isolated, since an Anglo-French defensive alliance, limited *ex hypothesi* to the contingency of direct aggression, would not apply to the far more probable hypothesis of indirect aggression. We may say, then, that such an alliance, at the best, would cover us, if not against another Charleroi, at least against a Sedan, but that it would not cover us against a Polish Sadowa, which, for Germany, would be the best preparation for another Sedan.'

Even between 1925 and 1930 France was not entirely happy. Her posture during the long discussions which had already started at Geneva to prepare the ground for the Disarmament Conference showed that. The main object of the Conference was to implement the undertaking implied in the opening paragraph of the Military, Naval, and Air Clauses of the Treaty of Versailles that the victors would round off the disarmament of the vanquished by reducing their own armaments. The paragraph runs:

'In order to render possible the initiation of a general limitation of the armaments of all the nations, Germany undertakes strictly to observe the military, naval and air clauses which follow.'

In Article 8 of the Covenant this was translated into a clause by which members of the League recognized that the maintenance of peace required 'the reduction of national armaments to the lowest point consistent with national safety and the enforcement by common action of international obligations'.

It soon became apparent that in practice the process of disarmament would be an arming down on the part of the victors and neutrals in the war and an arming up on the part of the vanquished. The French attitude to this programme never varied. It was that, in view of Germany's vast potential strength, France could not allow the gap between her armaments and those of Germany to be reduced, unless her security was increased. A few months before the Disarmament Conference opened, France published a memorandum in which she made it clear that she proposed to maintain this thesis at the Conference. She had, she said, already reduced her armaments 'to a level which appeared to her to represent the lowest point consistent with her national security in the present state of Europe and the world'. Further reductions therefore could only be affected in return for additional guarantees of security. At the opening of the Disarmament Conference she repeated this ultimatum. She said that she would like to see the creation of an international police force and that the Conference presented the 'best opportunity that has ever occurred to make a definite choice between a League of Nations possessing executive authority and a League of Nations paralysed by the uncompromising attitude of national sovereignty. France has made her choice. She suggests that other nations should make theirs.'

To this challenge, not devoid of an element of bluff, neither the British nor, of course, the American Government responded, and the Conference soon became enmeshed in an ever-growing maze of technicalities, from whose trammels it escaped from time to time to make unsuccessful attacks upon the major deadlock brought about by the fears of France and her friends, the natural desire of Germany to be allowed to escape from the long-drawn-out servitudes of the disarmament clauses of the Treaty of Versailles, and the refusal of the English-speaking nations to increase their commitments in Europe on behalf of collective security. Other factors, of course, contributed to the collapse of the Conference. The French more than once rejected German suggestions which merited consideration. In 1932 especially they rejected proposals made by Dr. Brüning, then Chancellor of Germany, the acceptance of which might conceivably have kept the German Republic in being.

All that, however, is spilt milk long since evaporated. What matters is that the Conference did collapse and that its collapse, together with the terrible reactions which the world depression had in Germany, and, it must be added, his own compelling personality, established Herr Hitler and his party in power and thus brought about the situation in Europe described in previous chapters by what now look like an inevitable series of events, each exalting the dictatorships at the expense of the democracies and of the League of Nations.

Such, very roughly, is the sequence of events which link the Abyssinian fiasco with the refusal of the United States to enter the League. It is a sequence so important to a correct understanding of contemporary international affairs as to merit brief recapitulation. The American withdrawal from Europe was followed by the decision of Great Britain not to quit the League but to limit her automatic responsibilities under it as much as possible. Great Britain's decision confirmed France in the suspicion which had always haunted her that it would be unsafe to rely upon the League for protection from the vengeance of Germany. France went back to her old policy, first practised in the seventeenth century, of ringing Germany round by alliances and otherwise weakening her. She later refused to surrender her Treaty superiority in armaments over Germany by allowing Germany to rearm and by reducing her own armaments. This made Germany, justly annoyed at the refusal of the ex-allies to carry out what she considered their Treaty promise to disarm, quit the League and challenge the League Powers and the Versailles Powers by tearing up the Disarmament Clauses of the Treaty of Versailles and re-arming. The League and the Versailles Powers gesticulated impotently in the face of this defiance. Signor Mussolini, who had long been meditating a coup in Abyssinia and had strong reasons for making it when he did, already encouraged by the impunity with which the Japanese had driven a coach and four through the Covenant in the Far East, found further encouragement in this spectacle, and acted with such vigour that, when the League tried after all to assert itself, it was too late for him to draw back, even if he had wanted to.

III

THE NATIONAL GOVERNMENT AND EUROPE

VARIOUS facts, not the less important because they are obvious, emerge from the story just sketched. First, the League is a co-operative institution and is thus as strong or weak as its members like to make it; secondly, in the affairs of Geneva as in those of the outer world it is the Great Powers that count; thirdly, the present deflated condition of the League, if the fault of the United States in the first instance, is now mainly the fault of Great Britain and France; fourthly, Great Britain and France have failed in their support of the League largely because of a superior loyalty to national self-interest, not always perhaps of that 'enlightened' variety, due recognition of which is a legitimate and indeed essential ingredient in a sound foreign policy.

The Abyssinian affair in particular compels these conclusions and for that reason its catastrophic story is worth further consideration. The collapse of the Disarmament Conference at the end of 1934 left the League, as we have seen, grievously weakened, in spite of the fact that France, already much alarmed at the growing strength of Germany, had persuaded us to join her in proposing Russia as a member of the League and in securing her election. For Russia as well as for us and France this meant a momentous change of policy; for, while co-operating with the League over disarmament and other specific tasks, this had never caused her to hide her contempt of it as a luckily inefficient organ of the capitalist States in their effort to exploit the world for their selfish ends. But she, on her side, was afraid of the new Germany, and was therefore prepared to join in her encirclement and to agree with Emerson that only small minds shrink from inconsistency. France was also doing her best to secure Italy, who had not yet come down on the German side, as another recruit to the encirclement group.

If France and Russia were afraid of Germany, Great Britain was very rightly afraid of the hostile *blocs and counter-*

blocs into which the Continent seemed to be slipping. But how was she to prevent their formation, how could she reassure France and Russia and the frightened countries, if she was not prepared to guarantee their security by deserting her habitual half-in-half-out attitude towards the League? This question, important enough in itself, had also a bearing upon the position of the National Government in home politics. For some time past the Labour and Liberal Oppositions, backed by progressive opinion throughout the country, had been growing more and more restless at what they considered to be the weak and wrong-headed diplomacy of Sir John Simon at the Disarmament Conference, and after the failure of the Conference and the resignation of Germany from the League they blamed the Government for the *débâcle*. They accused it of lack of real loyalty to the League of Nations and to the system of collective security which they wished to see established under the League.

Mr. Baldwin has told the House of Commons that at an early stage of its development this discontent which he described as 'pacifist feeling' had influenced the domestic plans of the Government. It is not therefore unfair to suppose that, in its later and more acute stage, combined with a genuine concern at the rapid deterioration of the European situation, it stimulated the Government after the failure of the Disarmament Conference to make an energetic effort to create in Europe an international system which would produce a sense of security and yet not demand further commitments from Europe.

Sir John Simon, at any rate, after the failure of the Disarmament Conference, came forward with a scheme to reinforce the League of Nations and to give the Continent the necessary security on essentially non-collective lines. He suggested that the countries in the east and south-east of Europe should sign regional pacts, under which members of the different groups would undertake to assist other members of their group should they be attacked. He said that Great Britain would be ready to make the Pact of Locarno bilateral so as to bring it into line with the other regional agreements. There was nothing new in the idea. It had been in Sir Austen

Chamberlain's mind ten years earlier when he suggested that the Pact of Locarno should be followed by other local treaties of mutual guarantee. It had been suggested in Geneva during the preparatory discussions on disarmament even before that and had figured in those days in the abortive draft of a treaty for giving Europe more security. Nor during the winter of 1934–5 did it come to anything in spite of the amount of time and travelling which Sir John Simon and Mr. Eden, who was then his subordinate, devoted to their efforts to 'sell' it abroad. The most important apparent effect of its resuscitation was, indeed, so to preoccupy Sir John Simon and his colleagues as to prevent them from grasping the full significance of the diplomatic and other preparations for the conquest of Abyssinia which Signor Mussolini started to make at the same juncture. Their preoccupation with a menacing European situation and desire to put right the results of the failure of the Disarmament Conference are at any rate the best explanation of their lack of alertness in regard to the cloud which was so obviously beginning to lower over the African horizon.

British lack of alertness was particularly unfortunate in view of the French attitude. France, in her efforts to tempt Italy into her camp, had given Signor Mussolini to understand that, so far as she was concerned, he might rely upon a fairly free hand in and about Abyssinia. Great Britain, it is true, indicated to Signor Mussolini more than once in the early months of 1935 that his threatening attitude towards Abyssinia caused her the gravest disquiet. But she had protested with equal emphasis against the successive moves taken by Japan in the seizure of Manchuria but had done nothing whatever to make her action square with her words, and Signor Mussolini therefore felt justified in ignoring her representations. Nor, when Sir John Simon and Mr. Ramsay MacDonald met Signor Mussolini in Stresa during the spring, was a single word said by either Minister to indicate that this time Great Britain was in earnest and that if Italy persisted in violating the Covenant against Abyssinia Great Britain would for her part throw all her weight on the side of sanctions when the breach of the Covenant was brought before the League of Nations. The Stresa meeting had been summoned in consequence of Germany's announcement that she was going to ignore the Treaty of Versailles and rearm. One of its chief objects was to range Italy with Great Britain and France in their protest against this illegality; and it is, therefore, to be presumed that the British Ministers were as loth as their French colleague to annoy Signor Mussolini by giving him a warning which it is possible might at that time have made him reconsider his venture.

No such warning was forthcoming; and again in the light of Mr. Baldwin's remarks regarding the subordination of foreign policy to the exigencies, real or imagined, of domestic party politics it is permissible to wonder whether Great Britain would have done anything more about Abyssinia than the French were then prepared to do and than she had herself done in the case of Manchuria, had not the National Government considered it advisable to present the electorate with further proof of its loyalty towards the League. Soon after the Stresa meeting public opinion gave another indication of the strength of its belief in the League. The results of the so-called Peace Ballot were published in May 1935. While it is easy to overestimate the significance of the Ballot, the fact does remain that the answers to the six questions posed by its promoters, returned by nearly 12,000,000 people out of a population of some 45,000,000, did seem to reveal a tremendous sentiment for the League and a considerable volume of approval for military sanctions if necessary. In June the Cabinet was reconstructed. The reconstruction itself was no surprise. It was known to have been planned long before. What did cause surprise was Sir John Simon's disappearance from the Foreign Office and reappearance at the Home Office, whose portfolio he had held as a young man before the War. The presumption was that he had been thrown to the Peace Ballot wolves. It was at any rate the fact that, in spite of his energetic and industrious efforts, his plans for the reconstruction of Europe by regional aggrements were making no progress.

Sir John Simon was succeeded as Foreign Minister by Sir Samuel Hoare, Mr. Eden remaining more or less under him as Special Minister for League of Nations Affairs. Almost immediately the League policy of the Government stiffened, and by the autumn we were committed to sanctions against Italy and to what looked like genuine support of a real collective security system for Europe. Sir Samuel Hoare, at the annual meeting of the Assembly of the League at Geneva, made his famous speech which seemed to imply that in future Great Britain would really act up to her obligations under the Covenant. The principal passage in his speech ran as follows:

'It is to the principles of the League . . . that the British nation has demonstrated its adherence. Any other view is at once an underestimate of our good faith and an imputation upon our sincerity. In conformity with its precise and explicit obligations the League stands and my country stands with it for the collective maintenance of the Covenant in its entirety and particularly for steady and collective resistance to all acts of unprovoked aggression.'

'At last after ten years England has seen the light', cried M. Herriot, one of the French Prime Ministers who had dealt with Sir John Simon at Geneva and elsewhere. M. Herriot and millions of others thought that the British Foreign Minister's speech meant that we had at last seen that the best way in which peace could be guaranteed in Europe was for us to be prepared to stand ready to protect it wherever it might be threatened instead of limiting our full responsibilities under the Covenant to Western Europe.

That was in September. In November the National Government, having in the meanwhile taken the lead in the invocation of economic sanctions against Italy, went to the country on a strong League of Nations platform, though it greatly weakened the effect of sanctions upon Italy by intimating that in no circumstances would it get the country into war and by proclaiming that 'there will be no great armaments'. Why it went to the country at that time and in that way was afterwards explained by Mr. Baldwin, in that speech of his which has already been alluded to, as follows:

'All I did was to take a moment perhaps less unfortunate than another might have been, and we won the election with a large majority but, frankly, I conceive that we should at that time by advocating certain courses have been a good deal less successful.'

Had the world been in possession of Mr. Baldwin's thoughts at the time it might have been less surprised, if not less shocked, by the Hoare-Laval episode in December and by the weakness, and therefore unsuccess, with which sanctions were pressed home after the election had been won.

Undeterred by the Abyssinian fiasco, Mr. Eden in the summer of 1936 tried to recapture the lead in European affairs from the dictatorships. After Germany had broken the Treaty of Versailles by sending her troops into her demilitarized zone, he had addressed to Herr Hitler a series of questions as to German policy which he intimated must be answered before there could be any real Anglo-German co-operation in regard to the future of Europe. These questions were ignored. Courageously ignoring this fresh rebuff, Mr. Eden presided in July at a meeting in London between France, Belgium, and Great Britain. Those three countries invited Germany and Italy to join them in an attempt to 'consolidate peace by means of a general settlement'. They hoped to negotiate with Germany and Italy another Locarno Pact to take the place of the one which Germany had broken by her demilitarized zone coup. After that they planned to call in the other European countries and try to negotiate some sort of security arrangement, or arrangements, for the rest of Europe.

Mr. Eden told the House of Commons soon afterwards that the Government still regarded the 'collective organization of peace' as the most important task before the Powers. He said that there were certain principles in the Covenant of the League of Nations which must be maintained. The most important of those principles was 'the prevention of war', a process which included a number of elements such as 'machinery for the peaceful settlement of disputes, machinery for the adjustment of grievances, the creation of a deterrent to war, and the establishment of an international agreement for the reduction and limitation of armaments'. Germany and Italy accepted the invitation to a Five Power Conference which was announced for October. But it soon became

apparent that Germany would not easily be induced to
negotiate a new Locarno if it was to be an integral part of
some security scheme for eastern Europe as well. The preliminary negotiations lagged, were eclipsed by the reactions
of the Spanish Civil War, and especially by the efforts of
Germany to confuse the issue by dividing Europe into the
new ideological camps of Fascists and Communists. It is by
no means certain whether she will enter into a Western Pact
for the mutual guarantee of frontiers. So bitterly does she
resent the Franco-Soviet Treaty that hints from Berlin that
she is not prepared to negotiate with France until that
Treaty is abandoned or modified cannot be entirely ignored.

Thus for the present the plans of the democratic countries
for the 'collective organization of Peace' are held up and
would seem to be in considerable danger. The outcome of
the deadlock would seem to depend very largely upon the
attitude of England. If she chose to throw her weight into
the organization of collective security as Sir Samuel Hoare
said in 1935 that she meant to do, then it might still be
possible to revive the League of Nations. The League might
then even become strong enough to impress the countries
which measure everything in terms of force that it really
counted according to their own standards instead of being,
as they consider it now, simply a factory of empty resolutions.
Germany, for instance, might be tempted back to Geneva on
account of the protection that it would give her against
Russia, if indeed her fear of Russia is genuine and not
largely a bogy erected to scare her own people into willing-
ness to finance rearmament and Frenchmen and Englishmen and other foreigners into sympathy with her. The
League would certainly be strong enough to make any one
country think twice before it broke the peace in Europe for
selfish ends.

There is, however, scant indication that we mean to try a
strong League policy. Mr. Neville Chamberlain, soon after
the failure of sanctions against Italy, beguiled the 1900 Club
by thinking aloud before it. The collective system, he said,
had been tried out and had failed over Abyssinia. Therefore
it might be wise 'to explore the possibilities of localizing the

T

danger spots of the world, and trying to find a more practical method of securing peace by means of regional arrangements which could be approved by the League but which should be guaranteed only by those nations whose interests were vitally concerned with those danger zones.' Mr. Chamberlain afterwards explained away his words as a purely personal indiscretion. But it was widely felt at the time that they could mean only one thing, namely, that opposition in the Cabinet to Mr. Eden's League of Nations policy had been strengthened by his failure to make it good and that there was every prospect that the Cabinet would return to its pre-Peace Ballot conception of British policy in Europe.

Mr. Eden himself somewhat confirmed this opinion. Speaking to his own constituents towards the end of 1936 he said, after a reference to rearmament:

'These arms will never be used in a war of aggression. They will never be used for a purpose inconsistent with the Covenant of the League or the Pact of Paris. They may, and if the occasion arose they would, be used in our own defence and in defence of the territories of the British Commonwealth of Nations. They may, and if the occasion arose they would, be used in the defence of France and Belgium with our existing obligations. They may, and, if a new Western European settlement can be reached, they would, be used in defence of Germany were she the victim of unprovoked aggression by any of the other signatories of such a settlement.

'Those, together with our Treaty of Alliance with 'Iraq and our projected treaty with Egypt, are our definite obligations. In addition our armaments may be used in bringing help to a victim of aggression in any case where, in our judgement, it would be proper under the provisions of the Covenant to do so. I use the word "may" deliberately, since in such an instance there is no automatic obligation to take military action. It is, moreover, right that this should be so, for nations cannot be expected to incur automatic military obligations save for areas where their vital interests are concerned.'

Mr. Eden was careful to explain that this did not imply the abandonment of Geneva. The principles of the League, he said,

'were entirely in accord with British ideas, and it would not be our nature to abandon them merely because in some parts of the world they had fallen on rocky ground, and we should certainly not do so. A league which did not include all the more powerful nations must necessarily be different, be less effective, than a universal league, but the fact that we knew that we could not do everything was no excuse for doing nothing.'[1]

It is true, also, that in a subsequent speech Mr. Eden reaffirmed his belief that our interests in peace are ubiquitous even if 'our vital interests are situated in certain clearly defined areas', that we cannot 'live secure in a Western European glass-house', and that therefore we must 'work for a comprehensive European settlement'.[2]

Nevertheless, it looked more than ever as if the effort which, mainly thanks to Mr. Eden's energy, England had made to strengthen her own policy towards the League and therefore the League itself had failed and as if while the dictatorships had in the interval steadily consolidated their positions often at the expense of the democracies, she was back to where she was at the end of the Disarmament Conference. Only in rearmament had there been progress and there various incidents and controversies caused heart-searching as to whether the lack of unanimity and drive so noticeable in the Cabinet's treatment of foreign affairs might not be contaminating its conduct of that important branch of domestic affairs as well. The situation caused disappointed anxiety and perplexity among the millions at home and abroad who twelve months before had hailed Mr. Eden as a new Castlereagh destined to regenerate British diplomacy and restore to it the influence which it had lost during the preceding years.

[1] Mr. Eden at Leamington as reported in *The Times* of 20 Nov. 1936.
[2] Mr. Eden at Bradford as reported in *The Times* of 15 Dec. 1936.

IV
ISOLATION OR CO-OPERATION

DISQUIET and perplexity as to British foreign policy and as to the future of the League have been increased by the sharp differences of opinion upon those subjects revealed by those from whom guidance is expected.

There are, roughly, three schools of opinion, of which two are important and one the reverse. They may be called the collectivists, the semi-isolationists, and the isolationists. There are two types of isolationist. There are the militant isolationists who would have the countries of the Empire, including Great Britain, let Europe stew in its own juice and rely for their trade and prosperity upon each other, upon the American hemisphere, the Far East, and other extra-European territories. They would have us boycott the political activities of the League, and, of course, the politics of Europe. In spite of the importance of the air in modern warfare, in spite of the range of modern guns, in spite of the submarine, they would have us take part in no European war even for the defence of France and the Low Countries. They favour rearmament but only as a means of defence, and are prepared to let Germany or any other Power lord it over the Continent. The only thing that would seriously disturb their complacency would be advance of Communism westward across Europe.

The other isolationists belong mainly to the Left. They are the complete pacifists who would have us disarm, wrap ourselves in our own virtue, and trust that the rest of the world would follow our good example, or at least refrain from taking advantage of our weakness. They would keep the League as an agency for international co-operation and conciliation. They were one of the causes of the damagingly paradoxical posture in which the Labour Party placed itself during the Italian invasion of Abyssinia by advocating drastic sanctions with one breath and opposing rearmament with the next, a posture which might well have been mentioned in the first part of this book as a factor in the slump of the prestige of our foreign policy. But since then they have lost weight in the party councils, with the result that their influence is probably as negligible as that of the militant isolationists who, though commanding a large newspaper circulation for the airing of their ideas, have palpably failed to impress them either on the country or on Parliament.

The semi-isolationists and the collectivists, on the other hand, are powerfully represented both inside and outside Parliament. The Dominions also are ranged in their conflicting ranks. New Zealand and South Africa are to-day collectivists, Australia and Canada semi-isolationist, according to the utterances of their spokesmen at Geneva when the reform of the League came up last autumn and was referred to the inevitable committee. At home the collectivists command the support of the majority of those on the Labour and Liberal benches and of the majority of the Labour and Liberal Press. Many progressive Conservatives subscribe to their creed. That creed is a simple one. It is that the League of Nations should, even at this late date, be given a real trial. In the Far East it obviously cannot be made to work, for the present anyhow. In the western hemisphere it is not needed. But in Europe it still might function, if only Great Britain would take the lead in its resuscitation. Mr. Eden has rightly said that if war is to be prevented there must be machinery for the adjustment of grievances, for the peaceful settlement of disputes, and for the reduction of armaments. The fate of the Disarmament Conference and the Abyssinian affair show that none of those things is possible without the full participation by Great Britain in the necessary continental system.

British Ministers have chided the world for being so mad as to risk ruining itself by another war. Cannot they realize that their own hesitation to protect peace where it is most threatened is not the least conspicuous ingredient in that madness? They say that the grievances of the discontented countries must be met. But if, even at the time of the Disarmament Conference, the frightened nations shrank from agreeing to changes which would have left them relatively weaker unless Great Britain came properly into the League and thus gave them security, how, as things stand now, can they be expected to agree to changes in the *status quo* which would strengthen the other side unless they are first made to feel reasonably safe? It is not only a question of economic readjustments, of lower tariff rates, currency stabilization, and so on, all of which would, in their eyes, tend to increase the economic strength of Germany and her grip on central Europe. There is also the question of treaty revision. Danzig, Memel, the various claims for frontier readjustments in central Europe and so on, none of these problems, all of which prevent the return of normality, can be approached so long as the frightened countries remain frightened. Then again, as has been shown in the case of Manchuria and Abyssinia, peace can only be adequately protected, and a sense of security consolidated, if there is an overwhelming alliance for its protection functioning with collective loyalty to the League of Nations, an alliance which makes it quite clear from the first that it will not hesitate to use force if necessary for the fulfilment of its object. The hard-headed politicians, lawyers, and diplomatists who were responsible for the groundwork of the Covenant were nearly all convinced that the League would not work unless prepared to fight for its principles, and that was in days when it was confidently expected that the world was going to be made safe for democracy and to a considerable extent disarmed. How much more, then, does the League need sanctions of force behind it now that armaments are again bigger than ever and the dictatorial countries spurn its authority and glorify the mailed fist?

The word 'alliance' was used just now to connote the effective organization of the League for the protection of peace. This does not mean that the collectivists desire to encircle Germany. On the contrary, they hope that Germany, if her grievances could be given sympathetic consideration, would rejoin the League and thus gain protection from Russia. If, on the other hand, she refused to return to Geneva and to avail herself of the opportunities which a strong League would offer her of righting her grievances, then she would have only herself to blame if she found herself isolated or standing with Italy and a few other European countries over against the League of Nations Powers. The latter group, the collectivists aver, would be strong enough to make their opponents think twice before going to war and to beat them if their third thought led to war. Even if Japan were allied with the dictatorships, the League of Nations Powers would still be a redoubtable combination, provided that they held together. The German-Japanese Treaty may, indeed, if the early reactions to it are any indication of its permanent effect, prove to have weakened Germany's position by the hint that it has given that the dictatorial *bloc* may become a world-encircling danger as well as a menace to free institutions in Europe. It might even bring home to Russia that, whether she likes it or not, her future is bound up in the strength or weakness of the democratic countries, and that therefore it is unintelligent on her part to work with them in high international affairs while trying at the same time to weaken their efficiency as partners in the League of Nations by the surreptitious corruption of their domestic affairs.

In any case, the League of Nations supported by France, Russia, Great Britain, the Little Entente, and (probably) Poland, not to mention the smaller democratic countries whose power to help might, for reasons to which we will return, be limited, with the Dominions behind them and with the benevolent and perhaps beneficent neutrality of the United States and the Latin American Republics farther in the background, would surely be strong enough to protect peace.

'If we wish to stop this coming war—if coming it is—we must in the year that lies before us—nay, in the next six months—gather together the great nations, all as well armed as possible and united under the Covenant of the League in accordance with the principles of the League, and in this way we may reach a position where we can invite the German people to join this organization of world security; where we can invite them to take their place freely in the circle of nations to preserve peace, and where we shall be able to assure them that we seek no security for ourselves, which we do not extend most freely to them.

'We should rally and invite under the League of Nations the greatest number of strongly armed nations that we could marshal.

Let us invite Germany to take her part among us. Then we should, I believe, sincerely have done not only our best but have succeeded in warding off from the world calamities and horrors the end of which no man could foresee.'

So spoke Mr. Winston Churchill at a great non-party meeting at the end of 1936 at the Albert Hall.

'Britain should organize within the League such a concentration of resources, economic and military, as will make it evident that aggression will not pay'

said a statement by the Liberal Party at about the same time.

'Labour supports the principles embodied in the Covenant of the League of Nations. These principles include the renunciation of war as an instrument of national policy; the settlement of all disputes by peaceful means; the obligation on all nations to take common action to prevent aggression; the reduction of national armaments to the lowest possible level.

'Armed force would be used only as a means of preventing and resisting aggression, and of ensuring security to all nations.

'A durable peace can only be secured by the establishment of a world commonwealth in which the nations shall act towards each other as citizens in an orderly community.

'As a step in that direction, British Labour supports the League of Nations which stands for order as against anarchy.

'The League is intended to be, and can be made, the instrument for peaceful change.

'In Labour's view, the breakdown of the world economic system which condemns millions to unnecessary poverty and distress can only be met by world co-operation between States and by a policy within each State of utilizing to the full for the benefit of all the people the potential wealth of the world.

'The fruits of the earth should not be denied, by private or State monopolies, or any other form of exclusive possession, to any other State.

'Labour's policy is that of collective security. Under this system instead of each nation depending for its defence on its own forces it relies upon the joint action of the forces of all peace-loving States to prevent aggression or to bring it to an end'

proclaimed the National Council of Labour a few months earlier.

The semi-isolationists are mainly to be found among the leaders and supporters of the National Government. Mr. Neville Chamberlain, as we have seen, belongs to them and, as we have also seen, Mr. Eden inclines towards them. They also command important Liberal support. Though many of them dislike to be told so, they have really reverted to the foreign policy which England traditionally adopted before the War, a policy which we have already described as being inspired by readiness to protect the coasts of the continent from an ambitious and aggressive Power, and also by determination to preserve a 'free hand' so far as intervention farther afield is concerned. They agree with the collectivists in two things: first that the activities of the League, for the present anyhow, cannot be world-wide and must be confined to Europe; secondly, that Great Britain cannot dissociate herself from Europe. But they do not think that we should play a full part on the continental stage. They would have us guarantee peace on the Rhine by renewing the Locarno Pact and by making it reciprocal, a policy that would oblige us to defend France and Belgium from a German attack or Germany from a French or Belgian attack. Many of them would also have us guarantee the French and Belgian frontiers, if Germany refuses to come into a new Locarno Pact. They would thus recognize modern conditions of warfare by pushing our defensive frontiers forward to the Rhine in exactly the same way as the Government would do. At the same time they would recognize the principles of the League and prevent Locarno from being a purely defensive alliance with France and Belgium by promising Germany that, if ever the French attacked across the Rhine, England would come to her side.

The semi-isolationists, again like the Government, would try to persuade the rest of Europe to ensure security and practise League of Nations principles by local treaties of mutual guarantee. They would, in fact, revert to the Regional Pact policy which Sir John Simon was trying to bring about at the time of his disappearance from the Foreign Office, though they would not, as he did, call it collective security. In order that a literal interpretation of the Covenant of the League of Nations should no longer clash with this localization of the defence of peace, they would cut out or modify those clauses in Articles 10 and 16 which call for the use of force. Many of them would also eliminate economic sanctions on the ground that the Abyssinian affair showed that, rigorously applied against a Great Power, they will almost certainly lead to war. They would thus, like the pacifists, be content if the League served as a sort of conciliation club which could meet in a crisis and try to devise ways out of it. They invoke in support of this project the remark of Lord Grey of Falloden that he might have been able to stop war in 1914 had the Council of the League existed. They recall the excellent work which, largely thanks to the leadership of Mr. Eden, the Council performed in 1934 in averting the dangerous crisis which threatened Europe as the result of the murder of King Alexander of Yugoslavia. The 'World Services' of the League they would, of course, again like the pacifists, leave untouched. They recognize that, whatever may be thought of the political functions of the League, there can be no doubt as to the excellence of the work which its secretariat does for the suppression of the white-slave traffic, for the regulation of the traffic in drugs, for the furtherance of international co-operation in regard to health and in many other administrative and advisory fields.

The collectivists say that semi-isolation simply would not work, that it would in effect mean no more than the continuance of that policy of modified participation in the responsibilities of the League, which, as we have seen, has characterized the British posture towards Europe ever since the United States withdrew from the Peace Settlement. They admit that this policy succeeded during the serene years after the signature of the Pact of Locarno. But, they argue, there can be no comparison between that period and the present one. Then everything was going relatively well. No dynamic expansionism existed; no *blocs* and *counterblocs* confronted each other. The state of Europe, in fact, almost justified the retirement of Great Britain behind her new defensive frontier of the Rhine in the same way as she used to retire behind the Channel when in the old days the political glass of the Continent registered 'set fair'. Now, however, everything is quite different. A state of emergency exists and it has never been the habit of Great Britain to cower behind her frontiers, defensive or other, when the stability of Europe was threatened.

The collectivists do not think that any system of regional pacts could guarantee peace without the support of a general collective security system in the background. They argue as follows. Even the most perfect network of regional pacts would not protect peace against infraction by a Great Power. It might prevent some local controversy from degenerating into war if no Great Power wished to use it as the pretext for armed adventure. But diplomacy would probably do it equally well, either inside or outside the League of Nations. What is wanted is something which would prevent a big war, deliberately planned, a cold-blooded attack upon peace and the rights of others like the Japanese attack on Manchuria or the Italian invasion of Abyssinia. That no amount of regional pacts could do. An eastern regional pact would not prevent Germany and Russia from flying at each other's throats. A mutual security pact between Germany, Italy, and the smaller countries of central Europe would not prevent Germany from attacking the Czechs or annexing Austria. A Locarno Pact might secure the countries whose frontiers it concerned from direct attack. But it would not secure France from being drawn into a war which started in central Europe, and it would not secure us from being dragged in if the war went badly for the French side and France was invaded.

The collectivists aver that for these and other reasons regional pacts would not stabilize things in times of peace, would not restore confidence sufficiently for Europe to settle down. They would tend to become centres of intrigue. The big countries would try to break them up or alter them or immobilize them for their own ends. Regional pacts would tend to degenerate into alliances of the old pre-War kind and might thus hinder rather than help the cause of post-War security. And, last but not least, it may not be possible even to conclude them. The history of Mr. Eden's efforts to initiate the negotiation of a new Locarno Pact and of other security arrangements for the rest of Europe shows what power the dictatorships have to stonewall when it seems profitable to them to do so. The old Locarno Pact, moreover, did nothing to quiet the nerves of Europe directly the situation began to get menacing at the beginning of this decade. Its existence failed to reassure the French and their friends to the extent of making them willing to disarm. Its existence up to the beginning of this year did nothing to prevent a steady aggravation of the fear neurosis and its menacing symptoms.

A regional security system would mean that our intentions would remain vague in regard to that part of Europe where a breach of the peace is most likely, namely, in the east and centre. Our insistence upon retaining a 'free hand' in regard to the equivalent danger spot in the last war, namely, the French frontier, must be regarded as one of the causes of that war. Of our behaviour in those days an eminent historian has written, 'The inability to take action which might conceivably have prevented the war was the result of lack oɪ precision in our relations with France. A policy of limited liability is easy to define but difficult to execute.'[1] We are ready now to define our responsibilities on the French frontier. That is something. But it is not enough now that the danger is patently elsewhere, and that everything points to the probability that the first steps towards the domination of Europe would, if taken, be in the east and south-east. Does not this, the collectivists ask, in itself afford a strong argument for the moving of our lines of defence even farther afield?

In any case considerations of Imperial security seem to do so. Our Empire has two frontiers so far as Europe is concerned. One is the Rhine, which protects its heart; the other is the Mediterranean, which protects the most important of its arteries. As was pointed out in the first part of this book, any hostile Power or group of hostile Powers, the present dictatorial *bloc* for instance, should it consolidate itself by peaceful or other means in central and south-eastern Europe,

[1] G. P. Gooch, *Cambridge History of British Foreign Policy*, vol. iii, p. 508.

might easily threaten our communications through the Mediterranean and the Suez Canal a great deal more effectively than Russia did in the last century. Russia, thanks to the alertness of our old Eastern security policy, was never able to set foot on the shores of the Mediterranean or the Aegean. And now there would seem to be even greater need of a new Eastern security policy, with Germany pressing down through south-eastern Europe, with Italy acting as her second, albeit perhaps an unwilling one, proclaiming herself as the predestined heir of the old Roman Empire, and with both countries trying to evolve from the troubles of Spain a *pied-à-terre* for their aggressive 'ideology' at the western entry of the Mediterranean as well. And, asks the collectivist, how is that eastern security policy to be efficient, unless composed according to his prescription? What local Mediterranean Pact would be strong enough if challenged by a Germany and an Italy controlling the shores of that sea and of the Adriatic from Genoa round to the Dardanelles, and perhaps Spain as well?

The collectivists do not agree with the semi-isolationists that, under a regional security system and robbed of the support of the sanctions clauses of the Covenant, the League of Nations could continue to exist as a useful agency in the high politics of Europe. Continue to exist it doubtless would, if only on account of the excellent work that it does in the social organization of the world. But as an agency for the consolidation of peace and as a solvent of the *blocs* and *counter-blocs* of the continent it would be next to useless. Marooned among the embattled nations, lacking concrete authority for the enforcement of its decisions, it would be no more than a talking-shop, settling perhaps small questions which could be as well dealt with elsewhere, serving as a useful club in which politicians and officials of different countries could learn to know each other, but impotent in the matters which really count.

V

THE EMPIRE AND THE WORLD

MANY of the semi-isolationists who now demand that the power of invoking sanctions should be taken from the League supported sanctions against Abyssinia and regretted at the time that the Government had not acted more quickly and more firmly. Now, however, they argue that the Abyssinian fiasco has finished the League as a peace-keeping machine backed by force. It has, for one thing, frightened the small countries away from sanctions.

The inability of France and Great Britain, they continue, to give the lead that might have made sanctions work against Italy, and the resultant obliteration of Abyssinia which 'trusted to the League', have demonstrated how unsafe it would be for any small country to participate in sanctions against a powerful neighbour. It might mean its obliteration by that neighbour because at the last moment the Great Powers shrank from putting really effective sanctions into effect, as in the case of Abyssinia, or because they were unable to protect them for reasons of geography or strategy. That has always been the fear of the Scandinavian States, who in spite of their intense loyalty to League principles have never been enthusiastic about sanctions. They have always doubted whether the extra safety which collective security might give them would counterbalance the extra liability which it would impose upon them of being drawn into other people's quarrels. Their fear has now been increased until it has become an inhibition, which is shared by Belgium, Holland, and probably some of the other small countries with exposed frontiers. There is the same shyness about economic sanctions because, as the Abyssinian affair also showed, strong economic sanctions against a Great Power would mean war almost as surely as the invocation of armed sanctions.

The semi-isolationists question, moreover, whether the full participation of Great Britain in a collective security system would in any case be feasible. They rightly contend that it would be folly to undertake to wage a collective war on the Continent without in these days of massed air attack making most adequate preparations for our own defence. It might happen that the aggressor would try first to paralyse us, knowing that in the collective war we should be in one way or another his most dangerous opponent. And if we had the necessary forces for that great double task, are we prepared, or indeed is any European nation prepared, to promise in advance to support the full terms of the Covenant of the League and to use force to stop a war anywhere in Europe? Are we or any other country really prepared to surrender our sovereignty to the extent of undertaking to go to war in some quarrel in which we have no direct and vital interest? Are we, as things stand, prepared to fight to protect Danzig, Memel, or Austria from a German attack? What would public opinion have said had the Government suggested the use of force to turn the Germans out of the demilitarized zone last spring?

And, even if collective security were feasible for us and for Europe, there are extra-European factors which might well prevent it from working. There is the American attitude. How could a blockade be instituted against a transgressor Power with the United States insisting upon her traditional doctrine of the 'freedom of the seas', upon the right, that is to say, to carry on the maximum amount of trade with both belligerents. Did not Mr. Balfour as early as 1920[1] adduce American non-membership as the principal reason for his suggestion that it might be necessary to weaken the sanctions, or blockade, clauses of the Covenant? Did not Mr. Baldwin say not so long ago that the collective system was impracticable 'in view of the fact that the United States is not yet a member of the League of Nations and that Germany and Japan have both retired from it'?[2] It is true that a few months later Mr. Baldwin altered his view and proclaimed that after many years of study he had come to the conclusion that the 'whole of Europe must get together and devise the means whereby this great end (collective security) can be

[1] At the first meeting of the Assembly.
[2] Speech at Glasgow, 23 Nov. 1934.

achieved'.[1] But the fact remains that the United States is still outside the League and has not as yet decided upon a neutrality policy which would assure the League of Nations Powers her recognition of any blockade that they might try to apply.

Last but not least there are the Dominions. Are they willing to have us pledge our word to go on crusades all over Europe for the protection of peace? Their opinion, as we have seen, is divided as to the merits of collective security, and there is nothing that any of them would like less than for us to implicate ourselves and possibly them in any war the waging of which was not absolutely vital to the Empire.

These are weighty objections and command weighty support. They gain force from the undeniable fact that the so-called League failure over Abyssinia and the growing gravity of the European situation have enhanced the public desire that our foreign commitments should not be greater than is demanded by considerations of the safety of ourselves and the other countries of the Commonwealth. Let us therefore examine them more closely. The unwillingness of many but not all of the small countries of Europe to pledge themselves to sanctions is obvious to any one who reads the newspapers. Even in France there has, as in England, been less enthusiasm for collective security since the black days of 1936. The collectivists, however, say that the smaller countries would lose their fear of the boomerang qualities of collective force, and that France would lay aside her hesitations, if Great Britain made up her mind in favour of a universal collective security system. They may be right. The lack of enthusiasm with which the Continent responded to Sir John Simon's efforts on behalf of a regional security system in 1935; the warmth with which France and the small countries greeted Sir Samuel Hoare's famous declaration of faith in collective security at Geneva later in the same year; the disillusionment and loss of heart caused firstly by his no less spectacular desertion of the League a few months later and then by the discomfiture of the League by Italy; these and other similar manifestations of European sentiment all

[1] Speech at Llandrindod Wells, 8 April 1935.

seem to support their view. So too, in the case of France, do the programmes of the political parties. During the electoral campaign of 1935 the Front Populaire put the automatic and universal application of sanctions in the forefront of their foreign programme and regional pacts at the end of it, evidently as a sort of second line in the defence of peace; and the Croix de Feu, who do not love the League, proclaimed that either 'illusions about it should be dissipated or it should be turned into an active force'. It should, moreover, be possible to reassure small countries inconveniently placed in relation to a powerful aggressor. The Council could, for instance, refrain from asking the Scandinavian countries to act, certainly in regard to armed sanctions and presumably in regard to economic sanctions against Germany or Russia. That would weaken sanctions but, as the success of our blockade during the War showed, by no means fatally.

British support is, on the other hand, essential to collective security if only because the forces behind it would be too weak otherwise. That brings us to the question whether the full participation of Great Britain in a continental peace system is feasible or desirable. The first point to decide is whether we have, or can have, sufficient forces to defend ourselves and at the same time play our part in the system. At first sight one is inclined to share the doubts of the semi-isolationists. Then come second thoughts. The Covenant makes it clear that we should not be compelled to use all our forces in any collective war, wherever it might be. Its framers obviously intended that the countries best placed to do so should provide the lion's share of the force. The constraint, therefore, of an aggression in farther Europe might not mean more than blockade duties for us and perhaps the dispatch of an air contingent or some relatively small force to the seat of the war. If the war spread to the West and if France or Belgium were invaded, then, of course, we should be fully involved, just as we should have been under our old European policy. In other words, if we are strong enough to guarantee the frontiers of France, Germany, and Belgium on the Rhine, we are strong enough to guarantee other frontiers farther afield, because on the Rhine will always be our maximum commitment.

There remains the danger that participation in collective war in farther Europe would cause the aggressor to turn upon us, the most powerful member of the collective alliance, the full fury of his air attack in order to put us out of action as quickly as possible. That is always a possibility. But is it a likely one? We still control the seas that surround us and propose to continue to do so. Unless preparations for air defence are completely fatuous, and there is happily no reason to suppose that they are, an attack from the air, however terrible it might be, would not put us out of action. On the contrary, it would be more likely to do on a large scale what the German attacks on our North Sea coast-towns did early in the last war, and stimulate us to grimmer efforts. One imagines that the aggressor, who would probably be out for the quickest possible attainment of his continental objectives, would have the sense to realize that and would leave us alone. He might attack us later if he triumphed in the European war. But he might do that anyhow and would, in fact, have to fight us, if his ambitions were anything like those of the countries which have recently tried to place Europe under their heels, like those of the France of Napoleon or the Germany of the Kaiser. All this is, of course, rank speculation. But the more one thinks about it the more one feels that readiness to participate in collective action against aggression in farther Europe would be less damaging to ourselves both now and in the future and more helpful to the general situation in Europe, upon which we depend so much, than the limitation of our responsibilities in the manner in which Mr. Eden now seems to suggest that they should be limited. Even if we could defend the Empire on the banks of the Rhine, which, as we have seen, we cannot safely do, to cower behind that river would seem to be a policy hardly safer or saner than the neutrality which some of Mr. Asquith's followers would have had him adopt in 1914 for the same reason, namely, that to go into a European war seemed too terrible and too dangerous a venture to contemplate.

The ultimate safety of Great Britain and of the Empire, together with our immediate prosperity, seem thus to demand the most serious consideration as to whether the only way in which we can continue to play our traditional role of a sort of balance-wheel in Europe is not now to be found in substituting for the spasmodic *ad hoc* interferences of the old days a steady participation in an alliance open to all countries in defence of the international system which the League of Nations was meant to inaugurate. If that is the case, then two of the other objections to our participation in collective security, namely, the points of view of the Dominions and the hesitations of our own public opinion, begin to lose force.

It is highly probable that, if we did join a general security system in Europe, the Dominions, or at any rate some of them, would elect to remain outside it. But there would be nothing catastrophic in that. It has long been recognized by the Dominions that our peculiar position demands that we take a more positive share in European politics than they need or ought to do. We, on our side, have long recognized the feasibility and justice of this attitude. No Dominion signed the abortive Treaty for the Guarantee of the French frontier in 1919, and none was expected to do so. No Dominion signed the Pact of Locarno in 1925, though it was left open for their adhesion. But this abstention did not in any way invalidate our responsibilities under the Treaty and still less did it mean that the Dominions objected to the commitments which we assumed under it. On the contrary, the Pact of Locarno was greeted throughout the Empire as a signal triumph for the diplomacy of Sir Austen Chamberlain and as a most meritorious contribution to the cause of peace. The Dominions are now, as their spokesmen frequently proclaim, intensely interested in the reconstruction of Europe. They realize that, for reasons which have already been sketched, a stable and prosperous Europe is only less important to them than it is to us, and that a European war would be only less disastrous to them. It is therefore unlikely that they would fail to applaud any new commitment that we might undertake in Europe provided that we could show that it radically increased the prospects of peace and prosperity in the Old World. The entry of Great Britain into any war, collective or other, would, of course, confront them with difficult questions and would involve difficult decisions. But so long as the British navy controlled the seas they would be immune from its direct repercussions and their contribution to the war would thus depend, as it ought to do, upon what each of them decided to make it.

It is difficult to think that public opinion in Great Britain would shrink from the responsibilities of collective security if the Government entered the system with the resolute intention of making it work and explained what it was doing. Low as the discomfitures of the League may have brought the stock of Geneva, it must be remembered that a fuller loyalty to the Covenant and participation in a collective security system remain the platform of both the Opposition parties. There are, too, constant indications that a large section of opinion, baffled and disheartened by the vagaries of the foreign policy of the National Government during the past years, would welcome a consistent and constructive lead.

It is true that, as the semi-isolationists say, no Englishman would march to the defence of Danzig or Memel or Austria from Germany, any more than he would have marched last year to turn her troops out of her demilitarized zone. But not the most ardent of collectivists suggests that we should pledge ourselves unconditionally to the protection of the *status quo* or even of peace everywhere. Our readiness to do so would depend upon the readiness of France and other countries to join with us in a real effort to meet the just grievances of Germany and the other discontented countries. If vitality is to be given to the force clauses of the Covenant, effectiveness must also be given to Article 19, which empowers the League to set in motion machinery for the revision of the peace settlement. There would also have to be a serious attack upon the trade and tariff and monetary restrictions which at present retard European prosperity.

The urgent necessity for some such programme indicates the answer to those who see in the recent failures of the League proof that it cannot work as an instrument for the protection of peace because complete allegiance to Articles 10 and 16 of the Covenant would imply an intolerable abdication of the rights of sovereign nations to decide when and how they should go to war. Proponents of that view argue that, in the present state of international society, countries are not ready to abandon in the common cause the sovereign right of saying when they will or will not fight; that, to put it differently, they will not consent to be obliged by their membership of the League to coerce a nation into desisting from a war in the prevention of which they have no direct interest. They quote Alexander Hamilton's saying that it is grotesque to imagine that a 'sovereign State will ever suffer itself to be used as an instrument of coercion'. Hamilton was arguing, and arguing successfully, against the inclusion of a sanctions clause in the American Constitution for the purpose of bringing to heel any State or States that might subsequently flout the Federal Government. The analogy, however, is hardly sound. Hamilton and his colleagues were engaged in making a nation out of a dozen States who had lived uncomfortably and dangerously together for some years under the inadequate control of a Government which had been hastily devised when they broke away from England.

There is no question of furnishing the League of Nations with the powers of a super-State Government. For a long time past international relations have consisted to a great extent of the gradual surrender by each nation of bits of its sovereignty in the common interests of international society. The international health and quarantine arrangements are an example of the excellent results which can be obtained by this method of co-operation between sovereign States. An international arrangement for the limitation of armaments is another instance of the same thing. At the Washington Naval Conference the United States and the British Empire consented to surrender their sovereign right to build as many and as large battleships as they liked. They thus laid the foundation for the only form of disarmament limitation, (since brought to an unfortunate end by the intransigence of Japan) that there has been since the War. For us it meant a tremendous surrender of sovereignty; for the

British naval supremacy was among the proudest of our inheritances, was regarded as an utterly essential national policy, and was hallowed by some of the most glorious names and triumphs of our history. The Washington Naval Treaty was signed at the beginning of 1922, and under it the British Navy was reduced to parity with that of the United States. Yet three years earlier at the Paris Peace Conference we had told the American delegation that 'Great Britain would spend her last guinea to keep a navy superior to that of the United States or any other Power' and that no Government could survive in England which took a different position. Thus does wise statesmanship sacrifice national sovereignty, national pride, and national tradition upon the altar of national self-interest.

Nor must it be forgotten that, though Alexander Hamilton may well have been right in his interpretation of their feelings in normal times, the American States which remained faithful to the Federal Government voluntarily and successfully applied armed sanctions against the Southern States and fought the Civil War against them, when they tried to secede in 1861, because they felt that the future of their country demanded such action.

In the same way the decision whether the sovereign right of keeping free to declare or not to declare war as expediency may dictate on each separate occasion should be sacrificed to collective security or not would seem to depend for us and for other countries far less upon whether such a thing has been possible or not possible in the past than upon whether it would pay us in the future.

Due regard must be paid to the attitude of the United States. American opposition to a League blockade would be a grave obstacle to successful collective action against an aggressor and especially to the share which our navy would presumably take in it. It would be equally prejudicial to the success of any war which we might be called upon to wage under a new Pact of Locarno, a fact which the semi-isolationists seem to forget when they adduce American opposition to a blockade as an argument against collective security but not against a western regional pact.

The right to trade with belligerents as freely as is consistent with the accepted rules of contraband and blockade was vigorously upheld by the United States against the British control of the seas during the period of American neutrality in the Great War. It was, as Mr. Balfour rightly took for granted in 1920, again the policy of Washington in the years following the War. It cannot, however, be taken for granted that it will be upheld with equal vigour in the case of another European contest. The neutrality policy temporarily adopted by Congress in 1936, during the Italian invasion of Abyssinia, curtailed the right of Americans to do business with the belligerents. It forbade loans or the sale of arms to either side. Congress thus reflected the intense anxiety of the American people to keep clear of the war which their Press now tells them is brewing in Europe. It was realized that insistence upon the Freedom of the Seas, as the old demand for the maximum amount of trade with all belligerents is called, had forced the United States into the only two great European conflicts that there have been since her birth, into the Napoleonic War to fight us and into the late war to fight Germany. Hence, when the Abyssinian war threatened to expand, the demand that everything possible should be done to insulate the United States from the danger. Hence the action of Congress.

Many Americans would like Congress to go farther and forbid all trade whatsoever with all parties in a war outside the American hemisphere, whatever the merits of the contest might be. They will make their voices heard when Congress again discusses neutrality. But it is by no means certain that they will have their way. Though the majority of Americans are for peace at almost any price, an influential minority of thoughtful people realize that the United States can no more insulate herself from the disastrous effects of another great war than we or the Dominions can. These people, of whom, as we have seen from his speeches, President Roosevelt is one, are intensely alarmed at the bellicose postures of the European dictatorships, and of the control which they now exercise over the march of events in the Old World. They feel that it will be a disastrous day for the whole world if the present slump in democracy is allowed to continue. Most of them hope that Great Britain and France will do what our collectivists wish them to do and make a supreme effort to bring the League of Nations into effective action in order to redress the European balance. Some of them even regret that the mass of American opinion makes it impossible for the United States to take active part in this work. All of them applauded the appeal which President Roosevelt and Mr. Hull made in 1935, in spite of the fact that Congress had given them no authority to do so, to American exporters not to sell oil and other raw materials for warfare to the Italians when they attacked Abyssinia. These people will oppose the perpetuation and strengthening of the present neutrality regulations, which lapse during the present year. They will argue that the United States, the author with France of the famous Kellogg Pact, which, concluded in 1928 and signed by nearly all the nations of the world, denounces war 'as an instrument of national policy', cannot in either decency or expediency adopt a rule of conduct which would prevent her selling means of defence to the victim of aggression. They would have on their side a large element of the industrialists and exporters who dislike the idea of boycotting the countries of Europe simply because a war breaks out among them and would, therefore, prefer a policy which would enable them to sell at any rate to one side, as they did while the United States was neutral in the Great War.

The interplay of isolationism, commercialism, and collectivism, to put the three schools of opinion in the order of their importance, may, in the event of another war, break up the old doctrine of the Freedom of the Seas, without, however, substituting for it anything so drastic as non-intercourse with belligerents. It is not likely that the friends of the League of Nations will be able to introduce a system which would allow official and automatic discrimination against the aggressor. But it is possible that the desire to avoid war and the desire to save some war trade might combine to create a situation favourable to the armed or even economic coercion of the aggressor. When the question of neutrality was under discussion in Washington at the beginning of 1936, much, for instance, was heard of the 'cash and carry' policy. That policy, also called 'the come and get it' policy, is simple in conception. It is that at the outbreak of war the Government should forbid all trade with belligerents in American ships but should authorize American citizens to sell to those belligerents who could pay cash and come and fetch their goods away. Such a policy would not prevent the collective system from functioning so long as Great Britain was on the right side and maintained control of the seas.

The United States, as we have already shown, believes in regional security organized on a continental scale. She is rightly optimistic about her own particular enterprise in that direction in her hemisphere. She is as pessimistic about the organization of the Far East as we are. In regard to Europe she is nervous but not without hope. In Europe, as was clear from the puzzled disappointment which the Hoare–Laval affair and its reactions in London caused her, she considers that the future of collective security rests principally with us. She pays us the compliment of attributing to us the same leadership in great affairs in the Old World as she has in the New World. The shaping of her neutrality policy will be a long process. It will continue whatever legislation may or may not be passed in Washington in the near future. It will depend largely upon how things go in Europe. The greater the fear of war, the greater the influence of the complete isolationists will be. But it will also depend upon the extent to which we seem to be taking the leadership in European reconstruction. To continue to protest our loyalty to the ideals of the League of Nations and to the cause of democracy, and at the same time only to work for what to oversea eyes resembles an old-fashioned alliance of the Western Powers against the dictatorships in the centre of Europe, would not strengthen the hands of those Americans who would like to help the cause of peace in Europe and hope to co-operate with us in the interests of world economic reconstruction. It would, on the other hand, increase the tendency noticeable in the United States at the time of the Buenos Aires Pan-American Conference to believe that for the present efforts at good neighbourship are likely to be unprofitable and indeed dangerous if pursued outside the Western Hemisphere. If, on the contrary, we could give fresh earnest of our determination to work for comprehensive European reconstruction, and could reassure American opinion that we have not forgotten our debt obligations and that we do wish to co-operate with Mr. Hull for the lowering of trade barriers the world over, then there would be a good chance that, if ever we had to fight some law-breaking country on behalf of the League or to protect ourselves, we should not find in the attitude of Washington an insuperable barrier to economic sanctions and blockade.

These considerations, together with the vital importance of good relations between the United States and the Empire, seem to enlist the American factor on the side of collective security rather than against it. Nor is it only in the United States that defeatism over the League, which as things are going would be interpreted by the world as continued surrender to the dictatorships, would hurt the standing of our diplomacy and cancel the credit which our recovery from the depression and our conquest of the recent constitutional crisis have given us as a nation. It would injure us everywhere. It would hamper us in the struggle which is before us to maintain our trade in Latin America against American and German competition. It would injure our 'face' and that of our traders in China. It would encourage Japanese nationalism to reach out into Asia and the neighbouring waters; it would encourage the 'Africa for the Africans' movement in Africa. It might even reverse the present more satisfactory march of events in India.

It is unfortunately quite possible that any effort we can now make to reinstate the League in Europe may fail; that, for instance, the smaller countries might still be too distrustful of British and French dependability in a crisis to join in it. But whatever is in store for us and for Europe the sympathy of the outside world and especially of the United States is more likely to be usefully forthcoming if trouble comes after a really convincing effort on our part to reassert the principles in which we believe and not after a further period of surrender to the initiatives and obstructions of those who desire to profit from troubled waters.

Apologists of the Government's present policy of semi-isolation say that public opinion would not allow the adoption of a more stalwart and constructive programme. They say that opinion here and in and among the Dominions is too deeply divided as to the merits of the League of Nations for collective security to be any longer practical politics. To use such an argument is to scold the cart for not being able to pull the horse. The Government has only itself to blame if puzzlement and defeatism are abroad here and throughout the Empire in regard to foreign policy. Neither by word nor by action has it given a clear or consistent lead. We have already glanced at the oscillations of our policy during the last two years from Sir John Simon's disconcerting prescription of collective security 'regionally' arrived at, through the extremes of Sir Samuel Hoare's Geneva speech on the one hand and of his surrender to M. Laval on the other, to Mr. Eden's apparent change from a hundred per cent. League of Nations man back to something very like an advocate of Sir John Simon's policy, less ambiguously formulated.

It is small wonder in these circumstances that Mr. Baldwin felt forced to complain in that speech of his already quoted that democracy is always two years late. It is likely to be even later than that as compared with the dictatorships unless the Government makes up its mind to a foreign policy and sticks to it and takes the public into its confidence. The dictatorships know exactly what they are after and how they propose to get it. They control the press and the other means of educating their publics and they control them with meticulous assiduity and great ability, though by methods utterly abhorrent to us with our devotion to freedom of thought, comment, and discussion. But there is no reason why our Government should not be able to persuade and educate just as successfully as Rome, Moscow, or Berlin bulldose and drug. The great majority of our newspapers are only too ready to report a member of the Cabinet who has something to say. There is also our broadcasting system, which, in spite of the stones thrown at it, is easily the best and most influential possessed by any country, especially since one of the results of the continual parrot-cries of the authoritarian radios is that hearers are apt to turn them off or stop their ears when they start on politics.

There is no good reason to suppose if the Government gave a lead the country would not support it in a strong League of Nations policy in the same way in which it was so evidently ready to support Sir Samuel Hoare when it was believed that his speech at Geneva really presaged an end to the timidities and compromises of which everybody was even then weary. There is no reason to suppose that, if properly enlightened, the British democracy would be slower to think in regard to foreign policy or would think less sensibly than it did in the two great domestic crises which the National Government has had to face, one last year and the other at the very outset of its administration. In both those crises the Government acted with firmness and imagination and on neither occasion did it have to complain of lack of support either in Parliament or in the country.

One thing the countries of the Empire should do and can do without reference to the outside world. They should insist upon a thorough examination of the publicity organization available for the explanation of British policies and points of view to the world. No nation is now properly equipped either for trade or for defence unless it has an efficient system to that end. Such a system consists roughly of two parts. There must be in the national capital efficient contacts between the Government and the press. The most important cogs in these contacts are the press departments of the Government offices and especially of the Foreign Office. Here the situation in London is satisfactory. The Foreign Office has a press department which, if smaller than those in the big continental capitals, is accessible and knows how to make the best of such information as it is allowed by its political superiors to vouchsafe. Other key Government departments also have their press services. It is in regard to the other side of national advertisement, namely, in the matter of news distribution abroad, that we are badly behind.

Germany, Japan, and even Italy have in the last years built up formidable news-distributing machines which stretch all over the world. So has France. They have done so largely through State-aided or State-controlled news agencies and by the intelligent and wholesale use of that great new medium of news distribution, wireless telegraphy.

A glance at the news-agency situation reveals what has happened. News agencies are now part of the equipment of all countries. As their name implies, they collect and distribute news to the newspapers. Probably between 80 and 90 per cent. of the telegraphic news that appears in the press comes, directly or indirectly, from them. They exist because the field in which news has to be collected is so immense that the richest of journals could only cover an infinitesimal part of it by means of its own correspondents and reporters. There are roughly two types of news agencies: those which are privately owned and managed and those which are more or less controlled and supported by Governments. The biggest private news agencies are to be found in Great Britain and the United States. They are run as commercial concerns and have to make both ends meet if they are to continue to exist. In England by far the most important agency, so far as foreign news is concerned, is Reuter. In the United States the leading agencies in the same field are the Associated Press and the United Press.

Havas, the great French agency, though maintaining a certain independence, is in very close contact with the Government and receives valuable assistance from it. The German agency, the Deutsches Nachrichtenburo, is of course part of the Government machine and presumably has the German propaganda fund at its disposal. The same holds true of Tass, the Moscow agency, and of Stefani, the Italian agency. The Domei agency in Japan is in an equally favourable position. The result of this is precisely what anybody would expect who knows the immense importance which the countries just mentioned place on national propaganda. Whereas until recently it pumped far more stuff than any of its rivals into the international news stream, Reuter is now working at a great and growing disadvantage, and month by month the proportion of British-made news, even of British affairs, that finds its way into that news stream is diminishing.

It was said above that the news agency exists because no newspaper can collect its daily bread single-handed. Even the big news agencies cannot do so. Hence many of the principal foreign agencies are grouped round Reuter in a loose news-collecting alliance. All the great agencies just named, except the American United Press, together with some thirty others in different countries, belong to this alliance. The gist of its terms is that each member has the use of the news collected by the other members in their own countries. Thus, in London, the representatives of Havas, the Deutsches Nachrichtenburo, &c., have the right to Reuter's news; and in Paris and Berlin the representatives of Reuter can use the Havas and Deutsches Nachrichtenburo news in the making of their messages. This co-operative arrangement is accompanied by a self-denying agreement on the part of each member of the alliance in regard to the distribution and sale of news in the countries of the other members. Thus no foreign news agency in the alliance can sell its wares in England, and Reuter keeps out of the French and German markets, and so forth.

Before the War Reuter, Havas, and Wolff (predecessor of the present D.N.B. in Germany) divided up the outer parts of the world between them. After the War a reshuffle took place which, with certain benevolent reservations, restricted Wolff to Germany; extended Reuter's already strongly established jurisdiction on the continent of Europe, and recognized the special claims of the Associated Press in South as well as North America. Until recently, under this arrangement, Reuter refrained from selling its news in Latin America, and Havas and the Associated Press recognized Reuter's monopoly in the Far East and elsewhere. When this part of the agreement came to an end a few years ago, Reuter was firmly established in the Far East and supplied the greater part of the foreign news published in China, Japan, and the Far East generally. In Latin America the only serious competitor that the Associated Press had was its American rival, the United Press. A 'news war' soon upset this comfortable state of affairs. In this war we were, and are, on the offensive in Latin America and on the defensive in the Far East. Our offensive has failed and our defence is threatened. In Latin America the French and German news agencies are proving more formidable competitors of the American agencies than Reuter can hope to be; in the Far East, though fighting hard, Reuter is severely pressed by the Japanese and French and German agencies. The reasons for Reuter's difficulties are the same in each continent. In spite of its strength and vigorous management, Reuter cannot compete with the Government-supported agencies.

In Latin America, as on the continent of Europe and in the Far East, Havas, helped by extremely generous treatment from the French Government wireless-sending stations, and probably in other ways, is distributing a large and well-edited wireless service which the newspapers can have for almost nothing, and the Germans are equally generous with a more tendentious and therefore less effective service. In the Far East Havas, the Nachrichtenburo, and particularly Transocean, another German subsidized service, are equally active. But there it is Japanese competition that most matters.

As things stand Domei, the Japanese agency, has practically ousted Reuter's news from Japan and is running it hard in China, where, as already said, Reuter used to have a monopoly. In other parts of the world the same thing is happening to a greater or less extent. The enormous news services of the Government-controlled or aided news agencies are running Reuter and the smaller British news-distributing mediums very hard. Even the American news agencies have the advantage of a company which is allowed by the American Government to transmit their messages, by wireless telegraphy, at a reduced rate. Reuter, in fact, is the only big news agency in the world which is given no help whatsoever by its Government in the business of distributing the news of the nation to which it belongs; or, to put it the other way round, Great Britain is the only Great Power that has not given practical recognition to the value in these days of keeping the large-scale distribution of its national news in the hands of its own nationals. The qualification 'large-scale' is used because the British Government does send out from the Foreign Office a well-edited wireless bulletin service. This service can be picked up free of charge by any newspaper or news agency anywhere and achieves considerable publicity. But it is not by summarized messages of only a thousand words or so sent out two or three times a day that public opinion is swung in these days of many-worded and variegated journalism.

For the best part of a century, and in growing measure during the past generation, Reuter has been carrying British news to the most remote parts of the earth. The British agency, thanks to the subsidies enjoyed by its foreign rivals, now finds itself in much the same situation as that of our great shipping companies, who, having like Reuter to balance revenue and expenditure, are finding it increasingly difficult to hold their own against the state-aided competition which confronts them; and it is not too much to say that, unless something is done, and done soon, to remedy this state of affairs, British news distribution throughout the world will be permanently damaged and, with it, British prestige. It is not suggested that we should copy the continental countries and flood the world with masses of tendentious propaganda. Still less is it suggested that Reuter or any other British agency should be turned into a State-controlled news agency. Such a procedure would be contrary to one of the soundest of our traditions, that of a free press, and certainly would not command the support of the great British newspapers in whom the main ownership of Reuter is now vested. Nor is it suggested that our official wireless service should be increased and 'gingered up' until it could compete in colourful variety with the services which pour out from the Government wireless stations of France or Germany. It is, however, suggested that the Governments of the Empire and especially the London Government should consider whether they could not aid Reuter and any other British agency which could qualify for assistance by at least extending to them equal facilities for cheap transmission of that copious stream of wireless messages which is more than ever becoming the recognized means of long-distance and large-scale press work.

Otherwise, if the challenge which other countries are making is allowed to go unanswered, our trade recovery is liable to suffer for want of national advertisement at a moment when more than ever it is true that trade follows the news, while in times of international crisis we shall find the channels of news distribution throughout the world more and more closed to us and more and more at the disposal of others. Some national advertisement is, of course, done, and competently done, by various organizations, and notably by a semi-official body called the British Council, which has a small official subsidy. These bodies deal with commercial and what is called cultural propaganda, that is to say, the popularization abroad of British products, from steel bridges and locomotives to art, literature, lecturers, and scenery. But their activities are on a humiliatingly small scale as compared with those of the national advertisement organizations of France or Germany and other continental countries, some of whose Governments spend scores of pounds on such activities where we hardly spend a pound. And even if the British Council and similar organizations were supported by the Government on the scale on which they ought to be, instead of having to depend partly upon inadequate private aid, they would not meet the needs of national advertisement unless reinforced by a steady and adequate flow of British press news from British sources through British channels, especially in the Far East and South America, where we are going to be forced to fight harder than ever for trade and where the right sort of British news is in danger of being swamped by the rising tide of foreign and therefore often unsatisfactory reports and interpretations of our politics and our problems.

We are again brought back to the issue of enlightened expediency. We have seen that neither American absence from the League nor the removal of the Far East from its sphere of influence need prevent its working in Europe. In Europe we have seen that the continuance of the present international anarchy cannot do us good and is bound to do us harm, perhaps to the fatal extent of involving us in another war; that Locarno and other regional Pacts, even if they can be consummated, which is doubtful, are not well calculated to improve things; that there seems to be no third course beside a drift back to the old Balance of Power system in circumstances none too favourable to ourselves, and a more vigorous effort to make the League of Nations work as it was originally meant to work than our faithfulness to old traditions has so far allowed us to make. We are, in other words, compelled to the conclusion that the Empire would be well advised to consider the possibility of taking the lead in another effort to create a real collective security system in Europe, of which the democratic Powers would be the nucleus and to which Germany and Italy and other countries now unsympathetic to the League would be most cordially and sincerely asked to join, but which would come into being as an alliance in the defence of peace whether they joined or not. An essential preliminary to such a system would, it must be repeated, be an undertaking on the part of the satisfied countries of Europe to examine most sympathetically the grievances of the dissatisfied Powers and to do their best to meet such demands as an impartial investigation might justify. Only so does there seem to be any real chance of stemming the dangerous drift towards the division of Europe into dictatorial and anti-dictatorial camps, with the advantage on the side of the dictatorships, of stopping the race in armaments, and of achieving the security and solid prosperity which we all so badly need.